First World War
and Army of Occupation
War Diary
France, Belgium and Germany

I0311144

34 DIVISION
Divisional Troops
208 Field Company Royal Engineers
9 January 1916 - 31 July 1919

WO95/2449/2

The Naval & Military Press Ltd
www.nmarchive.com
Published in association with The National Archives

Published by

The Naval & Military Press Ltd

Unit 10 Ridgewood Industrial Park,
Uckfield, East Sussex,
TN22 5QE England
Tel: +44 (0) 1825 749494

www.naval-military-press.com
www.nmarchive.com

Contents

Document type	Place/Title	Date From	Date To
Heading	WO95/2449 (2)		
Heading	208th Field Coy R.E. Jan 1916-Dec 1919		
Heading	208th F.C. R.E. Vol I		
Heading	208th Field Coy R.E. January 1916		
War Diary	Sutton Veny Wilts	09/01/1916	09/01/1916
War Diary	S Hampton	09/01/1916	09/01/1916
War Diary	Havre	10/01/1916	11/01/1916
War Diary	France	11/01/1916	11/01/1916
War Diary	Wardrecques	11/01/1916	23/01/1916
War Diary	Steenbecque	23/01/1916	31/01/1916
Heading	208th Field Coy. R.E. March 1916		
War Diary	La Chapelle d'Armentieres	01/03/1916	31/03/1916
Heading	208th Field Coy. R.E. April 1916		
War Diary	La Chapelle d'Armentieres	01/04/1916	06/04/1916
War Diary	Rue Marle Armentieres	06/04/1916	06/04/1916
War Diary	Erquinghem	07/04/1916	07/04/1916
War Diary	Vieux Berquin	08/04/1916	08/04/1916
War Diary	Morbecque	09/04/1916	09/04/1916
War Diary	Wardrecques	11/04/1916	11/04/1916
War Diary	Moringhem	12/04/1916	12/04/1916
War Diary	Muncq Nieurlet	13/04/1916	22/04/1916
War Diary	Boisdinghem	23/04/1916	30/04/1916
Heading	208th Field Coy. R.E. May 1916		
War Diary	Boisdinghem	01/05/1916	06/05/1916
War Diary	Longeau	07/05/1916	07/05/1916
War Diary	La Hussoye	07/05/1916	07/05/1916
War Diary	Dernancourt	08/05/1916	14/05/1916
War Diary	Dernanct	15/05/1916	26/05/1916
War Diary	Dernancourt	27/05/1916	31/05/1916
Miscellaneous	The 102nd (Tyneside Scottish) Brigade. Operation Order No. 23	03/05/1916	03/05/1916
Miscellaneous	Issued With Operation Order No. 23	03/05/1916	03/05/1916
Miscellaneous	Notes On Entrainment	19/04/1916	19/04/1916
Heading	208th Field Coy. R.E. June 1916		
War Diary	Dernancourt Nr Albert	01/05/1916	08/05/1916
War Diary	Dernancourt	09/05/1916	27/05/1916
War Diary	Albert	28/05/1916	28/05/1916
War Diary	Dernancourt	29/06/1916	30/06/1916
War Diary	Dernanct	29/06/1916	30/06/1916
War Diary	Usna-Tara Line	01/07/1916	01/07/1916
Heading	208th Field Coy. R.E. July 1916		
War Diary	Usna-Tara Line	01/07/1916	01/07/1916
War Diary	Becourt Wd	02/07/1916	04/07/1916
War Diary	Millencourt	05/07/1916	06/07/1916
War Diary	Baizieux	07/07/1916	07/07/1916
War Diary	Millencourt	08/07/1916	08/07/1916
War Diary	Dernancourt	09/07/1916	20/07/1916
War Diary	Bresle	21/07/1916	29/07/1916
War Diary	Dernanct	30/07/1916	30/07/1916
War Diary	Dernancourt	31/07/1916	31/07/1916

Miscellaneous	The 102nd (Tyneside Scottish) Brigade. Operation Order No. 36 Appendix A		
Miscellaneous	GOC 102nd Bde		
Miscellaneous	O C 208 Field Coy Appendix B	04/07/1916	04/07/1916
Operation(al) Order(s)	Operation Order No. 3 Appendix "C"	07/07/1916	07/07/1916
Miscellaneous	A Form Messages And Signals.	07/07/1916	07/07/1916
Miscellaneous	A Form Messages And Signals.		
Miscellaneous	A Form Messages And Signals. Appendix E	09/07/1916	09/07/1916
Miscellaneous	C.R.E's Operation Order No. 21 Appendix F	19/07/1916	19/07/1916
Miscellaneous	March Table.		
Miscellaneous	A Form Messages And Signals. Appendix G	28/07/1916	28/07/1916
Miscellaneous	O.C. 208th Field Co. Appendix H	28/07/1916	28/07/1916
Heading	208th Field Company R. E. August 1916		
Heading	208th Field Coy R. E. August 1916		
War Diary	Belle Vue Farm	01/08/1916	01/08/1916
War Diary	Albert	05/08/1916	05/08/1916
War Diary	Mametz Wood	07/08/1916	09/08/1916
War Diary	Fricourt	10/08/1916	14/08/1916
War Diary	Belle Vue Farm. Albert	15/08/1916	15/08/1916
War Diary	Bresle	16/08/1916	18/08/1916
War Diary	Hocquincourt	19/08/1916	20/08/1916
War Diary	Bailleul	21/08/1916	21/08/1916
War Diary	Estaires	22/08/1916	22/08/1916
War Diary	Rue Marle Armentieres	23/08/1916	31/08/1916
Operation(al) Order(s)	Operation Order No. 31	05/08/1916	05/08/1916
Operation(al) Order(s)	Operation Order No. 36	13/08/1916	13/08/1916
Miscellaneous	March Table "A"		
Operation(al) Order(s)	Operation Orders No. 38	15/08/1916	15/08/1916
Miscellaneous	101st Brigade Operation Order No. 50	17/08/1916	17/08/1916
Miscellaneous	O.C. 208th Field Co.	17/08/1916	17/08/1916
Miscellaneous	To Be Acknowledged By Wire. 34th Division Operation Order No. 47	17/08/1916	17/08/1916
Miscellaneous	34th Division Entrainment Table.	18/08/1916	18/08/1916
Heading	208th Field Company R.E. September 1916 Volume 9		
War Diary	Rue Marle Armentiers	01/09/1916	07/09/1916
War Diary	Rue Marle	01/09/1916	30/09/1916
Heading	208th Field Company R.E. October 1916 Volume 10		
War Diary	Rue Marle Armentiers	01/10/1916	31/10/1916
Heading	208th Field Company R.E. November 1916 Vol 1		
War Diary	Rue Marle Armentieres	01/11/1916	30/11/1916
Heading	208th Field Company R.E. December 1916		
War Diary	Rue Marle Armentiers	01/12/1916	11/12/1916
War Diary	Erquinghem Factory	12/12/1916	31/12/1916
War Diary	Erquinghem	12/12/1916	22/12/1916
Heading	January 1917 208th Field Coy R.E.		
War Diary	Erquinghem France	01/01/1917	26/01/1917
War Diary	Erquinghem Sun-la-Coy France	26/01/1917	31/01/1917
Heading	February 1917 208th Field Coy R.E.		
War Diary	Billets on Main Road Fletre-Caestre	01/02/1917	18/02/1917
War Diary	Molinghem	19/02/1917	21/02/1917
War Diary	Herlin-le-Vert	23/02/1917	23/02/1917
War Diary	Ecoivre Huts	25/02/1917	25/02/1917
War Diary	Arras	26/02/1917	28/02/1917
Heading	War Diary March 1917		
War Diary	Arras	01/03/1917	31/03/1917
War Diary	X Huts Ecoivre	16/03/1917	16/03/1917

Heading	208th Field Coy R E April 1917		
War Diary	Arras	01/05/1917	04/05/1917
War Diary	X Hutments. F.19.a.6.8	04/04/1917	06/04/1917
War Diary	X Hutments Ecoivres.	07/04/1917	08/04/1917
War Diary	In Line Roclincourt Valley	09/04/1917	13/04/1917
War Diary	Roclincourt Valley G10a 35 (57b. N.W.)	12/04/1917	22/04/1917
War Diary	G.12.a.3.5	23/04/1917	25/04/1917
War Diary	G.18.c.35.60	26/04/1917	26/04/1917
War Diary	La Laurent Blangy G18.c.35.60	27/04/1917	30/04/1917
Heading	208th Field Coy R.E. May		
War Diary	Camp at St Nicholas. (G.15b.4.3)	01/05/1917	02/05/1917
War Diary	Barly	03/05/1917	07/05/1917
War Diary	Ivergny	08/05/1917	08/05/1917
War Diary	Bouquemaison	09/05/1917	09/05/1917
War Diary	Vacquerie	10/05/1917	29/05/1917
War Diary	Couterelle	30/05/1917	30/05/1917
Heading	208th Field Company R.E. June		
War Diary	Vacquerie	30/05/1917	30/05/1917
War Diary	Railway Cutting (H.7.b.4.7)	31/05/1917	30/06/1917
Heading	208th Field Coy R.E. July 1917		
War Diary	Railway Cutting. H.7.b.4.7	01/07/1917	02/07/1917
War Diary	Hermaville	03/07/1917	05/07/1917
War Diary	Nr. Peronne	06/07/1917	06/07/1917
War Diary	Roisel K.16.d.8.8	07/07/1917	25/07/1917
War Diary	Nobescourt Wood. Q.1.a.8.8	26/07/1917	31/07/1917
Heading	208th Field Coy. R.E. August 1917		
War Diary	Nobescourt Wood Q.1.a.8.8	01/08/1917	02/08/1917
War Diary	K.35.b.8.2 Coy H.Q.	03/08/1917	14/08/1917
War Diary	Roisel. K.16.d.8.8	15/08/1917	25/08/1917
War Diary	Nobescourt Wood Q.1.a.8.8	26/08/1917	29/08/1917
War Diary	K.35.b.8.2. (Coy Hdqrs)	30/08/1917	31/08/1917
Heading	208th Field Coy R.E. September 1917		
War Diary	K35.b.8.2	01/09/1917	12/09/1917
War Diary	Q.1.a.8.8	13/09/1917	18/09/1917
War Diary	K.16.d.8.8	19/09/1917	30/09/1917
Heading	208th Field Coy R.E. October 1917 Vol XXII		
War Diary	Roisel K. 16.d.8.8	01/10/1917	04/10/1917
War Diary	Monchiet	05/10/1917	07/10/1917
War Diary	Pilgrim. Camp E.4.c.	08/10/1917	08/10/1917
War Diary	Parroy Farm B.16.c	09/10/1917	13/10/1917
War Diary	Canal Bank C.19.a.0.3	13/10/1917	23/10/1917
War Diary	Pilgrim Camp	24/10/1917	29/10/1917
War Diary	Argyle Camp 5.17. Central	30/10/1917	30/10/1917
War Diary	Sunken Rd. N.22.d.8.4	31/10/1917	31/10/1917
Heading	208th Field Coy R.E. November 1917		
War Diary	T.1.c.8.3.	01/11/1917	30/11/1917
Heading	208th Field Coy R.E. December 1917		
War Diary	T.1.c.8.8.	01/12/1917	31/12/1917
Heading	208th Field Coy R.E. January 1918		
War Diary	T.1.c.8.3	01/01/1918	28/01/1918
War Diary	Mory (B.28.a.4.6)	29/01/1918	31/01/1918
Heading	208th Field Coy R.E. February 1918		
War Diary	Mory B.28.a.4.6	01/02/1918	01/02/1918
War Diary	Henin Camp	02/02/1918	08/02/1918
War Diary	Henin Camp & Mary. B28.a.4.6	09/02/1918	09/02/1918
War Diary	Hendecourt Les-Ransart	10/02/1918	10/02/1918

War Diary	Bavincourt	11/02/1918	11/02/1918
War Diary	Villers-Sir Simon	11/02/1918	26/02/1918
War Diary	Humbercamp	27/02/1918	27/02/1918
War Diary	Hamelincourt	28/02/1917	28/02/1917
Heading	208th Field Company R. E. March 1918		
Heading	208th Field Coy R.E. March 1918		
War Diary	Hamelincourt	01/03/1918	01/03/1918
War Diary	St Ledger	02/03/1918	14/03/1918
War Diary	Boyelles	15/03/1918	21/03/1918
War Diary	Hamelincourt	22/03/1918	22/03/1918
War Diary	Boiry St Rictrude	23/03/1918	24/03/1918
War Diary	Blairville	25/03/1918	25/03/1918
War Diary	Bretencourt	26/03/1918	31/03/1918
Heading	208th Field Company R. E. April 1918		
Heading	War Diary April 1918 208th Field Coy R. E. Vol 28		
War Diary	Pont. De Nieppe	01/04/1918	10/04/1918
War Diary	Outersteen	10/04/1918	11/04/1918
War Diary	Ravelsburg	12/04/1918	12/04/1918
War Diary	Hille	13/04/1918	13/04/1918
War Diary	Croix De Poperinghe	14/04/1918	14/04/1918
War Diary	Farm. R24.a.0.5.	15/04/1918	15/04/1918
War Diary	Farm. H24.a.0.5.	16/04/1918	16/04/1918
War Diary	Boeschepe	17/04/1918	20/04/1918
War Diary	Abeele	21/04/1918	21/04/1918
War Diary	St Jans Ter Biezen	22/04/1918	25/04/1918
War Diary	Peselhoek	26/04/1918	30/04/1918
Heading	Maps To Accompany. 208th Field Company R. E. War Diary For April 1918		
Map			
Miscellaneous	208th Field C.R.E.		
Diagram etc			
Map			
Miscellaneous			
Map			
Miscellaneous			
Heading	208th Field Coy R.E. May 1918		
War Diary	Peselhoek	01/05/1918	11/05/1918
War Diary	Houtkerque	12/05/1918	12/05/1918
War Diary	Affringues	13/05/1918	31/05/1918
Heading	208th Field Coy R.E. June 1918		
War Diary	Affringues	01/06/1918	16/06/1918
War Diary	Secquieres	17/06/1918	20/06/1918
War Diary	Le Catelet	21/06/1918	27/06/1918
War Diary	Assinghem near Elnes	28/06/1918	28/06/1918
War Diary	Nieurlet	29/06/1918	29/06/1918
War Diary	Bambecque	30/06/1918	30/06/1918
Miscellaneous	Sanding Over Reports		
Heading	208th Field Coy. R.E. July 1918		
War Diary	Bambecque	01/07/1918	06/07/1918
War Diary	F27.b.8.5	07/07/1918	12/07/1918
War Diary	F27.b.8.5. Sheet 27	13/07/1918	17/07/1918
War Diary	Villemetrie (near Senlis N.E of Paris)	18/07/1918	18/07/1918
War Diary	Vaumoise	19/07/1918	20/07/1918
War Diary	Puiseux	21/07/1918	21/07/1918
War Diary	Moulin De Villers. Helon	22/07/1918	26/07/1918
War Diary	Bois De Nadon	27/07/1918	28/07/1918

War Diary	Billy. Sur Ourcq	29/07/1918	31/07/1918
Heading	208th Field Coy R.E. August 1918		
War Diary	Billy Sur Ourcq	01/08/1918	01/08/1918
War Diary	Bois de La Baillette.	02/08/1918	03/08/1918
War Diary	Chevreville	04/08/1918	05/08/1918
War Diary	La Plessy Belville	06/08/1918	06/08/1918
War Diary	Bergues	07/08/1918	07/08/1918
War Diary	Zeggers-Cappel	08/08/1918	11/08/1918
War Diary	Wormhouldt	12/08/1918	12/08/1918
War Diary	Poperinghe	13/08/1918	19/08/1918
War Diary	Ypres	20/08/1918	27/08/1918
War Diary	A.30 Central	28/08/1918	28/08/1918
War Diary	Wippenhoek	29/08/1918	31/08/1918
Miscellaneous	Weekly Works Report 208 Field Coy R.E. Week Ending	28/08/1918	28/08/1918
Miscellaneous	C R E 34th Div	12/08/1918	12/08/1918
Miscellaneous	Handing Over Notes 208 Field Coy R E	28/08/1918	28/08/1918
Miscellaneous	Stores	28/08/1918	28/08/1918
Miscellaneous	List Of Maps. Sketches Etc	28/08/1918	28/08/1918
Heading	208th Field Coy R.E. September 1918		
War Diary	Westoutre	01/09/1918	14/09/1918
War Diary	La Clytte	15/09/1918	29/09/1918
War Diary	Cheapside N.15.b.2.7	30/09/1918	30/09/1918
Miscellaneous	Weekly Works Report 208th Fld. Co. R.E. Week Ending		
Miscellaneous	Weekly Works Report 208th Fld. Co. R.E. Week Ending	26/09/1918	26/09/1918
Heading	208th Field Coy R.E. October 1918		
War Diary	Hollebeke	01/10/1918	15/10/1918
War Diary	Gheluwe	16/10/1918	18/10/1918
War Diary	St Anne	19/10/1918	22/10/1918
War Diary	Belleghem	23/10/1918	26/10/1918
War Diary	St Anne	27/10/1918	27/10/1918
War Diary	Oyghem	28/10/1918	31/10/1918
Heading	208th Field Coy. R.E. November 1918		
War Diary	Oyghem	01/11/1918	13/11/1918
War Diary	Rolleghem	14/11/1918	14/11/1918
War Diary	Quesnoy	15/11/1918	15/11/1918
War Diary	Beaufaux	16/11/1918	17/11/1918
War Diary	Bruyere	18/11/1918	30/11/1918
Heading	208th Field Coy R.E. December 1918		
War Diary	Bruyere	01/12/1918	11/12/1918
War Diary	Silly	12/12/1918	13/12/1918
War Diary	Soignies	14/12/1918	15/12/1918
War Diary	Hame St Paul	16/12/1918	16/12/1918
War Diary	Monceau	17/12/1918	17/12/1918
War Diary	Chatelet	18/12/1918	18/12/1918
War Diary	Lesves	19/12/1918	31/12/1918
Heading	208th Field Coy. R.E. January 1919		
War Diary	Lesves	01/01/1919	22/01/1919
War Diary	Bonn	23/01/1919	31/01/1919
War Diary	Troisdorf		
Heading	208th Field Coy R.E. February 1919		
War Diary	Troisdorf	01/02/1919	20/02/1919
Miscellaneous	D.A.G. 3rd Echelon		
War Diary	Wahlschied	01/03/1919	22/03/1919

War Diary	Wahlscheid Seelscheid	24/03/1919	31/03/1919
Miscellaneous	D.A.G. British Army Of The Rhine		
War Diary	Wahlsheid	01/04/1919	06/04/1919
War Diary	Seelsheid	07/04/1919	31/05/1919
War Diary	Orb-Zeit Near Seelscheid. Germany	01/06/1919	30/06/1919
War Diary	Seelscheid Germany	01/07/1919	31/07/1919

WO 95/2449
(2)

34TH DIVVISION

208TH FIELD COY R.E.

JAN 1916-~~DEC 1918~~

1919 JLY

208th F.C.R.E.
Vol I

TAIV

34

Jan '16
Dec '18

Instructions regarding War Diaries and Intelligence Summaries are contained in F. S. Regs., Part II. and the Staff Manual respectively. Title pages will be prepared in manuscript.

WAR DIARY
or
~~INTELLIGENCE SUMMARY.~~
(Erase heading not required.)

Army Form C. 2118.

Place	Date	Hour	Summary of Events and Information	Remarks and references to Appendices
			208th. Field Coy. R.E.	
			January 1916.	

T2134. Wt. W708–776. 500000. 4/15. Sir J. C. & S.

Instructions regarding War Diaries and Intelligence Summaries are contained in F. S. Regs., Part II. and the Staff Manual respectively. Title pages will be prepared in manuscript.

WAR DIARY
or
INTELLIGENCE SUMMARY.
(Erase heading not required.)

Army Form C. 2118.

1

Place	Date	Hour	Summary of Events and Information	Remarks and references to Appendices
Sutton Veny Wilts	9/1/16	2 am.	Leave R.E. Camp. Sutton Veny. Establishment and Transport Complete.	
S'hampton	"	7 am.	Arrive Dockside.	
		5 pm.	Embark on S.S. "Archimedes".	
		8 pm.	Leave S'hampton Docks.	
Havre.	10/1/16	4. am	At anchor 5 miles from Harbour.	
		10.30 am.	Disembark.	
		6.30 pm.	Leave for Station.	
		9. pm.	Leave Havre Station.	
			Arrive –	
France.	11/1/16	9.30 am.	Abbeville. 11. am. Etaples. 12 pm. Boulogne. 1.30 pm. Calais. 2.30 St. Omer.	
	"	7.30 pm.	Arrive Wardrecques. Transport parked along road ~~Ergna~~ Saint Omer – Aire. against La Belle Croix.	

T2134. Wt. W708–776. 500000. 4/15. Sir J. C. & S.

Instructions regarding War Diaries and Intelligence Summaries are contained in F. S. Regs., Part II. and the Staff Manual respectively. Title pages will be prepared in manuscript.

WAR DIARY
or
INTELLIGENCE SUMMARY.
(Erase heading not required.)

Army Form C. 2118.

7.

Place	Date	Hour	Summary of Events and Information	Remarks and references to Appendices
Wardrecques	11/1/16.	8.30.	Company settled in Billets along lane from La Belle Croix - Tile Factory.	
	11/1/16 to 22/1/16.		Overhauling Wagons & Equipment. Instruction in use of Gas Helmets. Route Marches. Entrenchments. Map Reading.	
	23/1/16	9.am	Leave for Steenbecque. Arrive noon. Company billetted.	
Steenbecque	23/1/16 to 31/1/16.		Overhauling Wagons & Equipment. Draining Camps occupied by Infantry. (Nos 1.2.3.4.5.6.) Attention to, and repair of Baths.	

J H Tupper [signature] Major R.E.
O.C. 208th Field Coy R.E.

T2131. Wt. W708–776. 500000. 4/15. Sir J. C. & S.

Instructions regarding War Diaries and Intelligence Summaries are contained in F. S. Regs., Part II. and the Staff Manual respectively. Title pages will be prepared in manuscript.

WAR DIARY
or
INTELLIGENCE SUMMARY.
(Erase heading not required.)

Army Form C. 2118.

208 F C RE Vol 3

Place	Date	Hour	Summary of Events and Information	Remarks and references to Appendices
			? XXXIV	
			208TH FIELD COY. R.E	
			MARCH. 1916.	

T2134. Wt. W708—776. 500000. 4/15. Sir J. C. & S.

Instructions regarding War Diaries and Intelligence Summaries are contained in F. S. Regs., Part II. and the Staff Manual respectively. Title pages will be prepared in manuscript.

WAR DIARY
or
INTELLIGENCE SUMMARY.
(Erase heading not required.)

Army Form C. 2118.

Place	Date	Hour	Summary of Events and Information	Remarks and references to Appendices
La Chapelle d'Armentières	1916 MAR 1.		Reclaiming WELLINGTON AVENUE. Revetting & boarding RUE de BOIS Work on S & S.S. Line. New Battn H.Q. Signal Huts. M.G. Emplact in FERME de BIEZ. Drainage.	
"	MAR. 2		Reclaiming WELLINGTON AVENUE. Revetting parapet and fixing fire-steps RUE de BOIS. Laying floor boards and draining PARK ROW. Laying floor boards to Dressing Station PARK ROW. Revetting & boarding S. & S.S. Lines. New Battn. H.Q. Signal Station (Rt. Battn) Signal Station (Left Battn). M.G. Emplacement Shelter FERME de BIEZ. Drainage.	
	MAR. 3.		Repairing, boarding, revetting & extending S. & S.S. Lines. Repairing RUE de BOIS. Repairing front line Left Battn. Reclaiming WELLINGTON AVENUE. New Signal Stations & Coy H.Q. M.G. Emplacement at FERME de BIEZ. Drainage.	

T2131. Wt. W708–776. 500000. 4/15. Sir J. C. & S.

Instructions regarding War Diaries and Intelligence Summaries are contained in F. S. Regs., Part II. and the Staff Manual respectively. Title pages will be prepared in manuscript.

WAR DIARY
or
INTELLIGENCE SUMMARY.
(Erase heading not required.)

Army Form C. 2118.

Place	Date	Hour	Summary of Events and Information	Remarks and references to Appendices
La Chapelle d'Armentières	1916 MAR. 4.		Extending boarding & revetting S. & S.S. Lines. Repairing RUE du BOIS. Reclaiming WELLINGTON AVENUE. New Signal Stats and Coy H.Q. M.G. Emplacements at FERME de BIEZ. Repairing PARK ROW AVENUE. Drainage.	
do.	MAR. 5.		Reclaiming WELLINGTON AVEN. & work on S.S. Line. Bridging stream at WELLINGTON AV. near S.S. Line. Continuing S. & S.S. Line.	
do.	MAR. 6.		Extending, boarding & revetting S. & S.S. Lines. Reclaiming WELLINGTON AVENUE. Repairing PARK ROW. Building new Signal Station and Coy H.Q. M.G. Emplacements Shelters at FERME de BIEZ. Drainage.	

T2134. Wt. W708—776. 500000. 4/15. Sir J. C. & S.

Instructions regarding War Diaries and Intelligence Summaries are contained in F. S. Regs., Part II. and the Staff Manual respectively. Title pages will be prepared in manuscript.

WAR DIARY
or
INTELLIGENCE SUMMARY.
(Erase heading not required.)

Army Form C. 2118.

Place	Date	Hour	Summary of Events and Information	Remarks and references to Appendices
	1916.			
La Chapelle d'Armentières	MAR. 7		Extending, boarding & revetting S. & S.S. Lines. Reclaiming WELLINGTON AVENUE. Repairing PARK ROW. Building new Signal Station and Coy. H.Q. M.G. Emplacements. Shelter at FERME DE BIEZ. Drainage.	
D°	MAR 8.		Extending, boarding & revetting S. & S.S. Lines. Draining and repairing boarding COWGATE AVENUE. Reclaiming WELLINGTON AVENUE. Draining & boarding PARK ROW. Building new Signal Station & Coy. H.Q. M.G. Emplacements. Shelter at FERME DE BIEZ.	
D°	MAR 9.		As MAR. 8: Also Signallers Hut Left Batn. H.Q.	
D°	MAR 10		As MAR. 8: Also repairing SALIENT, commencing new Traverses and draining. New Dug-outs in Front Line.	

Instructions regarding War Diaries and Intelligence Summaries are contained in F. S. Regs., Part II. and the Staff Manual respectively. Title pages will be prepared in manuscript.

WAR DIARY
or
INTELLIGENCE SUMMARY.
(Erase heading not required.)

Army Form C. 2118.

Place	Date	Hour	Summary of Events and Information	Remarks and references to Appendices
	1916			
La Chapelle d'Armentières	MAR. 11.		Draining & revetting COWGATE AV. Building traverses & firesteps in Front Line (Left Sector) Extending & revetting S. & S.S. Lines. Erecting Signallers' Huts – Left Batn HQ. Coy. H.Q. M.G. Emplacement at FERME de BIEZ. Repairing Dug-outs S.S. Lines R.H. Sector. Draining old Battn H.Q. Left Sector & repairing Dug-outs. Bridging Streams at Dead Cow Farm. Raising parapet boarding & repairing PARK ROW. Repairing & boarding CHORD LINE. Building traverses, boarding & revetting in front line to right of PARK ROW. Setting frames in WELLINGTON AVENUE. Draining SALIENT (water level reduced 9 inches). Building new traverses & boarding in SALIENT.	
Do.	MAR. 12		As above.	

T2134. Wt. W708—776. 500000. 4/15. Sir J. C. & S.

Instructions regarding War Diaries and Intelligence Summaries are contained in F. S. Regs., Part II. and the Staff Manual respectively. Title pages will be prepared in manuscript.

WAR DIARY
or
INTELLIGENCE SUMMARY.
(Erase heading not required.)

Army Form C. 2118.

Place	Date	Hour	Summary of Events and Information	Remarks and references to Appendices
La Chapelle d'Armentières	MAR 13.		Repairing PARK ROW. Raising & thickening parapet S. Line left of COWGATE AVENUE. Raising & thickening parapet at ORCHARD (left Battn. H.Q.). Repairing front line RIGHT & LEFT Sectors. Draining & repairing COWGATE AVENUE. Erecting Coy H.Q. Drainage.	
Do.	MAR 14.		Repairing PARK ROW. Work on S. Line left Battalion. Repairing parapet, front line. Repairing RUE de BOIS. Draining & revetting WINE AVENUE, COWGATE, & PARK ROW. Extending S. & S.S. Line.	
Do.	MAR 15.		Draining & revetting whole of FRONT LINE. Draining & building traverses in SALIENT. Extending & revetting S. & S.S. Lines & ORCHARD. Draining & revetting COWGATE AV. Boarding Dug-outs FRONT & S.S. Lines. Draining, rebuilding parapet & boarding PARK ROW. Making new bridges PARK ROW.	

Instructions regarding War Diaries and Intelligence Summaries are contained in F. S. Regs., Part II. and the Staff Manual respectively. Title pages will be prepared in manuscript.

WAR DIARY
or
INTELLIGENCE SUMMARY.
(Erase heading not required.)

Army Form C. 2118.

Place	Date	Hour	Summary of Events and Information	Remarks and references to Appendices
La Chapelle d'Armentières	MAR. 16		Draining, revetting, repairing FRONT LINE. Draining + building traverses in SALIENT. Extending S. + S.S. Lines. Repairing dug-outs, FRONT + S.S. Lines. Repairing COWGATE AV. PARK ROW.	
Do	MAR 17.		Draining, revetting + repairing FRONT LINE. Repairing SALIENT. Extending S. + S.S. Lines. Repairing dug-outs Front + S.S. Lines. Repairing COWGATE AV., PARK ROW, WINE AVENUE. Completing Screen on LILLE - ARMENTIERE Road. Strength Left Batn H.Q.	
Do	MAR 18.	19.	As above.	
Do.	MAR 20.	21.	Repairing parapet, revetting + draining; altering traverses, building firesteps, flooring dug-outs + boarding FRONT. LINE. Extending, repairing, inserting dug-outs, boarding + draining S. + S.S. Line. Draining.	

Instructions regarding War Diaries and Intelligence Summaries are contained in F. S. Regs., Part II. and the Staff Manual respectively. Title pages will be prepared in manuscript.

WAR DIARY
or
INTELLIGENCE SUMMARY.
(Erase heading not required.)

Army Form C. 2118.

Place	Date	Hour	Summary of Events and Information	Remarks and references to Appendices
La Chapelle d'Armentières	1916 MAR 22-23.		FRONT LINE: Building traverses & parapet. Laying trench boards repairing bays & traverses: flooring dug-outs & draining. S. & S.S. Lines: Extending, draining & repairing damage in PARK ROW & COWGATE AV. Reclaiming S.S. Line R of Rly. Line. Draining near FERME de BIEZ.	
Do.	MAR 24.		As above.	
Do.	MAR. 25.		FRONT LINE: Repairing parapet, revetting, boarding, building parados and fire steps: draining; & repairing M.G. Emplacements. S. & S.S. Lines: Extending, rebuilding parapets & parados. boarding draining & repairing dug-outs. Boarding & repairing revetment in PARK ROW. Reclaiming S.S. Line from Rly. to DEAD COW FARM.	

Instructions regarding War Diaries and Intelligence Summaries are contained in F. S. Regs., Part II. and the Staff Manual respectively. Title pages will be prepared in manuscript.

WAR DIARY
or
INTELLIGENCE SUMMARY.
(Erase heading not required.)

Army Form C. 2118.

Place	Date	Hour	Summary of Events and Information	Remarks and references to Appendices
	1916.			
La Chapelle d'Armentières	MAR 26.		Baths: Clean up Billets: Fatigues. Overhaul Tool Carts and Wagons: Inspection of Arms, Ammunition etc. Gas Helmet Drill.	
"	MAR. 27.		FRONT LINE: Repairing parapet: draining & revetting. Altering traverses & bays. M.G. Emplacement. Renewing top of PARK ROW. Laying Duck Walks. SALIENT: Repairs to parapet, traverses, & laying duck-walks S. & S.S. Lines: Revetments and repairs. Completing round ORCHARD; COWGATE AVENUE; WINE AVENUE; to LILLE ROAD.	
"	MAR. 28.		FRONT LINE: As MAR. 27. Repairs to Company H.Q. Building M.G. Emplacement. Mending parapet, revetting parados between SALIENT and WILLOW AVENUE. SALIENT: Traversing, mending parapet, M.G. Emplacement, revetment. S. & S.S. Lines: As Mar. 27. Revetting in QUEEN STR. Revetting parapet between RAILWAY and DEAD COW Farms.	

Instructions regarding War Diaries and Intelligence Summaries are contained in F. S. Regs., Part II. and the Staff Manual respectively. Title pages will be prepared in manuscript.

WAR DIARY
or
INTELLIGENCE SUMMARY.
(Erase heading not required.)

Army Form C. 2118.

Place	Date	Hour	Summary of Events and Information	Remarks and references to Appendices
	1916.			
La Chapelle d'Armentières	MAR 29		FRONT LINE : Repairs to traverses & laying walks, draining & revetting. Complete top end of PARK ROW. Flooring dug-outs and building traverses. M.G. Emplacement. SALIENT : Repairing parapet making communication trenches. S. & S.S. LINES. : Preparing M.G. Emplacement: revetting parapet, Completing COWGATE AVENUE to LILLE RD. Revetting in QUEEN STR. and N.W. of ORCHARD.	
Do	MAR. 30 - 31.		SALIENT : Repairing parapet in front of Examiner. M.G. Emplacement. Drainage. FRONT LINE : Altering traverses & parapet : revetting, building new traverses, new fire step, building new bridge ; boarding & draining. New . M.G. Emplacement. S. & S.S. LINES : Boarding & draining PARK ROW. Draining near DE BIEZ FARM. Extending & reclaiming : revetting and building fire-bays, & repairing dug-outs.	

J.W. Stephens Major RE
O.C. 208th Field Coy. R.E.

T2134. Wt. W708—776. 500000. 4/15. Sir J. C. & S.

ORIGINAL.

XXXIV

208 FCRE

Army Form C. 2118.

Vol 4

Instructions regarding War Diaries and Intelligence Summaries are contained in F. S. Regs., Part II. and the Staff Manual respectively. Title pages will be prepared in manuscript.

WAR DIARY
or
INTELLIGENCE SUMMARY.
(Erase heading not required.)

Place	Date	Hour	Summary of Events and Information	Remarks and references to Appendices
			208TH FIELD COY. R.E. — APRIL. 1916.	

T2134. Wt. W708—776. 500000. 4/15. Sir J. C. & S.

Instructions regarding War Diaries and Intelligence Summaries are contained in F. S. Regs., Part II. and the Staff Manual respectively. Title pages will be prepared in manuscript.

WAR DIARY
or
INTELLIGENCE SUMMARY.
(Erase heading not required.)

Army Form C. 2118.

Place	Date	Hour	Summary of Events and Information	Remarks and references to Appendices
La Chapelle d'Armentières	1/4/16.		FRONT LINE: Altering traverses & parapet: revetting: building new traverses, fire-steps, boarding, draining, repairing shell damage, new M.G. Emplacement. S. & S.S. LINES: Extending, reclaiming, revetting and repairing bays and dug-outs. PARK ROW: Boarding & draining.	
D°	2/4/16		FRONT LINE: Repairing broken traverses, building traverses and parados and boarding. Fixing dugouts, repairing parapet, revetting & draining, building M.G. Emplacements. S & S.S. LINES: Extending, reclaiming, repairing parapet, fixing dug-outs & firesteps, repairing dug outs.	
D°	3/4/16.		FRONT LINE: Building traverses & parados: boarding & fixing dug-outs, repairing parapet, fire-steps, draining. S. & S.S. LINES: As 2/4/16.	

T2134. Wt. W708—776. 500000. 4/15. Sir J. C. & S.

Instructions regarding War Diaries and Intelligence Summaries are contained in F. S. Regs., Part II. and the Staff Manual respectively. Title pages will be prepared in manuscript.

WAR DIARY
or
INTELLIGENCE SUMMARY.
(Erase heading not required.)

Army Form C. 2118.

Place	Date	Hour	Summary of Events and Information	Remarks and references to Appendices
La Chapelle d'Armentières	4/4/16		FRONT LINE: Building traverses, parados; boarding; fixing dug-outs. repairing parapet draining. S. & S.S. LINES: Extending reclaiming, repairing parapet; dugouts; and fixing M.G. Emplacements. PARK ROW: Boarding & draining.	
Do.	5/4/16		FRONT LINE: Repairing parapet. building parados: boarding; fixing dug-outs, building traverses and draining. S. & S.S. LINES: Extending, reclaiming, repairing parapet; dugouts building new M.G. Emplacements. PARK ROW: Boarding & draining.	
Do.	6/4/16		FRONT LINE: As 5/4/16. S. & S.S. LINES: Extending & reclaiming parapet. Building new M.G. Emplacements.	

Instructions regarding War Diaries and Intelligence Summaries are contained in F. S. Regs., Part II. and the Staff Manual respectively. Title pages will be prepared in manuscript.

WAR DIARY
or
INTELLIGENCE SUMMARY.
(Erase heading not required.)

Army Form C. 2118.

Place	Date	Hour	Summary of Events and Information	Remarks and references to Appendices
La Chapelle d'Armentières	6/4/16	8 am	FRONT LINE ; S & S.S. LINES ; PARK LINE :- Introduction of 7th Australian Field Coy R.E. in situation of stores, dug-outs, trenches, etc.	
RUE MARLE ARMENTIÈRES	"	12 Noon to 5 pm	Packing stores etc. in readiness for move, under orders of 102nd Brigade. 34th Division.	
	"	5.30.	Leave RUE MARLE : Arrive ERQUINGHEM at 6.30 pm.	
ERQUINGHEM	7/4/16	9 am.	Ref. Map. 5A. HAZEBROUCK. (BELGIUM). Leave ERQUINGHEM. March CROIX-DU-BAC, DOULIEU, BLEU to VIEUX BERQUIN. Arrive. 3. 0 pm.	
VIEUX BERQUIN	8/4/16	9 am.	Leave. March LA MOTTE ; PAPOTIE ; MORBECQUE to STEENBECQUE. Arrive 1. 30. pm. Coy. Hdqrs. at MORBECQUE.	
MORBECQUE	9/4/16	9. am	Leave. March LA BELLE HOTESSE ; LE CROQUET to WARDRECQUES. Coy Hdqrs. at LA BELLE CROIX. Arrive. 1. 0 pm.	

Instructions regarding War Diaries and Intelligence Summaries are contained in F. S. Regs., Part II. and the Staff Manual respectively. Title pages will be prepared in manuscript.

WAR DIARY
or
INTELLIGENCE SUMMARY.
(Erase heading not required.)

Army Form C. 2118.

Place	Date	Hour	Summary of Events and Information	Remarks and references to Appendices
WARDRECQUES	11/4/16.	9.0 am.	Leave WARDRECQUES. March to CAMPAGNE, ARQUES, TATINGHEM, CORMETTIE to MORINGHEM.	
MORINGHEM	17/4/16.	9.0 am.	Leave MORINGHEM. March via MORNECOVE, WESTROVE, LE COMMUNAL, LA CALIFORNIE TO MUNCQ NIEURLET. (4.0 pm.).	
MUNCQ NIEURLET.	13/4/16.		Cleaning up billets. Inspection of transport, equipment, clothing, stores. Rifle and gas helmet inspection.	
Do.	14/4/16 to 19/4/16.		Training in 2nd Army Training Area, with 3rd Division. 1st Period:— Dismounted Men: Physical Drill; Musketry Training; Close Order Drill. Bayonet Exercise & Charging. Practice in Rapid Defence Works. Mounted Men: Inspection of Men and Transport & Animals. Physical Drill: Musketry Training. Riding Drill.	

T2134. Wt. W708—776. 500000. 4/15. Sir J. C. & S.

Instructions regarding War Diaries and Intelligence Summaries are contained in F. S. Regs., Part II. and the Staff Manual respectively. Title pages will be prepared in manuscript.

WAR DIARY
or
INTELLIGENCE SUMMARY.
(Erase heading not required.)

Army Form C. 2118.

Place	Date	Hour	Summary of Events and Information	Remarks and references to Appendices
MUNCQ NIEURLET	20/4/16 to 21/4/16		Training in 2nd Army Training Area. 2nd Period. As from 14/4/16 – 19/4/16.	
Do.	22/4/16		March to BOISDINGHEM via EPERLECQUES.	
BOISDINGHEM	23/4/16 to 26/4/16		3rd Period – Company Training. Field Training. Close Order Drill. Exercises in attacks; preparations for protection of other advancing troops; night assaults; counter attacks.	
Do	27/4/16 to 30/4/16		3rd Period:– Company Training, in connexion with Brigade and Divisional Exercises: as 23/4/16 – 26/4/16.	

J H Hopkins [signature]
Major RE.
O.C. 208th Fld. Coy RE

T2134. Wt. W708—776. 500000. 4/15. Sir J. C. & S.

Instructions regarding War Diaries and Intelligence Summaries are contained in F. S. Regs., Part II. and the Staff Manual respectively. Title pages will be prepared in manuscript.

WAR DIARY
or
~~INTELLIGENCE~~ SUMMARY.
(Erase heading not required.)

Army Form C. 2118.

Place	Date	Hour	Summary of Events and Information	Remarks and references to Appendices
			208TH FIELD COY. R.E.	
			MAY. 1916.	

T2134. Wt. W708—776. 500000. 4/15. Sir J. C. & S.

Instructions regarding War Diaries and Intelligence Summaries are contained in F. S. Regs., Part II. and the Staff Manual respectively. Title pages will be prepared in manuscript.

WAR DIARY

~~or~~

~~INTELLIGENCE~~ SUMMARY.

(*Erase heading not required.*)

Army Form C. 2118.

Place	Date	Hour	Summary of Events and Information	Remarks and references to Appendices
	MAY 1916		2nd ARMY TRAINING AREA:	
BOISDINGHEM	1/5/16 to 3/5/16		Divisional Training: Practise in Trench Attacks: CULEM - NORTBÉCOURT - INGLINGHEM Area.	
			208th Field Coy. working under instructions of 102nd Brigade.	
BOISDINGHEM	4/5/16 5/5/16		Squad Company training. Overhauling Stores, Tool carts etc.	
BOISDINGHEM	6/5/16	6 am.	Ref. 102nd (T.S.) Brigade O.O. No. 23 of 3/5/16: * Leave BOISDINGHEM 6 am. March to SAINT OMER arriving 9 am.	* Attached.
		11.45 am.	Leave SAINT OMER. Proceed by rail via CALAIS, BOULOGNE, ABBÉVILLE and AMIENS to	
		11 pm.	LONGEAU: Detrain and load up.	

T2134. Wt. W708—776. 500000. 4/15. Sir J. C. & S.

Instructions regarding War Diaries and Intelligence Summaries are contained in F. S. Regs., Part II. and the Staff Manual respectively. Title pages will be prepared in manuscript.

WAR DIARY

~~or~~

~~INTELLIGENCE SUMMARY.~~

(Erase heading not required.)

Army Form C. 2118.

Place	Date	Hour	Summary of Events and Information	Remarks and references to Appendices
LONGEAU.	7/5/16	1 a.m	Leave LONGEAU: March via AMIENS - QUERRIEU to LA HUSSOYE. Arriving 11. am.	
LA HUSSOYE	7/5/16	6 p.m.	Leave LA HUSSOYE March via RIBEMONT-sur-ANCRE and BUIRE to DERNANCOURT Arriving 11. 0 p.m.	
DERNANCOURT	8/5/16	9 am to 8 pm	Cleaning up camp equipment. Inspection of transport stores.	
			Preparation of RE. Dump at DERNANCOURT. Work in Reserve Trenches at BÉCOURT WOOD.	
D°.	9/5/16 to 14/5/16	8 am to 8 pm	Preparation of, and work in, RE. Dump, DERNANCOURT. Making Tramway E. of ALBERT.	
			Making cross-road between DERNANCOURT - ALBERT Road and DERNANCOURT - VIVIER MILL - ALBERT Rd.	

Instructions regarding War Diaries and Intelligence Summaries are contained in F. S. Regs., Part II. and the Staff Manual respectively. Title pages will be prepared in manuscript.

WAR DIARY

~~or~~

~~INTELLIGENCE SUMMARY.~~

(Erase heading not required.)

Army Form C. 2118.

Place	Date	Hour	Summary of Events and Information	Remarks and references to Appendices
DERNANC[T].	15/5/16 16/5/16		Work on R.E. Dump. Communication Roadway at E.10.c. Tramway E. of ALBERT.	
D°.	17/5/16 to 20/5/16		Work on R.E. Dump. Dernancourt. Communication Road at E.10.c. Tramway E. of ALBERT. Dug-Outs at MOULIN VIVIER. Work on Quarries near Dernancourt. Preparation of Baths at BRESLE. Work in trenches near USNA REDOUBT.	
D°	21/5/16 to 26/5/16		Work on R.E. Dump, Dernancourt. Divisional H.Q. Dug-Outs at MOULIN VIVIER. Cross Roads at E.10.c., near MOULIN VIVIER. Tramway E. of ALBERT. Work in trenches near USNA REDOUBT. Wire Entanglements and Defences of ALBERT — near Hospital. Work on roads at DERNANCOURT. Repairing Baths at ALBERT.	

Instructions regarding War Diaries and Intelligence Summaries are contained in F. S. Regs., Part II. and the Staff Manual respectively. Title pages will be prepared in manuscript.

WAR DIARY
~~or~~
~~INTELLIGENCE SUMMARY.~~
(Erase heading not required.)

Army Form C. 2118.

Place	Date	Hour	Summary of Events and Information	Remarks and references to Appendices
DERNANCOURT	27/5/16 to 31/5/16.		Work on R.E. Dump at DERNANCOURT.	
			Divisional H.Q. Dug-Outs at MOULIN DU VIVIER.	
			Cross Roads at E.10.c. near MOULIN DU VIVIER.	
			Tram Line EAST of ALBERT.	
			Preparation of Emergency Roads between DERNANCOURT and M. VIVIER.	
			Wiring and Defence Works near Hospital, ALBERT.	
			Sanitary Work and Coy. Miscellaneous Duties at DERNANCOURT.	

208TH FIELD CO.
1 JUN 1916
R. E.

J H Stephens
Major RE.
O.C. 208th Fld Coy. RE.

T2134. Wt. W708—776. 500000. 4/15. Sir J. C. & S.

S E C R E T. COPY NO. 4.

The 102nd (TYNESIDE SCOTTISH) BRIGADE.

OPERATION ORDER NO... 23.

3rd MAY, 191[illegible].

1.. The Brigade will entrain at ST.OMER on the 5th and 6th MAY, for [illegible].
Order of entrainments and roads to be used, are shewn on attached Table "A".

ROUTES - 2... Routes from the Detraining Station to the new Billetting Area will be allotted on arrival at Detraining Station.
Arrangements are being made for guides to meet units and conduct them to their billets.

BILLETTING PARTIES. 3.. Billetting parties - strength as under - will proceed from ST.OMER Station by the 2.43 a.m. train on the 5th inst.
Billetting parties to be at ST.OMER Station at 1 a.m.

	Offrs.	O.R.
Brigade Headquarters) Signal Section.) 102 Machine Gun Coy.)	1	6
20th N.F. (1st Tyneside Scottish)........	1	6
21st " (2nd " ")........	1	6
22nd " (3rd " ")........	1	4
23rd " (4th " ")........	1	4
102 Field Ambulance	1	2
No. 3 Coy Train		1
20[illegible]th Field Coy. [illegible]		1

RATIONS ....4.. All units will entrain with the unexpended portion of the day's rations - and rations for the day following that of entrainment.
The Billetting parties mentioned in para.3 will take 3 days rations with them.
All Units including Billetting parties will carry Iron Rations on the man, extra to the rations referred to above.
The 3 days rations for billetting parties will be conveyed in a G.S. Limbered wagon to ST.OMER Station under Battalion arrangements.

BAGGAGE AND SUPPLY WAGONS. 5. Baggage and Supply wagons will entrain with units and not with Train Companies.

SUPPLIES ... 6. Units which entrain between midnight 4/5th and midnight 5/6th will draw supplies for consumption on the 5th at Refilling Point as usual - i.e. on the 4th.
The Supply Wagons when unloaded will return to the Refilling Point at 3 p.m. on the 4th inst., and draw supplies for consumption on the 6th. These wagons will then return to their units and entrain "loaded" on the 5th.

Units which entrain between midnight 5/6th and midnight 6/7th will draw supplies for consumption on the 6th at Refilling Point as usual - i.e. on the 5th.
The Supply wagons when unloaded will return to the Refilling Point at 3 p.m. on the 5th inst., and draw supplies for consumption on the 7th. These wagons will then return to their units and entrain "loaded" on the 6th.

/2..

STAFF OFFICERS AT ENTRAINING & DETRAINING STATIONS. 7.. There will be a Staff Officer at Entraining and Detraining Stations for the whole period during which units of the Brigade will be either entraining or detraining.

The Brigade Major will be at the Entraining Station
The Staff Captain will be at the Detraining Station

ROAD CONTROL.... 8.. The O.C. 23rd N.F. (4th Tyneside Scottish) will detail an officer to be present to control traffic at the T Roads at ST MARTIN AU LAERT during the whole period that various units of the Brigade are passing that point for ST.OMER Station.
This Officer will rejoin his unit when the last portion of his Battalion has passed that point.

LIGHT TRENCH MORTAR BATTERIES 9.. The personnel of the 102/1 and 102/2 Trench Mortar Batteries will for the purposes of this move be attached to units to which they originally belonged, but will be kept as far as possible as a distinct unit during the move.

BILLETS....... 10.. On arrival in the new area - the Brigade will be billetted in the area of ST GRATIEN and RAINNEVILLE. Brigade Headquarters will be at ST.GRATIEN.

RAILHEAD...... 11.. The Railhead at WATTEN will remain open up to and including 5th MAY, 1916, and a new Railhead will be opened at HERICOURT on that day.

GENERAL INSTRUCTIONS. 12.. The instructions "Notes on Entrainment" issued to Units of the Brigade - 34th Div No. 806/Q dated 19:4:1916, are to be strictly complied with.

REPORT CENTRE...13.. Brigade Headquarters will close at POLINCOVE at 12 noon on 5th MAY, 1916, and reopen at ST.GRATIEN at the same hour.

Major.
BRIGADE MAJOR.
102nd (TYNESIDE SCOTTISH) BRIGADE.

102 B.H.Q.
3:5:1916.
Issued at p.m.
Copies 1 & 2 retained.
3 20th N.F. (1st Tyneside Scottish)
4 21st " (2nd " ")
5 22nd " (3rd " ")
6 23rd " (4th " ")
7 208th Field Coy. R.E.
8 102 Machine Gun Coy.
9 No.3 Coy. A.S.C.
10 War Diary.

S E C R E T.

Issued with Operation Order No. 23.

TRAIN NO.	CONVEYING.	LEAVES.	AT	ON	DUE AT LONGEAU.	ON	R E M A R K S.
95	20th N.F. (1st TYNESIDE SCOTTISH)	ST OMER.	5:53 p.m	5th	1.31 a.m.	6th.	Any road.
96	102nd Bde. Head Qrs.) Signal Section......) Machine Gun Coy.....)	ST OMER.	8:43 p.m	5th	4.31 a.m	6th	Any road.
97	21st N.F. (2nd TYNESIDE SCOTTISH)	ST OMER.	11:43 p.m.	5th	7.31 a.m.	6th	Any road.
[illegible]	22nd N.F. (3rd TYNESIDE SCOTTISH)	ST OMER.	2.43 a.m	6th	10.31 a.m.	6th	Via CALAIS--ST OMER road.
[illegible]	23rd N.F. (4th TYNESIDE SCOTTISH)	ST OMER.	5.43 a.m.	6th	1.31 p.m.	6th	Via CALAIS--ST OMER road.
[illegible]	102nd Field Ambulance) No. 3 Coy. A.S.C. D.T.)	ST OMER.	8.33 a.m.	6th	4.31 p.m.	6th	Any road.
[illegible]	208th Field Coy. R.E.	ST OMER.	11.43 a.m.	6th	7.32 p.m.	6th	Any road - North of [illegible].

[illegible]1916.

Major

BRIGADE MAJOR

102nd (TYNESIDE SCOTTISH) BRIGADE

NOTES ON ENTRAINMENT 34 Div /806/Q

1.. COMPOSITION OF TRAINS — Trains are composed of Officers' carriages, covered trucks (to carry 40 men or 8 horses), flat trucks(to carry 4 axles), and Brake- vans (in which neither personnel or stores are to be placed).

2.. ROUTES. — Routes to the entraining stations are to be reconnoitred.

Places will be selected by Units where train-loads can halt clear of traffic, until the R.T.O. is ready to receive them.

3.. MEDICAL. — The number of sick unable to march will be notified to the nearest Field Ambulance, by whom they will be collected.

4.. VETERINARY. — Sick Horses unable to march will be sent to Mobile Veterinary Section; if they cannot be moved or time does not admit, they will be handed in to the nearest farm, and a receipt obtained from the Mairie; A.D.V.S. will be notified of numbers of horses so left and their location.

5.. SUPPLY WAGONS. — Supply wagons will be filled with rations for the day following day of entrainment.

6.. WATER CARTS. — Water Carts will be entrained full.

7. OFFICER FOR CONTROL OF TRAFFIC. — At each entraining station an Officer will be detailed by the Headquarters of the Infantry Brigade or Brigade Group entraining at that station, to control the traffic on the road approaches; no troops or vehicles are to enter the station till the R.T.O. is ready.

8. MARCHING IN STATES. — A complete marching-in-state showing the numbers of men, horses, 4-wheeled and 2-wheeled wagons, and bicycles, should be sent down <u>with the first portion</u> of every Unit, and handed to the R.T.O. by the Officer in charge of the party.

9. TIME OF ARRIVAL AT ENTRAINING STATION.

<u>(a) Infantry Battalions.</u>

The transport and 1 Company will arrive at the entraining station three hours before the departure of the trains; remaining 3 companies one hour before departure of the train.

<u>(b) Other Units</u>

will arrive three hours before the departure of the trains.

(c) The entrainment of all Units must be completed half an hour before the scheduled time of departure.

P.T.O.

10. FATIGUE PARTIES. (a) When Infantry Battalions entrain, the Company arriving with the transport will detail two working parties each of 1 Officer and 25 men ; one is required for loading wagons, the other for entraining horses.

(b) When the Divisional Ammunition Column is being entrained the personnel of one ~~of the~~ Medium Trench Mortar Battery is to detailed at each Station at which the D.A.C. entrains. The personnel of the Trench Mortar Battery (and guns if in possession) will proceedi in the last train of the D.A.C. FROM EACH STATION.

11. WAGON POLES. Are only interchangeable in theory. Actually the pole of one wagon ~~does not~~ frequently does not fit another wagon. It is therefore necessary that all poles should bear marks by which they can be indentified as belonging to a particular wagon of the Unit.

12. BREAST ROPES. Breast-ropes for horse trucks must be provided by the Units themselves: ropes for lashing vehicles on the flat trucks will be provided by the Railway. Picketing ropes can be used as breast ropes and should be put on vehicles so that they can be easily reached.

13. SWINGLE BARS. Should be made fast to the wagons to which they belong.

14. WAGON-PINS. Should be put in a place of safety where they cannot fall out or be lost.

15. CAMP-KETTLES. Will be placed in the trucks with the men, so that at stations where hot water is available, no delay will occur in obtaining it.

16. SURPLUS BAGGAGE. will either be :-

(a) Taken to the entraining stations, and stacked some time before the Unit arrives.

(b) Taken to the entraining stations [illegible] the same day as the Unit arrives.

(c) Moved direct by M.T.

In all cases the necessary guards and loading parties will be detailed by the Group Commanders, Divisional Headquarters in case of Divisional Troops not included in any group.

17. DUTIES OF O.C. TRAIN. The O.C. Train will be responsible that :-

(a) Railway regulations are complied with and that the running of trains and Railway services are not interfered with.

(b) No one travels on roofs or steps of carriages or in the Guards Brakes.

(c) THERE WILL BE NO SMOKING IN HORSE TRUCKS.

(d) A picquet is detailed with orders to detrain at every ~~hat~~ halt to prevent men leaving the train. If number of troop trucks is considerable, half the picquet should travel in front part of Train and half in rear.
Men attempting to leave train should be severely dealt ~~with~~ with. The O.C. Train should ascertain when long stops are likely to take place and troops should be informed.

(d) *Continued* A report to be made to R.T.O. that this has been done

(e) A Guard is posted on the door of every refreshment room en-route, to prevent men entering.

19/4/16

sd/ O.K. Chance Lt. Col.
A.A. & Q.M.G. 34th Division

~~DUPLICATE.~~

Instructions regarding War Diaries and Intelligence Summaries are contained in F. S. Regs., Part II. and the Staff Manual respectively. Title pages will be prepared in manuscript.

WAR DIARY
or
INTELLIGENCE SUMMARY.
(Erase heading not required.)

208 F. C. R.E.

Army Form C. 2118.

Vol 6

Place	Date	Hour	Summary of Events and Information	Remarks and references to Appendices
			208TH FIELD COY. R.E.	
			JUNE 1916.	

Instructions regarding War Diaries and Intelligence Summaries are contained in F. S. Regs., Part II. and the Staff Manual respectively. Title pages will be prepared in manuscript.

WAR DIARY
or
~~INTELLIGENCE~~ ~~SUMMARY~~.
(Erase heading not required.)

Army Form C. 2118.

Place	Date	Hour	Summary of Events and Information	Remarks and references to Appendices
DERNANCOURT Nr. ALBERT.	1/VI/16 to 8/VI/16.		Work on R.E. Dump, DERNANCOURT. Construction of Divisional Headquarters Dug-outs at MOULIN VIVIER. Cross Roads at E.10.C. (ALBERT - DERNANCOURT : MEAULTE - ALBERT). Tram Line E. of ALBERT. Defences of ALBERT - wiring. Emergency roads near ALBERT. Camp Road at DERNANCOURT.	
DERNAN-COURT.	9/VI/16 to 16/VI/16		As above. Preparation of Laundry and Baths at Hospital, ALBERT. Observation Post at DERNANCOURT. Work with H.A.G. - Sanitary work and drainage.	

Instructions regarding War Diaries and Intelligence Summaries are contained in F. S. Regs., Part II. and the Staff Manual respectively. Title pages will be prepared in manuscript.

WAR DIARY
or
INTELLIGENCE SUMMARY.
(Erase heading not required.)

Army Form C. 2118.

Place	Date	Hour	Summary of Events and Information	Remarks and references to Appendices
DERNAN-COURT.	17/VI/16 to 19/VI/16.		Work on R.E. Dump. Work in Trenches - A.D. Station: Repairs to Dug-Outs. Making Cook House. Work on Tramway near ALBERT. Div. Hdq. Dug-Outs, and R.A.M.C Dug-Outs at MOULIN VIVIER. Work at Hospital ALBERT; and with 10" Siege Battery. Repairs to R.A. Hut at MOULIN VIVIER.	
DITTO.	20/VI/16. to 24/VI/16.		As above. Work in Trenches - repairs to Dug-Outs, and Regimental Aid-Posts. Casting for 209th Field Coy. RE.	

Instructions regarding War Diaries and Intelligence Summaries are contained in F. S. Regs., Part II. and the Staff Manual respectively. Title pages will be prepared in manuscript.

WAR DIARY
or
INTELLIGENCE SUMMARY.
(Erase heading not required.)

Army Form C. 2118.

Place	Date	Hour	Summary of Events and Information	Remarks and references to Appendices
DERNANCOURT.	25/VI/16.		Move to Camp at E.11.a (Ref Map 57 D. SE. 4) near DERNANC^T. Work in R.E. Yard. Overhauling equipment, stores, arms etc.	
D^o.	26/VI/16.		Camp Fatigues: Work in R.E. Yard. Inspection of Arms, Ammunition etc. by. under orders 102nd Brig.*	* Ry. "A".
D^o.	27/VI/16.		General Fatigues and rest during Day. 11.0 a.m. Parade. 11.30 p.m. March to FIR WOOD (Ref. Map 57 D. SE. 29 b central). All sections with exception of Mounted Section and Company Headquarters, under orders from 102nd Brigade. March via ALBERT to billets in dug-outs.	

Instructions regarding War Diaries and Intelligence Summaries are contained in F. S. Regs., Part II. and the Staff Manual respectively. Title pages will be prepared in manuscript.

WAR DIARY
or
INTELLIGENCE SUMMARY.
(Erase heading not required.)

Army Form C. 2118.

Place	Date	Hour	Summary of Events and Information	Remarks and references to Appendices
ALBERT.	28/VI/16.	4 am.	Coy. arrive at FIR WOOD. 1/4 am.	
			Rest in dugouts and stand by in readiness for attack (Vide Appendix B. – Operation Orders by C.R.E. 34th Division.)§	§ "B"
		2.30 pm.	Operations postponed for 48 hours. – Vide "C".# – under instructions from Brigade Major, 103rd Brigade.	# "C"
		8.0 pm.	Return to Camp (Coy Hdq.) near DERNANCOURT. – vide "D"§§	§§ "D"
DERNANCOURT.	29/6/16		Rest in Camp at DERNANCOURT. General fatigues, overhauling, ammunition, equipment, stores etc.	

T2134. Wt. W708—776. 500000. 4/15. Sir J. C. & S.

Army Form C. 2118.

Instructions regarding War Diaries and Intelligence Summaries are contained in F. S. Regs., Part II. and the Staff Manual respectively. Title pages will be prepared in manuscript.

WAR DIARY
or
INTELLIGENCE SUMMARY.
(Erase heading not required.)

Place	Date	Hour	Summary of Events and Information	Remarks and references to Appendices
DERNANCOURT	30/VI/16	6.0 am.	Coy. (as on 27/VI/16) march to FIR WOOD. Rest in dug-outs during Day.	

L. J. Murphy. Capt. RE.
for O.C. 208 Field Coy RE.

T2134. Wt. W708–776. 500000. 4/15. Sir J. C. & S.

Instructions regarding War Diaries and Intelligence Summaries are contained in F. S. Regs., Part II. and the Staff Manual respectively. Title pages will be prepared in manuscript.

WAR DIARY

~~or~~

~~INTELLIGENCE~~ SUMMARY.

(*Erase heading not required.*)

Army Form C. 2118.

Place	Date	Hour	Summary of Events and Information	Remarks and references to Appendices
DERNANCT.	JUNE 29.		Dismounted Sections leave Camp. March to Rendez Vous at FIR-WOOD.	
	30.	10 pm.	Under orders received from the G.O.C. 102nd Brigade, the Company proceeded to a position in ST ANDREW'S AVENUE for "Y" night, with instructions to move forward on the morning of Z Day (1st July), after the 103rd Brigade had passed; to pick up R.E. Material from the R.E. Dump; and to act under the orders of O.C. 22nd N.F. (3rd Tyneside Scottish), and O.C. 23rd N.F. for work in the construction of strong points. One half Company, comprising Nos. 1 and 2 Sections was under the orders of 23rd N.F. (4th Tyneside Scottish) which was the Left Reserve Battalion of the Brigade; and the other half Company, comprising Nos. 3 and 4 Sections, was under the orders of the 22nd N.F. (3rd Tyneside Scottish), the Right Reserve Battalion of the Brigade. The orders received by the Section Officers from the Battalion Commanders were, after the 103rd Brigade had passed, to collect the material and proceed to the respective battalion objectives, and assist in consolidation.	
USNA-TARA LINE	JULY 1.		When the 103rd Brigade had gone by, No 1 and 2 Sections collected their material, and attempted to cross NO MAN'S LAND, but owing to heavy shell and M/G fire, were unable to do so, and retired.	

VOLUME 7.

Instructions regarding War Diaries and Intelligence Summaries are contained in F. S. Regs., Part II. and the Staff Manual respectively. Title pages will be prepared in manuscript.

WAR DIARY

~~or~~

~~INTELLIGENCE SUMMARY.~~

(*Erase heading not required.*)

Army Form C. 2118.

ORIGINAL.

Vol 7

Place	Date	Hour	Summary of Events and Information	Remarks and references to Appendices
			208TH. FIELD. COY. R.E.	
			JULY. 1916.	

Instructions regarding War Diaries and Intelligence Summaries are contained in F. S. Regs., Part II. and the Staff Manual respectively. Title pages will be prepared in manuscript.

WAR DIARY
~~or~~
~~INTELLIGENCE SUMMARY.~~
(Erase heading not required.)

Army Form C. 2118.

Place	Date	Hour	Summary of Events and Information	Remarks and references to Appendices
USNA-TARA LINE	JULY 1.		Several casualties were sustained, and the Sections became somewhat scattered. About 40 men were collected, and remained in our lines under 2/Lt. C.A. ABLETT, until 2 p.m., when they were utilised to carry bombs and water to the South Mine Crater, via the tunnel, until 9.30 p.m.	
			Nos 3 and 4 Sections also collected R.E. Material, and moved forward with it, but owing to both their Sections Officers and several O.R. being wounded by shell fire, they did not get into NO MAN'S LAND, and were ordered by their officers to go into dug-outs. They became scattered, and were not collected until 8 p.m. Orders were received from the G.O.C. for the Company to proceed to Dug-outs in BECOURT WOOD, and the Company was reassembled there – Nos 3 and 4 Sections marching, to be joined later by Nos 1 and 2 Sections.	

2353 Wt. W2544/1454 700,000 5/15 D. D. & L. A.D.S.S./Forms/C. 2118.

Instructions regarding War Diaries and Intelligence Summaries are contained in F. S. Regs., Part II. and the Staff Manual respectively. Title pages will be prepared in manuscript.

WAR DIARY

or

~~INTELLIGENCE~~ ~~SUMMARY.~~

(Erase heading not required.)

Army Form C. 2118.

Place	Date	Hour	Summary of Events and Information	Remarks and references to Appendices
BECOURT. W^d	2/VII/16		Coy. resting in dug-outs in BÉCOURT WOOD - cleaning arms, equipment etc.	
D^o.	3/July/16		As 2/7/16. Work on Emergency Road leading thro' Becourt wood.	
D^o.	4/July/16	9am	Leave BÉCOURT WOOD. March to camp at E.14.d. Under 34 Div/Operation Order/No. 20 - Leave camp E.14.d. March via Quarry E.14.c. Cross-roads at E.7.c.1.9. to MILLENCOURT. Arrive 3pm. Billets.	Map. 62D.NE.
MILLENCOURT	5/July/16	8am	March from Billets at MILLENCOURT via HENNENCOURT to BAIZIEUX. Rest in Billets.	Map "B".
Ditto	6.		Camp Fatigues. Cleaning up arms, ammunition, stores transport etc.	

T2134. Wt. W708—776. 500000. 4/15. Sir J. C. & S.

Instructions regarding War Diaries and Intelligence Summaries are contained in F. S. Regs., Part II. and the Staff Manual respectively. Title pages will be prepared in manuscript.

WAR DIARY

~~or~~

~~INTELLIGENCE SUMMARY.~~

(Erase heading not required.)

Army Form C. 2118.

Place	Date	Hour	Summary of Events and Information	Remarks and references to Appendices
	JULY			
BAIZIEUX.	7.	9 a.m.	Camp Fatigues: Cleaning up arms, equipment etc.	"C"
		9 p.m.	Leave BAIZIEUX. March via HENNENCOURT to MILLENCOURT. Arrive 10.30 p.m. Billets.	
MILLENCOURT.	8.	8 a.m.	March via LAVIÉVILLE – D. 17.a. 1.1. – E. 7.c. 1.9 – DERNANCOURT. Take up camp at E. 9. A. – Dismounted Sections. Mounted Sections bivouac at E. 14. a. Arriving noon. Rest in camp, and cleaning up arms, equipments.	"D"
DERNANCOURT.	9.	7 a.m.	Work on New Road in SAUSAGE VALLEY. " " Tramway Extension from BÉCOURT WOOD to GORDON POST.	
		5 p.m.	Move to Camp at E. 14. b. – Dismounted Sections only. Mounted Section and Transport remain at E. 14. a.	"E"

Instructions regarding War Diaries and Intelligence Summaries are contained in F. S. Regs., Part II. and the Staff Manual respectively. Title pages will be prepared in manuscript.

WAR DIARY
or
~~INTELLIGENCE~~ ~~SUMMARY~~.
(Erase heading not required.)

Army Form C. 2118.

Place	Date	Hour	Summary of Events and Information	Remarks and references to Appendices
	JULY			
DERNANCOURT	10.		Work on NEW ROAD in SAUSAGE VALLEY.	
	11.		" " Tramway Extension towards GORDON POST.	
Do.	12th to 16th		Work on New Road in SAUSAGE VALLEY.	
			Extension of BÉCOURT TRAMWAY to GORDON POST.	
			Transport and loading of stores at "G" Dump.	
			Maintenance Party at work on Tramway.	
Do.	17th to 19th		Extension of Tramway from BECOURT WOOD through SAUSAGE VALLEY towards GORDON POST.	
			Alteration of Tramway in BECOURT WOOD.	
			Maintenance of existing Tramway.	
			Work on "G" Dump, DERNANCOURT - ALBERT ~~[illegible]~~ ROAD.	
			Extension of Tramway from BECOURT WOOD through GORDON POST to X. 15 b. 0. 2½.	

T2134. Wt. W708—776. 500000. 4/15. Sir J. C. & S.

Instructions regarding War Diaries and Intelligence Summaries are contained in F. S. Regs., Part II. and the Staff Manual respectively. Title pages will be prepared in manuscript.

WAR DIARY
or
~~INTELLIGENCE SUMMARY~~.
(Erase heading not required.)

Army Form C. 2118.

Place	Date	Hour	Summary of Events and Information	Remarks and references to Appendices
	1916.			
DERNANCOURT	JULY 20.	10 am	In accordance with C.R.E. 34th Div. O.O. No. 21. of 19/7/16. Company leave camp at E.14.b and march via BOOMERANG and X ROAD - D.17.a.1.1 - ALBERT-AMIENS ROAD to camp near BRESLE. Arrive noon.	F.
			Remainder of Day spent fixing camp, and removing stores etc	
BRESLE.	21.		Inspection of arms, Equipment; repairing deficiencies in stores, clothing; overhauling technical stores, transport etc.	
	22. to 26.		Squad Drill with and without arms; physical exercises etc. Trench exercises; lectures; map-reading.	
BRESLE	27.		As above (22nd to 26th). Inspection by C.R.E 34th Division. (10.15 am)	
D°.	28.		As above. General Inspection by Major-General C. Nicholson CMG. G.O.C. 34th Division. (10.15 am.)	

T2134. Wt. W708—776. 500000. 4/15. Sir J. C. & S.

Instructions regarding War Diaries and Intelligence Summaries are contained in F. S. Regs., Part II. and the Staff Manual respectively. Title pages will be prepared in manuscript.

WAR DIARY
or
INTELLIGENCE SUMMARY.
(Erase heading not required.)

Army Form C. 2118.

Place	Date	Hour	Summary of Events and Information	Remarks and references to Appendices
	JULY			
BRESLE.	29. 7.16.	7 am.	Under C.R.E. 3rd Division Orders (R.E. 158) Company marched via AMIENS - ALBERT Road to Camp in E. 9. a. 5. 0. - between ALBERT and DERNANCOURT.	G.
			Work on erection of Camp for Div. H.Q. (3rd Divn).	H.
DERNANCt.	30.	6 am. to 8 pm.	Work on D.H.Q. camp in E. 9. central.	
DERNANCOURT	31.	6 am.	Work on D.H.Q. Camp in E. 9. central.	
		5 pm.	March to bivouac near BELLE VUE FARM. ALBERT. (E. 5. d. central)	I

[signature]
Major R.E.
O.C. 208th Fd Coy. R.E.

Appendix A

SECRET
Ref. Sheet 62D
N.E., 1/20,000.

COPY NO... 9

The 102nd (TYNESIDE SCOTTISH) BRIGADE.
OPERATION ORDER NO.. 36.

1.. The following moves will take place on the night of JUNE 30th/JULY 1st, 1916. :-

2.. 2 Companies of the 22nd N.F. (3rd Tyneside Scottish) will move from the USNA/TARA Line to their position of assembly via PERTH AVENUE, to be clear of the USNA/TARA Line by 10:15 p.m.

2 Companies of the 23rd N.F. (4th Tyneside Scottish) will move from the USNA/TARA Line to their position of assembly via ST. ANDREWS AVENUE, to be clear of the USNA/TARA Line by 10:30 p.m.

The 208th Field Co. R.E. will move from the FIRWOOD to their position of assembly at 10:15 p.m. - to be clear of the USNA/TARA Line by 11 p.m.

3.. On completion of these moves - the whole of the 102nd (Tyneside Scottish) Brigade with the 102 Machine Gun Coy. and the 208th Field Coy. R.E. will then be in their respective positions of assembly.

4.. Battle Headquarters will be as under :-

Brigade Headquarters	W.29.b.5.1
20th N.F. (1st Tyneside Scottish)..	KEATS REDAN.
21st N.F. (2nd " ")..	Junction of KERRIMUIR STREET & MERCIER STREET.
22nd N.F. (3rd " ")..	- do -
23rd N.F. (4th " ")..	ST.MONANS STREET.
102 Machine Gun Coy	DALHOUSIE STREET.

5.. The O.C., 23rd N.F. (4th Tyneside Scottish) will police PERTH and ST.ANDREWS AVENUES, where these intersect the USNA/TARA Line - from 10 p.m. to 12 midnight JUNE 30th,1916, so as to prevent any block in the forward movement of troops. At 12 midnight the police will rejoin their unit.

6.. Units will report to Brigade Headquarters by telegraphing the word "TYNESIDE" when they are in their respective assembly positions.

7.. Acknowledge.

102 B.H.Q.
29:6:1916.
Issued at 11:30 p.m.

[signature] Major.
BRIGADE MAJOR.
102nd (TYNESIDE SCOTTISH) BRIGADE.

Copies to -
1 & 2 retained.
3 20th N.F. (1st T.S.)
4 21st " (2nd ")
5 22nd " (3rd ")
6 23rd " (4th ")
7.. 34th Division.
8.. 102 M.G. Coy.
9.. 208th Field Coy. R.E.
10.. 102 T.M. Battery.
11.. 101st Inf. Bde.
12.. 103rd Inf. Bde.

GOC 10 Inf Bde

1. Can we wait till reinf[?] ?
2. I'm instructed to remain with him, receive reports from Officers & then obtain his instructions to withdraw
3. Position fought.
4. Officers dugouts.
5. Bde HQ advanced.

C & D roads

Fetch maps.

advanced Bde. H.Q.

X.14 d 1.8

Appendix B

Secret

OC
208 ~~Field~~ Coy. 4/7/16

The following extracts from 34 Dw OO 21 are forwarded for information and necessary action

(1) All tents and tarpaulins now in use in the Long valley will be struck and stacked by the side of the MILLENCOURT–BOUZINCOURT Rd by 8.30 am tomorrow

(2) Units will march tomorrow as in attached march table (x)

3 Baggage wagons of all units will join the Divisional Train by 8 am ~~tomorrow~~ on the day following completion of the move.

4 Acknowledge

(x)

Unit.	Time	Route.	Destination
208 Field Coy RE	7.40 a.m.	via HENENCOURT.	BAIZIEUX.

10/30 pm.

[signature] Major
B M 102 Bde.

Appendix "G".

SECRET. R/903.

~~O.C. 207th Field Co.~~
O.C. 208th do.
~~O.C. 209th do.~~

OPERATION ORDER No.3.

1. The 207th, 208th and 209th Field Cos. will move immediately on receipt of this order to MILLENCOURT.

2. They will billet there for the night, and each Company should immediately send an officer ahead to the Town Major, MILLENCOURT, to make the necessary arrangements for billets.

3. The Companies may move off indepdndently of one another.

4. On arrival at MILLENCOURT, O.C.Cos. will immediately report their time of arrival by telegram to the C.R.E. 34th Division.

5. The estimated hour of arrival at MILLENCOURT as reported by the C.R.E. to Divisional Headquarters is 10.30 p.m. to-night.

6. Transport will move with Companies. Men will carry packs, but O.C.Cos. will make arrangements for leaving their packs at MILLENCOURT to-morrow. This should be done through the Town Major, who will allot storage space for them. Each Company should leave one man in charge of packs.

7. Instructions for to-morrow's move will be issued on receipt.

8. Acknowledge.

[signature]
Lieut.& Adjutant, R.E.
34th Division.

7-7-16.

"A" Form. Army Form C. 2121.

MESSAGES AND SIGNALS.

No. of Message

Prefix ...... Code ...... m.	Words	Charge	This message is on a/c of:	Recd. at ...... m.
Office of Origin and Service Instructions.		Sent	Appendix	Date
Secret		At ...... m.	W	From
		To	...... Service.	
		By	(Signature of "Franking Officer.")	By

TO O.C. 208 Field Company

*Sender's Number.	Day of Month	In reply to Number	AAA
R.E. B 24	7-7-16	—	

207	208	and	209	Field
Companies	will	march	tomorrow	8th
inst	so	as	to	reach
Camp	at	E 9 A	and	B
map	62 D N.E.	by	10	a.m.
aaa	route	to	be	taken
via	LAVIEVILLE —		D 17 a 1.1	—
E 7 c 1 9	and	DERNANCOURT		aaa
The	transport	of	each	Company
will	bivouac	at	E 14 a	aaa
Sufficient	shelter	can	be	taken
from	the	camp	at	E 9 A & B
for	the	mounted	sections	and
erection	at	E 14	aaa	the
number	of	shelter	taken	for
this	purpose	should	be	reported
at	once	to	the	CRE

From

Place

Time

The above may be forwarded as now corrected. (Z)

Censor. Signature of Addressor or person authorised to telegraph in his name.

* This line should be erased if not required

(4193) Wt. W1-042—1444. 500000 Pads. 12/15. Sir J. C. & S.

"A" Form. Army Form C. 2121.

MESSAGES AND SIGNALS.

No. of Message

Prefix ... Code ... m. | Words | Charge

Office of Origin and Service Instructions.

Sent
At ... m.
To
By

This message is on a/c of:
... *Service.*
(Signature of "Franking Officer.")

Recd. at ... m.
Date
From
By

TO 2

Sender's Number. | Day of Month | In reply to Number | AAA
*

aaa acknowledge

From C R E 7th Div

Place

Time

The above may be forwarded as now corrected.

Censor.

(Z) [illegible signature] Lt Capt RE 7th

Signature of Addressor or person authorised to telegraph in his name.

* This line should be erased if not required

(4198) Wt. W1.042—M44. 900000 Pads. 12/15. Sir J. C. & S.

Appendix E

"A" Form.

Army Form C. 2121

MESSAGES AND SIGNALS.

No. of Message

Prefix .... Code .... m. | Words | Charge

Office of Origin and Service Instructions.

Sent At .... m. To .... By ....

This message is on a/c of: .... *Service.*

(Signature of "Franking Officer.")

Recd. at .... m. Date .... From .... By ....

TO 208th Fld Co

Sender's Number.	Day of Month	In reply to Number	AAA
* RE B6	9-7-16	–	

Wire	from	DHQ	begins	aaa
All	RE	personnel	now	under
canvas	at	E.9	and	all
RE	transport	is	to	move
to	valley	E.14	this	afternoon
aaa	Canvas	now	in	use
may	be	retained	but	in
the	event	of	another	Brigade
coming	into	this	area	it
may	be	necessary	to	withdraw
a	large	portion	of	it
aaa	Watering	for	horses	at
E 20				

From CRE 34th

Place

Time 12/15 pm

[illegible signature]

The above may be forwarded as now corrected. (Z) [illegible signature] RE

Censor. Signature of Addressor or person authorised to telegraph in his name.

* This line should be erased if not required.

(4198) Wt. W14042—M44. 300000 Pads. 12/15. Sir J. C. & S.

APPENDIX F

S E C R E T.

C.R.E's OPERATION ORDER No. 21.

19-7-16.

1. The Division is to be relieved by the 1st Australian Division on the night 19th/20th.

2. Copies of the 34th Division Operation Order No.34 relating to this have been sent to all concerned.

3. Relief of the Field Companies, R.E. takes place to-night and they will move their camp to BRESLE to-morrow in accordance with attached March Table.

4. All other ranks employed in Tramway maintenance will remain at their present posts until relieved by the C.R.E. incoming Division. This will be arranged as early as possible. They will be rationed by O.C. Supplies, to whom lists and localities should immediately be sent.

5. Field Companies will at 8 a.m. 20th instant prior to leaving hand over 2 pontoon wagons with mules and drivers, and an N.C.O. in charge, to "D" Company, 2nd Labour Battalion.

The third pontoon wagon will be used for transporting canvas, &c. and on completion of this duty will be returned before night to "D" Company, 2nd Labour Battalion, with mules and drivers.

All pontoon and trestle wagon personnel and animals will be rationed by the "D" Company, 2nd Labour Battalion, and work under Chief Engineer IIIrd Corps.

Bridging material may also be left in charge of "D" Company.

6. Advance parties with cnavas should meet the Adjutant as shewn on March Table at 10 a.m.

7. Canvas now in possession of the Companies is all that is available for camping the three Companies, and will be arranged as follows:-

The 207th Field Co. will hand one small Tarpaulin Shelter and 4 tents to the O.C. 209th Field Co.

The 208th Field Co. will hand 6 small Tarpaulins and 3 tents to the 209th Field Co.

The O.C. 209th Field Co. will arrange to draw these from the 207th and 208th Field Companies at 7.30 a.m. to-morrow 20th instant.

For information it is noted that the capacity of tents and tarpaulins is laid down as follows by the Corps:-

Tent	=	16 men.
Tarpaulin Large	=	40 men.
do. Small	=	16 men. (!?)

[signature]

Lieut.& Adjutant, R.E.
34th Division.

Issued at 9.15 p.m.

To 207th Field Co.
208th do.
209th do.

MARCH TABLE.

Unit.	Route.	Destination.	Time of Arrival.	Remarks.
Advance Parties from each Company with 1 Pontoon Wagon per Company loaded with tents, Tarpaulin Shelters &c.	BOOMERANG Road and X. Road to D.17.a.11 along Main ALBERT Road to D.21.a.46 - then to BRESLE.	207th at D.9.c.31 208th at D.14.b.82 209th at D.15.b.39	10 a.m.	To meet Adjutant R.E.
207th Field Co. 9.30 a.m.	Via BOOMERANG and X. Road to D.17.a.11 thence along main AMIENS-ALBERT Road to D.21.a.46 then through BRESLE.	Pitch camp at D.9.c.31.		
208th Field Co. 10 a.m.	ditto.	Pitch camp at D.14.b.82.		
209th Field Co. 9.30 a.m.	E.5.a.48. - HOSPICE, Tram Base and MACMAHON BRIDGE, BOOMERANG and X. Road (picking up its transport as it passes), thence to D.17.a.11 along AMIENS-ALBERT Road to D.21.a.46 to BRESLE.(not to pass through ALBERT).	Pitch camp at D.15.b.39. with horse lines at D.9.d.22.		

"A" Form. Army Form C. 2121.

MESSAGES AND SIGNALS. No. of Message

Prefix .... Code .... m. | Words | Charge | This message is on a/c of: .... Service. | Recd. at .... m.

Office of Origin and Service Instructions. APPENDIX

Sent At .... m. To .... By ....

(Signature of "Franking Officer.")

Date .... From .... By ....

TO O.C. 208th Field Co.

Sender's Number.	Day of Month	In reply to Number	AAA
* R.E. 158	28-7-16	—	

Your company will move to DERNANCOURT to-morrow 29th inst at 7 a.m. aaa You will take with you all the tentage and shelters you brought to BRESLE extra transport will be provided of which you will receive details later. aaa Further details relating to route, locality &c will be sent to you later aaa Acknowledge

From CRE 34th

Place

Time 8-30 pm

The above may be forwarded as now corrected. (Z)

Censor. Signature of Addressor or person authorised to telegraph in his name. [illegible] Lt. & Adjt. R.E. 34th

* This line should be erased if not required.

(4198) Wt. W14042—M14. 300000 Pads. 12/15 Sir J. C. & S

APPENDIX H.

R/959

SECRET.

O.C. 208th Field Co.

1. With reference to my R.E.158 of this date, your destination to-morrow is E.9.a.5.0. between DERNANCOURT and ALBERT.

2. You will be prepared on arrival to start your sappers working at once.

3. The work to be carried out is the erection of a camp for Division H.Q. Plans and material will be handed to you on arrival on the ground.

4. You will send an officer in advance to the point E.9.a.5.0. to meet the C.R.E. at 10 a.m. sharp there.

5. Your Company should arrive on the ground not later than 10.30 a.m. and your sappers should be ready at once to startxwork.

6. The road you take from BRESLE to DERNANCOURT will be selected by yourself.

7. ACKNOWLEDGE.

J. Shepherd.
Lt.& Adjutant, R.E.

28-7-16.

34th Divisional Engineers

208th FIELD COMPANY R. E.

AUGUST 1 9 1 6::::::

34

Army Form C. 2118

Vol 8

Instructions regarding War Diaries and Intelligence Summaries are contained in F. S. Regs., Part II. and the Staff Manual respectively. Title Pages will be prepared in manuscript.

WAR DIARY

or

~~INTELLIGENCE SUMMARY~~

(Erase heading not required.)

Place	Date	Hour	Summary of Events and Information	Remarks and references to Appendices
			208TH FIELD COY. R.E.	
			AUGUST. 1916.	

1875 Wt. W593/826 1,000,000 4/15 J.B.C. & A. A.D.S.S./Forms/C. 2118.

Instructions regarding War Diaries and Intelligence Summaries are contained in F. S. Regs., Part II. and the Staff Manual respectively. Title Pages will be prepared in manuscript.

WAR DIARY
or
~~INTELLIGENCE SUMMARY~~
(Erase heading not required.)

Army Form C. 2118

Place	Date	Hour	Summary of Events and Information	Remarks and references to Appendices
BELLE VUE FARM.	AUG.		Work on W.H.Q. Camp near DERNANCOURT.	
ALBERT	1st to 5th		Extension of Tramway in MAMETZ WOOD.	
			Construction of Advanced Dressing Station in BOTTOM WOOD.	
			Repairs to Road N. of MAMETZ WOOD.	
			Repairing and Ballasting Tramway in MAMETZ WOOD.	
DITTO.	6th		Coy. Hdq. and Mounted Section complete remain at BELLE VUE FARM.	
		4 pm.	Dismounted Sections move to billets at N.W. end of MAMETZ WOOD.	B.
MAMETZ WOOD.	7th		Improvements to Shelters and Dugouts in MAMETZ WOOD.	
			Improvements to Brigade Hdq. Repairing, revetting and putting in firesteps in Trench at BAZENTIN LE PETIT WOOD.	
	8th 9th		Making Communication Trench from Brigade Hdq. at S.W. end of BAZENTIN LE PETIT WOOD along side of wood.	
			Wire entanglements along SOUTH end of BAZENTIN LE PETIT WOOD.	

1875 Wt. W593/826 1,000,000 4/15 J.B.C. & A. A.D.S.S./Forms/C. 2118.

Instructions regarding War Diaries and Intelligence Summaries are contained in F. S. Regs., Part II. and the Staff Manual respectively. Title Pages will be prepared in manuscript.

WAR DIARY
or
~~INTELLIGENCE SUMMARY~~
(Erase heading not required.)

Army Form C. 2118

Place	Date	Hour	Summary of Events and Information	Remarks and references to Appendices
	AUG.		Coy. Dug-Outs heavily shelled with HE and gas shells.	
			Dug-Outs and Trench ruined – 36 Casualties.	
MAMETZ WOOD.	9th	5pm	Dismounted Sections move to billets at FRICOURT.	
FRICOURT	10th		Strengthening and repairing dug-outs in Brigade Hdq. Trench.	
			Revetting and repairing Trench, and making fire-bays.	
	to		Wiring on SOUTH front of BAZENTIN LE PETIT WOOD practically completed.	
	14th.		Communication Trench from N.W. corner of BAZENTIN LE PETIT WOOD to N. end of BAZENTIN LE PETIT Village Sector completed.	
			Clearing breaches in Communication Trench W. of BAZENTIN LE PETIT WOOD.	
			Clearing damaged Communication Trench from Support Line near NORTH end of Village Sector to front line.	
DITTO.	14	7pm.	Dismounted Section rejoin Coy. Hdq. at BELLE VUE FARM, ALBERT.	
BELLE VUE FARM, ALBERT.	15.	6am.	Company march via MACMAHON BRIDGE, main ALBERT–AMIENS Road, to BRESLE – arriving 9. am.	C.

Army Form C. 2118

Instructions regarding War Diaries and Intelligence Summaries are contained in F. S. Regs., Part II. and the Staff Manual respectively. Title Pages will be prepared in manuscript.

WAR DIARY
or
~~INTELLIGENCE SUMMARY~~
(Erase heading not required.)

Place	Date	Hour	Summary of Events and Information	Remarks and references to Appendices
BRESLE	AUG. 16.		Coy. at rest – overhauling and repairing equipment, clothing, stores etc.	
"	17.		Mounted Section and Transport march to POULAINVILLE (near ABBÉVILLE) and remain there for night. Dismounted Sections remaining at rest in camp at BRESLE.	D.
"	18.		Mounted Section and Transport march from POULAINVILLE to HOCQUINCOURT, and there join Dismounted Sections at 8. 0 pm.	D.
"		3.30 am.	Dismounted Sections leave Camp at BRESLE: march via RIBEMONT to MÉRICOURT. Entrain at 6. am.	E. F.
"		11. am.	Arrive LONGPRÉ. March via HALLENCOURT to HOCQUINCOURT. Arriving 4 pm.	
HOCQUINCOURT	19.		Coy. resting in billets – Camp Fatigues.	
"	20.	1. pm.	Leave HOCQUINCOURT. March via GRANDSART and DUNCQ to Station at PONT RÉMY – arriving 2.40 pm. Entrain.	
		3.40 pm.	Leave PONT REMY, for BAILLEUL.	

1875 Wt. W593/826 1,000,000 4/15 J.B.C. & A. A.D.S.S./Forms/C. 2118.

Army Form C. 2118

Instructions regarding War Diaries and Intelligence Summaries are contained in F. S. Regs., Part II. and the Staff Manual respectively. Title Pages will be prepared in manuscript.

WAR DIARY
or
~~INTELLIGENCE SUMMARY~~
(Erase heading not required.)

Place	Date	Hour	Summary of Events and Information	Remarks and references to Appendices
	AUG.			
BAILLEUL	21.	2.0 am.	Arrive and detrain. March via DOULIEU to ESTAIRES, arriving 8.0 am.	
ESTAIRES.	22	3.0 pm.	March via CROIX DU BAC and ERQUINGHEM to RUE MARLE, ARMENTIÈRES – arriving 6.0 pm.	
RUE MARLE, ARMENTIÈRES	23		One Section engaged on Camp Fatigues, and work at Brigade Hdqrs., and at Soldiers' Club, RUE MARLE.	
	24		Three Sections engaged on following work –	
	25		Repairing and revetting, and clearing S.S. line between WINE AVENUE and HAYSTACK AVENUE. Repairing and clearing PARADISE ALLEY. Revetting, gridding and firestepping Wing Trench left of RUE DE BOIS, and Wing Trench to right of WILLOW AVENUE. Repairing S line to left of RUE DE BOIS. Finishing Reserve line to the rear of DEAD COW FARM. Repairing RUE DE BOIS between firing and S. LINE.	

1875 Wt. W593/826 1,000,000 4/15 J.B.C. & A. A.D.S.S./Forms/C. 2118.

Instructions regarding War Diaries and Intelligence Summaries are contained in F. S. Regs., Part II. and the Staff Manual respectively. Title pages will be prepared in manuscript.

WAR DIARY
or
~~INTELLIGENCE SUMMARY.~~
(Erase heading not required.)

Army Form C. 2118.

Place	Date	Hour	Summary of Events and Information	Remarks and references to Appendices
	AUG			
RUE MARLE,	26.		One Section engaged on Camp Fatigues, and work at Brigade Hdq., and at SOLDIERS' CLUB, RUE MARLE.	
ARMENTIÈRES	27.		Three Sections employed as follows –	
	28.		Repairing front line traverses and parapet left of BRICK STR.	
			Relaying Trench Boards in front line from LEITH WALK.	
			Draining LEITH WALK and PARADISE ALLEY.	
			Repairing parapet and traverses in PARADISE ALLEY.	
			Revetting and Repairing right and left flanks of SALIENT.	
			Repairing RUE DE BOIS, and wing trench to left of RUE DE BOIS.	
			Completing Reserve Line in rear of DEAD COW FARM.	
			Repairing WILLOW AVENUE	
			Repairing and relaying trench boards in LEITH WALK, COWGATE AVENUE and WELLINGTON AVENUE.	
	29		As for 26. 27. 28 August, and –	
Ditto			Draining and Sandbagging PARADISE ALLEY.	
	30		New Battalion Hdq. in Subsidiary Line, near entrance to WELLINGTON AV.	
			Draining and boarding SALIENT.	
	31.		Constructing parados, and draining Trench on L flank of SALIENT.	
			Clearing COURANT DE LA CHAPELLE	

J. H. Kyffin[?] Major R.E. O.C. 20th Field Coy R.E.

2353 Wt. W2544/1454 700,000 5/15 D. D. & L. A.D.S.S./Forms/C. 2118.

SECRET

B

OPERATION ORDER No.31.

5-8-16.

1. Following the relief of the 101st Brigade by the 112th Bde. the 208th Field Co. will relieve the 207th Field Co. on the night of the 6th/7th under arrangements made between the O.C. 207th and the O.C. 208th Field Cos.

2. The 208th Field Co. will come under the orders of the G.O.C. 112th Brigade on completion of the relief and will report to the G.O.C. 112th Brigade.

3. The 208th Field Co. will billet in the places vacated by the 207th Field Co. The 208th Co. transport will not be moved.

4. On relief the 207th Field Co. become the Company in reserve, and will work under the orders of the C.R.E. and will billet in the camp vacated by the 208th Field Co. who will leave all large tarpaulins, tents, small tarpaulins and bivouac shelters for use of the 207th Field Co.

5. The O.C. and all Company officers of each Company will immediately proceed to make themselves acquainted with the work being carried on by the other company, and arrange that all works in hand are continued without break.

6. The O.C. 207th Field Co. will report completion of the relief to the C.R.E.

7. The 208th Field Co. transport will remain as before at the disposal of the C.R.E.

8. The O.C. 207th Field Co. may use his discretion as to whether he moves his transport lines to his Company camp or not.

9. The N.C.O. I/c TRAM BASE dump, detailed by the O.C. 208th Field Co., will remain there.

10. ACKNOWLEDGE.

AFB

J. Shepherd

Lt.& Adjutant, R.E.

Issued at 8 p.m.

~~O.C. 207th Field Co.~~
O.C. 208th do.
~~O.C. 209th do.~~

C

OPERATION ORDER NO. 36 - 13th August 1916.

1. This Division is to be relieved by 1st Division. The relief commences on 14th instant and will be complete by 6 a.m. 16th inst.

2. Field Cos. R.E. will be relieved by Field Cos. of the 1st Division, who are sending advance parties on the 13th instant to start taking over.

3. The O.C's 208th and 209th Field Cos. will arrange to hand over all the work in their own Brigade Section to the incoming Field Cos. The O.C. 207th Field Co. will hand over all work in the Reserve Co's area to the O.C. 26th Field Co. including work on the Tram Line, Roads, &c.

4. R.E. material at BAZENTIN Dump and MAMETZ Divisional Dump is being handed over under Divisional arrangements. The MAMETZ R.E. Dump and FRICOURT R.E.Dump will be handed over by C.R.E. who will make arrangements for the relief of personnel of these dumps.

5. On relief Field Cos. will march to the Back Area in accordance with attached table "A".

6. Billetting parties should be sent ahead as follows:-

By 207th Field Co. Early on 14th to BRESLE.
Early on 15th to BEHENCOURT.

6 A.M. 15.8.16

By 208th Field Co. Early on 15th to BRESLE to take over billets from 207th Field Co.

NOTE Advance party

By 209th Field Co. Early on 14th to BRESLE and early on 15th to BEHENCOURT with one day's rations.

7. Supplies. Railhead for all services other than ammunition will be at FRECHENCOURT from 12-8-16 inclusive.
Refilling point will change from W.20. to C.23. on 16th inst. on which date the latter refilling point will be used.
All personnel rejoining their units from Dumps, Salvage Co. &c. will be rationed for the day following that on which they rejoin their units.

8. Tunnellers attached to 207th Field Co. will rejoin the Salvage Co. by 6 p.m. 15th inst. rationed for 16th instant.

9. Field Cos. will hand over to their relieving Field Cos. 1st Division all tents, tarpaulins and shelters in their possession, except those allowed by A.F. G.1098 for a Field Co. Receipts must be obtained and the same forwarded to C.R.E.

10. Completion of all reliefs will be reported to C.R.E.

11. Field Cos. will be prepared to move from the Corps Area as follows:-
Transport on 17th and 18th.
Dismounted Personnel by Tactical Train on 18th.

12. ACKNOWLEDGE.

AHB

[signature]
Lt.& Adjutant, R.E.

Issued at 1 p.m.

O.C. 207th Field Co.
O.C. 208th do.
O.C. 209th do.

M A R C H   T A B L E   "A".

Date.	Unit.	Move From	Move To	To be relieved by	Route.	Remarks.
14th	209th Field Co.	Present billets FRICOURT	Transport lines at Mill ALBERT.	A Field Co. 1st Divn.	As arranged by O.C. 209th Field Co.	To be carried out in small numbers not exceeding 1 section at a time, after 8 p.m.
14th	207th Field Co.	BELLE VUE FARM	BRESLE	C Field Co. 1st Divn.	BELLE VUE Farm - CEMETERY Mill (E.4.c.) - MACMAHON Bridge - main ALBERT-AMIENS Road.	To reach BRESLE by 9 a.m.
15th	208th Field Co.	Present billets FRICOURT	BRESLE	B Field Co. 1st Divn.	As above.	Sections at FRICOURT will move in small numbers not exceeding 1 section at a time, the first leaving FRICOURT at 3 a.m. The Coy. will assemble at its transport lines to move off with the transpor To reach BRESLE by 9 a.m. To take over billets at BRESLE vacated by 207th Field Co.
15th	207th Field Co.	BRESLE	BEHENCOURT	--	BAISIEUX	To reach BEHENCOURT by 9 a.m.
15th	209th Field Co.	Mill, ALBERT	BRESLE	--	MACMAHON Bridge. Main ALBERT-AMIENS Road.	To reach BRESLE by 9 a.m. To bivouac night at BRESLE.
16th	209th Field Co.	BRESLE	BEHENCOURT	--	BAISIEUX	To beach BEHENCOURT by 9 a.m.

East of a North and South line through ALBERT units to march by ~~platoons~~ *sections*, 200 yards distance to be maintained between ~~Platoons~~ *Sections*

West of the above line not less than 5 minutes interval to be left between Companies: 10 minutes interval between Battalions.

SECRET

D

OPERATION ORDERS NO. 38.

15-8-16.

1. The Division is moving from the BRESLE - LA HOUSSOYE - BEHENCOURT Area to Area 5 (round HALLENCOURT) by road and rail.

2. R.E. units will move as follows:-
   Riding Horses and Transport of all Companies by road on 17th and 18th.
   Dismounted Personnel R.E. by Tactical Trains on 18th.

3. Horses, Mounted Personnel, and Transport of Field Cos. will march under the orders of O.C. Divisional Train in groups.
   No.1 Group includes Horses and Transport &c. of 208th F.Co.
   No.2 Group do. do. do. do. of 207th F.Co.
   No.3 Group do. do. do. do. of 209th F.Co.
   Headquarter Group - includes H.Q., R.E.

   The 1st day's march has destinations as follows:-
   No.1 Group to POOLAINVILLE) Billets will be allotted
   No.2 Group to CARDONETTE) by O.C. Train.
   No.3 Group to ALLONVILLE)
   Second day's march - Destination of R.E. is HALLENCOURT - HOCQUINCOURT.

4. Dismounted R.E. personnel will entrain on the 18th instant:-
   No.1 Group at MERICOURT.
   No.2,3, and Headquarter Group at FRECHENCOURT.

   The ultimate destination of Field Cos. R.E. is HOCQUINCOURT.
   Times &c. to be notified later.

5. A Bus will leave Divisional Headquarters at 12 noon on 17th instant to convey billeting parties to the new area. O.C.Cos. will each arrange to send one N.C.O. and the O.C. 208th Field Co. will also detail one officer who will report to the C.R.E. for instructions prior to departure. Billeting parties should be at R.E. H.Q., BAISIEUX at 11 a.m. on 17th.

6. Instructions regarding the conveyance of heavy baggage will be issued later.

7. Subsequent to the arrival at Area 5 the Division is to be transferred by ~~rail~~ rail to the 2nd ANZAC Corps, 2nd Army.
   The entraining of the Division will commence, after 6 p.m. August 19th at PONT REMY and LONGPRE (W. of CONDE)
   No.1 and Div.H.Q. Groups entrain at PONT REMY.
   Nos. 2 & 3 Groups at LONGPRE.

8. R.E. H.Q. will close at BAISIEUX on 18th and open on same day at HALLENCOURT.

9. ACKNOWLEDGE.

[signature]

Lt.& Adjutant, R.E.
34th Division.

Issued at 4.45 p.m.

O.C. 207th Field Co.
O.C. 208th do.
O.C. 209th do.

E

SECRET. COPY NO. 10

101st BRIGADE OPERATION ORDER
NO. 50.

Ref. 1/40,000, 62D. 17.8.16.

---

1. No.9 Group, consisting of 101st Inf.Bde. and 208 Fd. Coy.R.E. will entrain tomorrow morning at MERICOURT Stn. in two Columns -
   Column "A" - Will proceed by train leaving at 6 am
   Column "B" - " " " 8 am
   Both Columns will detrain at LONGPRE Station where they will be met by guides from billeting parties.
   The journey is timed to take about four hours.

2. MARCH TO ENTRAINING STATION.

   Column "A" (in order of march):
   10th Lincolns
   11th Suffolks
   208 Fd.Coy.R.E.
   Starting Point: Junction of road, B.29.d.7.7.
   Route; Via cross roads S. of BRESLE (D.20.b)
   Head of column to pass starting point at 3.30 a.m
   208 Fd.Coy.R.E. will join column at cross roads S. of BRESLE (D.20.b)

   Column "B" (in order of march):
   15th R.Scots
   16th R.Scots
   Brigade H.Q.
   101 M.Gun Coy.
   101 T.M.Battery.
   Starting Point: Junction of road, B.29.d.7.7.
   Route: Via cross roads S.of BRESLE (D.20.b)
   Head of column to pass starting point at 5.30 a.m

   An interval of 20 yards will be maintained between units.

3. ENTRAINING OFFICERS.

   Units will send a representative to report to R.T.O. MERICOURT Station as follows :-
   Units of Column "A" - 4.45 a.m
   Units of Column "B" - 6.45 a.m.

4. BAGGAGE.

   Baggage will go by lorry and will be handed over at Brigade H.Q. -

   Units of Column "A" - 2.30 a.m
   Units of Column "B" - 4.30 a.m.

5. ACKNOWLEDGE. ✓ ARB

E.A. Boone(?)
Major,
Brigade Major,
101st Infantry Brigade.

Issued at 9.45 p.m.

Copies to -

1 & 2 retained
3 16 R.Scots
6 11 Suffolks
7 101 M.Gun Coy.
8 101 T.M.Batty.
9 34th Div.
10 208 Fd.Coy.R.E.

F

O.O.39.

~~O.C. 207th Field Co.~~
O.C. 208th do.
~~O.C. 209th do.~~

Herewith instructions for entrainment to-morrow, 18th instant, which I think, taken in conjunction with instructions already issued ~~tax~~ to you, explain themselves.

The area in which your Company will billet is HOCQUINCOURT.

Please acknowledge.
According to attached orders you will receive order as to exact time of train departure from G.O.C. Brigade Group.

J.Shepherd.
Lt.& Adjutant, R.E.

17-8-16.

COPY.
SECRET.

Copy No.11.

TO BE ACKNOWLEDGED BY WIRE.

34th DIVISION OPERATION ORDER NO.47.

Reference:
Map AMIENS 17, &
Sheet 3 Administrative
Map.

17-8-16.

1. In continuation of para. 3 of Addendum No.1 to this Division Operation Order No.45, Brigade Groups will entrain on the 18th inst., under orders to be issued by the G.Os.C. Brigade Groups in accordance with the attached Entrainment Table. The Camp Commandant, Divisional Headquarters, will issue orders for No. 4 (Headquarters) Group Details.

2. Routes:
   (a) To entraining Stations.
   No.1 Group ..... BAISIEUX - BEHENCOURT.

   No.2 Group ..... All available routes.

   No.3 Group ..... Direct from LA HOUSSOYE and BEHENCOURT.

   (9th Bn. North Staffordshire Regt. to proceed via BAISIEUX and BEHENCOURT).

   No.4 Group ..... BEHENCOURT.

   (b) From Detraining Stations Groups may use all available Roads.

3. Units will arrive at the Entrainment Station 45 minutes before the advertised hour of departure of their trains and they will send a representative to report to the R.T.O. half-an-hour before they are timed to arrive at the Station.

4. The journey is timed to take about 4 hours.

5. O.C. Groups will arrange that units are met at the Detraining Station by one of the billeting party, who will guide them to their billets.

6. Stokes Mortars will be dumped under a guard at the Detraining Station.

sd/.........Major,
for Lt.Col.G.S.
34th Division.

Issued at 7 p.m.

34th DIVISION ENTRAINMENT TABLE.

18th August, 1916.

No.	Train. Description.	Accommodation.	Station of departure.	Hour of departure.	Station of arrival.	Unit to entrain.	Billeting Area.	Remarks.
1	Tactical	2,000 men	MERICOURT	6 a.m.	LØNGPRE	(No.2 (101st Bde) (Group less 102nd (Fd.Amb. less 207 (Fd.Coy.R.E. plus (208th Fd.Coy.R.E.	"A"	R.E. Coy. to billet HOCQUINCOURT.
2	Goods	50 trucks to take 2,150 men.	MERICOURT	8 a.m.	LONGPRE			
3	Goods	ditto	FRECKENCOURT	10 a.m.	ARAINES	(No.1 Group (111th (Bde) less 104th Fd (Amb. less 2 Coys. (9th N.Staffs, less (208th Fd.Coy.R.E. (plus 207th Fd.Coy. (R.E.	"C"	9th N.Staffs billet HALLENCOURT. R.E.Coy. HOCQUINCOURT.
4	Goods	ditto	ditto	12 noon	ARAINES			
5	Tactical	2,000 men	ditto	3 p.m.	LONGPRE	(No.3 (112th Bde) (Group plus 102nd (and 104th Fd.Ambs (& 2 Coys 9th N. (Staffs & 100 * (Divisional Hd. (Qrs. details.	"B"	102nd Fd.Amb. billet Area "A". 104th Fd.Amb. billet Area "C". 9th N.Staffords billet HALLENCOURT. Field Coy.R.E. billet HOCQUINCOURT. *These to proceed by 5-0 p.m. train.
6	Goods	50 trucks to take 2,150 men.	ditto	5 p.m.	ditto			

To accompany 34th Division Operation No.47.

Instructions regarding War Diaries and Intelligence Summaries are contained in F. S. Regs., Part II. and the Staff Manual respectively. Title pages will be prepared in manuscript.

WAR DIARY
~~or~~
~~INTELLIGENCE SUMMARY.~~
(Erase heading not required.)

Army Form C. 2118.

Vol 9

Place	Date	Hour	Summary of Events and Information	Remarks and references to Appendices
ORIGINAL			208th — Field Company R.E. — September 1916.	
			Volume 9.	

T2131. Wt. W708—776. 500000. 4/15. Sir J. C. & S.

Instructions regarding War Diaries and Intelligence Summaries are contained in F. S. Regs., Part II. and the Staff Manual respectively. Title pages will be prepared in manuscript.

WAR DIARY
or
INTELLIGENCE SUMMARY.
(Erase heading not required.)

Army Form C. 2118.

Place	Date	Hour	Summary of Events and Information	Remarks and references to Appendices
Rue Marle Armentieres	Sept 13th 16 – [illegible]		Company in billets at Rue Marle.	
			Work on trenches as under:-	
			Repairing Rue-de-Bois between firing and S line.	
			Revetting and clearing Paradise Alley from Wine Avenue, and repairing traverses and dug-outs.	
			Repairing front line traverses and parapet left of Brick Street.	
			Relaying trench boards in front line from Leith Walk to Lille Road.	
			Revetting and repairing trenches on right and left flanks of Salient; relaying duck walks and building parados to trench on flank of Salient.	
			Repairing parapet near top of Cowgate Avenue.	
			Repairing front line near Willow Avenue.	
			Revetting, boarding and putting fire steps to new trench left of Willow Avenue.	
			Repairing front line trench left of Brick Street.	
			Repairing breaches in parapet of Salient.	

Instructions regarding War Diaries and Intelligence Summaries are contained in F. S. Regs., Part II. and the Staff Manual respectively. Title pages will be prepared in manuscript.

WAR DIARY
or
INTELLIGENCE SUMMARY.
(Erase heading not required.)

Army Form C. 2118.

Place	Date	Hour	Summary of Events and Information	Remarks and references to Appendices
Rue Marle	Sept 1st/4th		Repairing, revetting and clearing S.S. line between Wine Avenue, and Haystock Avenue.	
			Revetting, gridding and fire-stepping wing trench and Support Trench left of Rue-de-Bois, and wing trench to left of Willow Avenue.	
			Repairing S. line to the left of Rue-de-Bois.	
			Finishing Reserve line to the rear of Dead Cow Farm.	
			Repairing, revetting and boarding Rue-de-Bois, and wing trench to left of Rue-de-Bois.	
			Excavating for new Dug-outs for Battalion H.Q. in Subsidiary line, near Wellington Avenue.	
			Repairing parapet in S. line, left of Brick Street.	
			Repairing Willow Avenue.	
			Relaying and relaying trench boards, and draining, in Leith Walk and Wellington Avenue.	
			Revetting and boarding parts of Leith Walk and Wellington Avenue, and repairing trench walks.	

T2134. Wt. W708—776. 500000. 4/15. Sir J. C. & S.

Instructions regarding War Diaries and Intelligence Summaries are contained in F. S. Regs., Part II. and the Staff Manual respectively. Title pages will be prepared in manuscript.

WAR DIARY
or
INTELLIGENCE SUMMARY.
(Erase heading not required.)

Army Form C. 2118.

Place	Date	Hour	Summary of Events and Information	Remarks and references to Appendices
Rue Marle	Sept 1st–4th		Repairing trench boards and drainage in Cowgate Avenue and Wine Avenue.	
			Draining Leith Walk, Paradise Alley, Wellington Avenue, Cowgate Avenue, Wine Avenue etc.,	
			Draining Suffolk line left of Partick Street.	
			Clearing Coureau-de-la Chapelle.	
do.	Sept 5th–14th		Repairing front line traverses and parapet left of Partick Street.	
			Repairing, boarding and [illegible] left of Willow Avenue.	
			Revetting [illegible] parapet of Salient.	
			[illegible] and repairing [illegible] on right and left flanks of Salient [illegible] duckwalks and building parados [illegible] Salient.	
			Repairing [illegible] top of Cowgate Avenue.	
			Repairing and clearing Paradise Alley from Wine Avenue, and repairing	

Instructions regarding War Diaries and Intelligence Summaries are contained in F. S. Regs., Part II. and the Staff Manual respectively. Title pages will be prepared in manuscript.

WAR DIARY
or
INTELLIGENCE SUMMARY.
(Erase heading not required.)

Army Form C. 2118.

Place	Date	Hour	Summary of Events and Information	Remarks and references to Appendices
Rue Marle	Sept 8th-14th		Traverses and dug-outs.	
			Repairing Rue de-Bois between firing and S. line.	
			Relaying trench boards in Front line from Leith Walk to Lille Road.	
			Revetting and repairing Front line trench left of Brick Street.	
			Constructing Dug-Outs at Lille Post	
			Revetting and boarding Park Row.	
			Laying trench walks in Reserve trench in rear of Dead Cow Farm	
			Excavating for new dug-outs for Battalion Headquarters in Subsidiary line, near Wellington Avenue.	
			Repairing, revetting and clearing S.S. line between Wine Avenue.	
			Repairing S. line to left of Rue-de-Bois.	
			Draining between Leith Walk and Brick Street.	
			Clearing site for Dug-Outs at Willow Avenue.	
			Revetting and repairing Wellington Avenue.	
			Revetting and draining Avondale Avenue.	
			Repairing and revetting Leith Walk, and sandbagging same.	

T2134. Wt. W708—776. 500000. 4/15. Sir J. C. & S.

Instructions regarding War Diaries and Intelligence Summaries are contained in F. S. Regs., Part II. and the Staff Manual respectively. Title pages will be prepared in manuscript.

WAR DIARY
or
INTELLIGENCE SUMMARY.
(Erase heading not required.)

Army Form C. 2118.

Place	Date	Hour	Summary of Events and Information	Remarks and references to Appendices
Rue Marle	Sept 8th-11th		Levelling and repairing trench walks in Wellington Avenue.	
			Repairing, revetting, and laying duck-walks in Willow Avenue.	
			Repairing and laying trench walks in Park Row.	
			Repairing trench walks and drainage in Wine Avenue and Cowgate Avenue.	
			Rebuilding between [illegible] line and Miners Lane.	
			Draining Paradise Alley, Wellington Avenue, Leith Walk, Wine Avenue, Cowgate Avenue etc..	
			Clearing Coureau-de-la-Chappelle.	
			Draining Chards Farm and Salop Avenue.	
do.	11th-22		Excavating, pumping out and concreting dug outs in Front Line.	
			Renewing duck boards, repairing and draining in Wine Avenue.	
			Repairing and revetting broken parapet in Chards Farm Salient.	
			Repairing and laying trench walks in Rue-de-Bois and support trench left of same.	

T2134. Wt. W708—776. 500000. 4/15. Sir J. C. & S.

Instructions regarding War Diaries and Intelligence Summaries are contained in F. S. Regs., Part II. and the Staff Manual respectively. Title pages will be prepared in manuscript.

WAR DIARY
or
INTELLIGENCE SUMMARY.
(Erase heading not required.)

Army Form C. 2118.

Place	Date	Hour	Summary of Events and Information	Remarks and references to Appendices
Rue Marle	Sept 18th-22nd		Boarding and repairing Willow Avenue.	
			Repairing traverses and parapet in Front Line.	
			Revetting and repairing trenches on right and left flanks of Salient, refixing duck-walks and building up parados.	
			Relaying trench boards in Front Line from Leith Walk to Lille Rd.	
			Revetting and draining Avondale Avenue.	
			Constructing Dug-Outs at Lille Post.	
			Repairing top of Leith Walk in rear of Front Line.	
			Clearing site for Dug-outs at Willow Avenue.	
			Repairing and revetting Wellington Avenue.	
			Laying duck-boards and putting fire-step in Orchard Trench.	
			Revetting and repairing in Park Row.	
			Repairing, revetting, and laying duck-walks in Willow Avenue.	
			Revetting and repairing trench walks in Wellington Avenue.	
			Repairing and revetting Leith Walk.	
			Making new trench and revetting Miners Lane.	

T2134. Wt. W708—776. 500000. 4/15. Sir J. C. & S.

Army Form C. 2118.

WAR DIARY
or
INTELLIGENCE SUMMARY.
(*Erase heading not required.*)

Instructions regarding War Diaries and Intelligence Summaries are contained in F. S. Regs., Part II. and the Staff Manual respectively. Title pages will be prepared in manuscript.

Place	Date	Hour	Summary of Events and Information	Remarks and references to Appendices
Rue Marle	Sept 15th – 22nd		Repairing and laying trench walks in Park Row.	
			Repairing trench boards and drainage in Wine Avenue and Cowgate Avenue.	
			Draining Paradise Alley, Wellington Avenue, Leith Walk, Wine Avenue, Cowgate Avenue, Willow Avenue etc.	
			Clearing and widening Coureau-de-la-Chapelle.	
			Draining Chards Farm and Salop Avenue.	
Rue Marle	Sept	25th	1 Section moved into billets at ERQUINGHEM, for work under le S. to.	
	Sept 23rd – 30th		Excavating, pumping out and concreting dug-outs in Front-Line and Salient.	
			Repairing and revetting damages in Salient, and in trenches on the right and left of same, repairing duck walks and building up parados.	
			Repairing and revetting trench parapet in Chards Farm Salient.	

T2134. Wt. W708—776. 500000. 4/15. Sir J. C. & S.

Instructions regarding War Diaries and Intelligence Summaries are contained in F. S. Regs., Part II. and the Staff Manual respectively. Title pages will be prepared in manuscript.

WAR DIARY
or
INTELLIGENCE SUMMARY.
(Erase heading not required.)

Army Form C. 2118.

Place	Date	Hour	Summary of Events and Information	Remarks and references to Appendices
Rue Marle	Sept 23rd - 30th.		Repairing traverses and parapet, and relaying trench walks in Front Line.	
			Renewing duck-boards, repairing and draining in Wine Avenue.	
			Constructing Dug-Outs at Lille Post.	
			Revetting, draining, and building up in Avondale Avenue.	
			Revetting and sandbagging top of Keith Walk, and filling in.	
			Reconstructing bridge traverse near Leith Walk.	
			Sandbagging Officers Dug-Out in S. Line by Willow Avenue.	
			Repairing trench near Knightsbridge, and relaying duck-walks in same.	
			Revetting & repairing Wellington Avenue.	
			Laying duck-boards and revetting in Orchard Trench.	
			Lining C.O's Dug-Out, S.C.O.Q. near Wellington Avenue.	
			Repairing damages in Paradise Alley.	
			Revetting and repairing in Park Row.	
			Renewing duck-boards, repairing and draining in Wine Avenue.	

Army Form C. 2118.

Instructions regarding War Diaries and Intelligence Summaries are contained in F. S. Regs., Part II. and the Staff Manual respectively. Title pages will be prepared in manuscript.

WAR DIARY
or
INTELLIGENCE SUMMARY.
(Erase heading not required.)

Place	Date	Hour	Summary of Events and Information	Remarks and references to Appendices
Rue Marie	Sept 23rd–30th		Repairing and revetting Willow Avenue.	
			Reduting and repairing trench walks in Wellington Avenue.	
			Revetting and draining Avondale Avenue.	
			Making new trench and revetting Miners Lane.	
			Repairing and revetting in Leith Walk.	
			Draining Wellington Avenue, Wine Avenue, Leith Walk, Willow Avenue, Paradise Alley, and Cowgate Avenue.	
			Clearing and widening Coureau-de-la-Chapelle.	

208TH FIELD CO. R. E.

[signature] Major R.E.
O.C. 208th Field Coy. R.E.

T2134. Wt. W708—776. 500000. 4/15. Sir J. C. & S.

Instructions regarding War Diaries and Intelligence Summaries are contained in F. S. Regs., Part II. and the Staff Manual respectively. Title pages will be prepared in manuscript.

WAR DIARY

~~or~~

~~INTELLIGENCE SUMMARY.~~

(Erase heading not required.)

Army Form C. 2118.

Vol 10

Place	Date	Hour	Summary of Events and Information	Remarks and references to Appendices
			208th FIELD Company R.E. October 1916. VOLUME 10.	

T2134. Wt. W708—776. 500000. 4/15. Sir J. C. & S.

Instructions regarding War Diaries and Intelligence Summaries are contained in F. S. Regs., Part II, and the Staff Manual respectively. Title pages will be prepared in manuscript.

WAR DIARY
or
INTELLIGENCE SUMMARY.
(Erase heading not required.)

Army Form C. 2118.

Place	Date	Hour	Summary of Events and Information	Remarks and references to Appendices
Rue Marle Armentières	Oct. 1st–6th		3 sections working in trenches. No. 3 section working under C.R.E. Mounted sections billeting at Croix-du-Bac. Excavating, framing out, covering and roofing dug-outs in front line and salient; strengthening existing dug outs. Repairing and revetting broken parapet, Chords Farm salient; clearing [illegible] Repairing and revetting damages in Salient, and in trenches on right and left, relaying duck walks and building up parados. Revetting traverses and parapet and relaying trench-walks in front line. Removing duck boards, repairing and draining in [illegible] Avenue. Repairing [illegible] trench Rue-de-Bois. Constructing Dug-Outs at [illegible] Post. Levelling, draining, building up in Avondale Avenue. Constructing, repairing, and strengthening Officers' Dug out in Hollow	

T2134. Wt. W708–776. 500000. 4/15. Sir J. C. & S.

Instructions regarding War Diaries and Intelligence Summaries are contained in F. S. Regs., Part II. and the Staff Manual respectively. Title pages will be prepared in manuscript.

WAR DIARY
or
INTELLIGENCE SUMMARY.
(Erase heading not required.)

Army Form C. 2118.

Place	Date	Hour	Summary of Events and Information	Remarks and references to Appendices
Rue Marle	Oct		Avenue, Park Row, and Land Point.	
Armentières	1st-6th		Repairing and duck walking trench in Knightsbridge	
			Revetting and sand-bagging side of Leith Walk and filling in.	
			Reconstructing bridge traverse near Leith Walk.	
			Laying duck boards and revetting in Orchard trench.	
			Repairing damages in Paradise Alley	
			Revetting and repairing in Park Row.	
			Laying duck boards and revetting Orchard trench and clearing away damage	
			Revetting and repairing trench walks in Wellington Avenue	
			Repairing and revetting Willow Avenue.	
			Renewing duck boards, repairing and draining in Wine Avenue.	
			Revetting and drainage Avondale Avenue.	
			Repairing and revetting in Leith Walk.	
			Revetting and making new trench in Miners' Lane	
			Draining Wellington Avenue, Leith Walk, Wine Avenue, Lovers Walk,	

T2134. Wt. W708—776. 500000. 4/15. Sir J. C. & S.

Instructions regarding War Diaries and Intelligence Summaries are contained in F. S. Regs., Part II. and the Staff Manual respectively. Title pages will be prepared in manuscript.

WAR DIARY
or
INTELLIGENCE SUMMARY.
(Erase heading not required.)

Army Form C. 2118.

Place	Date	Hour	Summary of Events and Information	Remarks and references to Appendices
Rue Marle Armentières	Oct 1st-6th 7th-12th		Willow Avenue, and Cowgate Avenue. Clearing and widening Corean and Rue-de-Bois. Renewing and refixing dug-outs in Front Line and Salient, strengthening existing dug-outs. Relaying and revetting broken parapet and traverse Chards Farm Salient, clearing drainage. Repairing fire bays, and revetting in trenches right and left of Salient; refixing duck-walks and building parados. Putting in "A" Frames, repairing traverses and parapet in Front line; relaying trench-walks. Repairing wing trench Rue-de-Bois. Sandbagging, strengthening and repairing Dug-outs in Willow Avenue, Park Row and Lanel Point. Constructing Dug outs at Lille Post Levelling and sandbagging top of Leith Walk. Reconstructing bridge traverse near Leith Walk.	

T2134. Wt. W708—776. 500000. 4/15. Sir J. C. & S.

Instructions regarding War Diaries and Intelligence Summaries are contained in F. S. Regs., Part II. and the Staff Manual respectively. Title pages will be prepared in manuscript.

WAR DIARY
or
INTELLIGENCE SUMMARY.
(Erase heading not required.)

Army Form C. 2118.

Place	Date	Hour	Summary of Events and Information	Remarks and references to Appendices
Rue MARLE Armentières	Oct 6th-13th		Repairing and draining in Willow Avenue.	
			Laying duck-boards and revetting Orchard trench.	
			Repairing Aid Post roof.	
			Building new fire bay Right of Miners Road.	
			Clearing, revetting and repairing Park Row.	
			Repairing Wing trench Rue-de-Bois.	
			Rebuilding damaged traverse between Brick St and Cowgate.	
			Constructing drying-room at Chapelle-d-Armentiers.	
			Revetting and repairing trench walks in Wellington Avenue.	
			Repairing and revetting Willow Avenue.	
			Repairing duck-boards, repairing and draining in Wine Avenue.	
			Revetting and making new trench in Miner's Lane, revetting in Miners Road.	
			Repairing and revetting in Avondale Avenue, and Leith Walk.	
			Repairing Trenchwalks, and forming fire-bay in Salop Avenue.	
			Draining Wellington Avenue, Leith Walk, Wine Avenue, Miners Walk,	

T2134. Wt. W708—776. 500000. 4/15. Sir J. C. & S.

Army Form C. 2118.

Instructions regarding War Diaries and Intelligence Summaries are contained in F. S. Regs., Part II. and the Staff Manual respectively. Title pages will be prepared in manuscript.

WAR DIARY
or
INTELLIGENCE SUMMARY.
(Erase heading not required.)

Place	Date	Hour	Summary of Events and Information	Remarks and references to Appendices
Rue Marle Armentières	Oct 6th-13th		Willow Avenue, Cowgate Avenue.	
			Clearing ditch Nunnery Lane.	
			Clearing Rue-de-Bois.	
	14th-20th		Concreting and roofing dug-outs in front-line and Salient, strengthening existing dug-outs.	
			Putting in A frames, repairing traverses and parapet in front line, relaying trench walks.	
			Repairing fire bays and revetting in trenches right and left of Salient; refixing duck walks and building parados.	
			Repairing and strengthening listening post.	
			Sandbagging, strengthening and repairing Dug-outs in Willow Avenue, Park Row, and Sand Point.	
			Constructing new dug-outs in Switch-line, and in 1st Supports	
			Constructing Dug-outs at Lille Post.	
			Laying duck-boards and revetting Orchard trench.	
			Repairing and strengthening Aid Post roof.	

T2134. Wt. W708—776. 500000. 4/15. Sir J. C. & S.

Instructions regarding War Diaries and Intelligence Summaries are contained in F. S. Regs., Part II. and the Staff Manual respectively. Title pages will be prepared in manuscript.

WAR DIARY
or
INTELLIGENCE SUMMARY.
(Erase heading not required.)

Army Form C. 2118.

Place	Date	Hour	Summary of Events and Information	Remarks and references to Appendices
Rue Marle Armentières	Oct 14th–20th		Repairing and revetting in Willow Avenue. Building new fire bay and repairing Right of Miners Road. Rebuilding damaged traverse right of Brick Street. Repairing and relaying duck walks in Queen Street. Repairing Reserve line by Dead Cow Farm. Constructing drying room at Chapelle-d'-Armentières. Constructing store room for boots in 's line. Revetting and repairing french walks in Wellington Avenue. Repairing and Revetting Willow Avenue. Repairing, relaying duck walks and draining in Wine Avenue. Revetting and making new trench in Miners Lane, revetting in Miners Road. Repairing and revetting in Avondale Avenue and Leith Walk. Draining Wellington Avenues, Leith Walk, Wine Avenue, Miners Walk, Willow Avenue, Cowgate avenue. etc. Clearing ditch Nunnery Lane.	

Instructions regarding War Diaries and Intelligence Summaries are contained in F. S. Regs., Part II. and the Staff Manual respectively. Title pages will be prepared in manuscript.

WAR DIARY
or
INTELLIGENCE SUMMARY.
(Erase heading not required.)

Army Form C. 2118.

Place	Date	Hour	Summary of Events and Information	Remarks and references to Appendices
Rue Marle Armentières	Oct 11th-20th 21st-31st		Making new drains by Rue-de-Bois and draining ditches near Rue-de-Bois road. Concreting and roofing Dug-Outs in Front-line, left and right of Plank and Willow Avenues. Putting in "A" Frames, repairing traverses and parapet in Front line, relaying trench walks. Repairing fire bays and revetting in trenches right and left of Salient, repairing duck-walks and building parados. Repairing and strengthening listening post, and building new fire bay near by. Work on construction of New Coy Headquarters in Front line. Repairing damaged traverse and drainage in Chards Farm salient. Constructing new cupola dug-outs in Switch-line and 1st Supports. Sandbagging, strengthening and repairing Dug-Outs in Willow Avenue, Park Row, and Lanel Point. Constructing dug-outs at Lille Post.	

Instructions regarding War Diaries and Intelligence Summaries are contained in F. S. Regs., Part II. and the Staff Manual respectively. Title pages will be prepared in manuscript.

WAR DIARY
or
INTELLIGENCE SUMMARY.
(Erase heading not required.)

Army Form C. 2118.

Place	Date	Hour	Summary of Events and Information	Remarks and references to Appendices
Rue Marle Armentières	Oct 21st-31st		Revetting, relaying duck-boards and draining in Orchard trenches.	
			Repairing and strengthening Aid Post roof.	
			Building new fire bay and repairing at Juncture of Miners Road and Front line.	
			Repairing, draining and relaying duck-walks in Queens Street.	
			Making and rebuilding Parados left of Brick Street, also new fire bay and traverse. Rebuilding damaged traverse right of Brick St.	
			Repairing reserve line by Dead Cow Farm.	
			Constructing drying room at Chapelle-d'-Armentiers.	
			Constructing store room for books in Support line.	
			Repairing Signals Dug Out in Reserve line.	
			Draining and clearing trench from Lille Post to Support line.	
			Revetting near by Battalion Headquarters in Rue-de-Bois.	
			Working on Coy. Headqrs in Close Supports.	
			Relaying duck-walks and repairing sides of trench in Paradise Alley.	

T2134. Wt. W708—776. 500000. 4/15. Sir J. C. & S.

Instructions regarding War Diaries and Intelligence Summaries are contained in F. S. Regs., Part II. and the Staff Manual respectively. Title pages will be prepared in manuscript.

WAR DIARY
or
INTELLIGENCE SUMMARY.
(Erase heading not required.)

Army Form C. 2118.

Place	Date	Hour	Summary of Events and Information	Remarks and references to Appendices
Rue Marle Armentières	Oct. 21st-31st		Constructing concrete floor to pump at Burnt Farm.	
			Building new traverse left of Leith Walk.	
			Levelling and repairing trench walks in Wellington Av.	
			Repairing and levelling Willow Avenue.	
			Relaying duck-walks and draining in Wine Avenue.	
			Repairing, relaying duck walks and draining in Salop Avenue.	
			Constructing new loophole for M. G. emplacement in front line by Park Row	
			Draining Wellington Avenue, Willow Avenue, Orchard Trench, Wine Avenue, Miners Road, Cowgate Avenue etc.	
			J. Stephens Major R.E. O.C. 208th Field Coy R.E.	

T2134. Wt. W708—776. 500000. 4/15. Sir J. C. & S.

Instructions regarding War Diaries and Intelligence Summaries are contained in F. S. Regs., Part II. and the Staff Manual respectively. Title pages will be prepared in manuscript.

WAR DIARY

or

~~INTELLIGENCE SUMMARY.~~

(Erase heading not required.)

Army Form C. 2118.

Vol XI

Place	Date	Hour	Summary of Events and Information	Remarks and references to Appendices
			208th Field Company R.E. November 1916. Vol 1	

T2134. Wt. W708—776. 500000. 4/15. Sir J. C. & S.

1

Instructions regarding War Diaries and Intelligence Summaries are contained in F. S. Regs., Part II. and the Staff Manual respectively. Title pages will be prepared in manuscript.

WAR DIARY
~~or~~
~~INTELLIGENCE~~ SUMMARY.
(Erase heading not required.)

Army Form C. 2118.

Place	Date	Hour	Summary of Events and Information	Remarks and references to Appendices
Rue Marle Armentieres	Nov. 1st/10th		No's 1, 2 + 4 Sections working in trenches.	
			No 3 Section working under instructions from C.R.E.	
			Transport lines at Croix-du-Bac.	
			Work in Front Line & Breastworks:-	
			Concreting and roofing Dug-Outs in Front Line, left and right of Wine and Willow Avenues.	
			Construction of New Company Headquarters in Front Line, by Willow Avenue.	
			Constructing new concrete dug-out in the Salient.	
			Revetting Front Line by Willow Avenue dug-out.	
			Revetting fire-bay in T. Head Sap.	
			Repairing revetments and damage done in front trench of Chards Farm Salient.	
			Repairing fire bays and revetting in trenches right and left of Salient; relaying duck-walks and building parados.	

T2131. Wt. W708—776. 500000. 4/15. Sir J. C. & S.

Instructions regarding War Diaries and Intelligence Summaries are contained in F. S. Regs., Part II. and the Staff Manual respectively. Title pages will be prepared in manuscript.

WAR DIARY
~~or~~
~~INTELLIGENCE SUMMARY.~~
(Erase heading not required.)

Army Form C. 2118.

Place	Date	Hour	Summary of Events and Information	Remarks and references to Appendices
Rue Marle Armentieres	1 Nov. 1st/10th		Putting in "A" frames, repairing traverses and parapet in Front Line, relaying trench walks.	
			Constructing new drain right of Salient.	
			Revetting around dug-outs in Front Line.	
			Work on Support and Reserve Breastworks:-	
			Constructing new Cupola dug-outs in Switch-Line, and in 1st Supports.	
			Draining and repairing Leith Walk.	
			Construction of concrete dug-outs at Lille Post.	
			Repairing and building new roofs to C.O's and R.A. signal dug-outs in Reserve Line.	
			Draining, revetting and repairing in Switch-Line.	
			Revetting, relaying trench-walks, draining and clearing Miners Lane.	
			Repairs by Knightsbridge.	
			Revetting + repairing entrance to Adjutant's Dug-Out, Rue-de-Bois.	
			Clearing and revetting right of Dead Cow Farm.	

3

Instructions regarding War Diaries and Intelligence Summaries are contained in F. S. Regs., Part II. and the Staff Manual respectively. Title pages will be prepared in manuscript.

WAR DIARY

~~or~~

~~INTELLIGENCE SUMMARY.~~

(Erase heading not required.)

Army Form C. 2118.

Place	Date	Hour	Summary of Events and Information	Remarks and references to Appendices
Rue Marle	Nov		Draining and laying duck walks in First Supports.	
Armentières	1st-10th		Draining north of Cowgate Avenue.	
			Draining ditch and clearing trench from Lille Post to Support Line.	
			Draining and repairing duck-walks in Reserve Line.	
			Repairing and relaying trench-walks in Park Row.	
			Retaining screen for railway near subsidiary line.	
			Draining, engine room, overhauling and running engine in Gunnery Lane.	
			Repairing, revetting and draining in Rue-de-Bois.	
			Repairing and revetting Paradise Alley.	
			Building new fire bay in Leith Walk.	
			Draining and repairing Queen Street, cutting new drain and repairing trench. Repairing, revetting, draining, and rebuilding in Brick St. and constructing new fire bay.	
			Revetting & draining rough tracks in Support Line.	
			Setting in and fixing 2 water tanks at Burnt Farm.	

T2134. Wt. W708—776. 500000. 4/15. Sir J. C. & S.

Instructions regarding War Diaries and Intelligence Summaries are contained in F. S. Regs., Part II. and the Staff Manual respectively. Title pages will be prepared in manuscript.

WAR DIARY

~~or~~

~~INTELLIGENCE SUMMARY.~~

(Erase heading not required.)

Army Form C. 2118.

Place	Date	Hour	Summary of Events and Information	Remarks and references to Appendices
Rue Marle. Armentieres	Nov. 1st/10th		Constructing new concrete Dug-out for Company Headqrs in Close Supports.	
			Draining, revetting and repairing trench walks in Wellington Avenue.	
			Constructing staging for water storage tank in Cowgate Avenue.	
			Revetting and sand-bagging Cowgate Avenue, and clearing drains.	
			Repairs to well.	
			Putting in additional tank. Sandbagging around tanks.	
			Clearing drains in Wellington Avenue.	
			Draining and relaying duck-walks in Wine Avenue.	
			Revetting, repairing and clearing drainage in Nunnery Lane.	
			Relaying duck-walks and repairing drainage in Salop Avenue.	
			Draining Wellington Av., Willow Av., Wine Av., Miners Road, Nunnery Lane, Cowgate Av., Salop Av., etc.	
			Clearing drain from T. Head Sap to Support Line.	
			Drainage of Knightsbridge, and Reserve line in Dead Cow Farm.	
			Clearing drain to Lakes of Killarney.	

T2134. Wt. W708—776. 500000. 4/15. Sir J. C. & S.

5

Instructions regarding War Diaries and Intelligence Summaries are contained in F. S. Regs., Part II, and the Staff Manual respectively. Title pages will be prepared in manuscript.

WAR DIARY
or
INTELLIGENCE SUMMARY.
(Erase heading not required.)

Army Form C. 2118.

Place	Date	Hour	Summary of Events and Information	Remarks and references to Appendices
Rue Marle, Armentières	Nov 1st [illegible]		Concreting and roofing Dug-Outs in Front Line, left and right of Wine and Willow Avenues.	
			Constructing new concrete Dug-Out in the Salient.	
			Revetting around dug-outs in Front Line.	
			Putting in "A" frames, repairing traverses and parapet in Front Line, relaying trench-walks.	
			Work on construction of New Company Headquarters in Front Line, by Willow Avenue.	
			Constructing new drain right of Salient.	
			Repairing fire-bays and revetting in trenches right and left of Salient, relaying duck-walks and building up parados.	
			Constructing new concrete dug-outs in Switch-Line and in 1st Supports.	
			Work on construction of concrete dug-outs at Lille Post.	
			Repairing and building new roof to C.O's and R.A signal dug-out in Reserve Line.	
			Draining and repairing Leith Walk.	

Instructions regarding War Diaries and Intelligence Summaries are contained in F. S. Regs., Part II. and the Staff Manual respectively. Title pages will be prepared in manuscript.

6

WAR DIARY
or
~~INTELLIGENCE SUMMARY.~~
(Erase heading not required.)

Army Form C. 2118.

Place	Date	Hour	Summary of Events and Information	Remarks and references to Appendices
Rue Marle Armentieres.	Nov. 11th/15		Revetting, relaying trench-walks, clearing and draining Miners Lane.	
			Repairs by Knightsbridge.	
			Clearing and revetting right of Dead Cow Farm.	
			Draining right of Cowgate Avenue.	
			Draining, refixing trenchwalks, and repairing Park Row.	
			Constructing concrete Dug-Out for New Coy Headquarters in Close Supports.	
			Repairing and revetting Paradise Alley.	
			Draining and repairing Queen Street, cutting new drain and repairing trench.	
			Taking up and fixing 2 water tanks at Burnt Farm.	
			Draining engine room, overhauling and running engine in Nunnery Lane.	
			Repairing, revetting and draining in Rue-de-Bois.	
			Repairs to drying-room racks in Support Line.	
			Draining and refixing duck-walks in Reserve Line.	
			Draining, revetting and repairing trench-walks in Wellington Avenue.	

T2131. Wt. W708—776. 500000. 4/15. Sir J. C. & S.

Instructions regarding War Diaries and Intelligence Summaries are contained in F. S. Regs., Part II. and the Staff Manual respectively. Title pages will be prepared in manuscript.

WAR DIARY

~~or~~

~~INTELLIGENCE SUMMARY.~~

(Erase heading not required.)

Army Form C. 2118.

Place	Date	Hour	Summary of Events and Information	Remarks and references to Appendices
Rue Marle Armentières	Nov. 11th. 17th.		Levelling and sandbagging Cowgate Avenue, and clearing drains.	
			Repairs to well in Cowgate Avenue, putting in additional tank and sandbagging around it.	
			Draining and relaying duck-walks in Wine Avenue.	
			Levelling in Willow Avenue.	
			Levelling, repairing, and clearing drainage in Nunnery Lane.	
			Draining Wellington Av., Willow Av., Wine Av., Cowgate Av., Miners Road, Rue-de-Bois, Nunnery Lane etc..	
			Draining by Knightsbridge and Reserve Line by Dead Cow Farm.	
			Clearing drain to Lakes of Killarney.	
do.	Nov. 18th/24th		Concreting and roofing Dug-outs in Front Line, left and right of Wine and Willow Avenues.	
			Constructing new concrete dug-out in Salient.	
			Work on construction of New Centre Company Headquarters in Front Line, by Willow Avenue.	

T2134. Wt. W708—776. 500000. 4/15. Sir J. C. & S.

Instructions regarding War Diaries and Intelligence Summaries are contained in F. S. Regs., Part II. and the Staff Manual respectively. Title pages will be prepared in manuscript.

8

WAR DIARY
or
~~INTELLIGENCE SUMMARY.~~
(Erase heading not required.)

Army Form C. 2118.

Place	Date	Hour	Summary of Events and Information	Remarks and references to Appendices
Rue Marle Armentières	Nov. 18th/24th		Remodelling bays in Front Line.	
			Draining left of Salient.	
			Putting in "A" frames, repairing traverses and parapet in Front Line, relaying trench-walks.	
			Draining from Salient to Miners Road.	
			Repairing fire-bays and revetting in trenches right and left of Salient, refixing duck-walks and building up parados.	
			Constructing new concrete dug-outs in Switch-Line and in 1st Supports.	
			Work on construction of concrete dug-outs at Lille Post.	
			Constructing concrete dug-out for Coy. Headquarters in Close Supports.	
			Constructing Light Trench Mortar emplacement in Park Row.	
			Relaying duck-walks near Lille Post.	
			Draining and repairing Leith Walk.	
			Clearing and revetting right of Dead Cow Farm.	
			Draining from Nunnery Lane to Supports.	
			Clearing drain from engine in Nunnery Lane, and clearing trench	

Instructions regarding War Diaries and Intelligence Summaries are contained in F. S. Regs., Part II. and the Staff Manual respectively. Title pages will be prepared in manuscript.

WAR 9 DIARY
or
~~INTELLIGENCE SUMMARY.~~
(Erase heading not required.)

Army Form C. 2118.

Place	Date	Hour	Summary of Events and Information	Remarks and references to Appendices
Rue Marle Armentières	Nov. 18th/24th		to Front Line.	
			Draining engine room, overhauling and running engine in Nunnery Lane.	
			Draining in Switch-Line.	
			Draining and repairing Queen Street.	
			Relaying trench-walks at Burnt Farm. Repairing tank at Burnt Farm.	
			Revetting, relaying trenchwalks and repairing damage in Miners Lane.	
			Constructing drying room at Chapelle-d'-Armentières.	
			Draining, revetting and repairing trench-walks in Wellington Avenue.	
			Revetting and clearing drainage in Cowgate Av.	
			Repairs to well in Wine Av.	
			Revetting in Willow Av. Draining in Salop Av.	
			Draining Wellington Av., Willow Av., Wine Av., Cowgate Av., Miners Road., Nunnery Lane., etc..	
			Draining ditch at Lille Road.	
	Nov. 25th/26th		Constructing [illegible] dug-outs in Front-Line, right of Willow Avenue	
			[illegible] fire-bays and revetting around concrete dugouts [illegible]	

Instructions regarding War Diaries and Intelligence Summaries are contained in F. S. Regs., Part II. and the Staff Manual respectively. Title pages will be prepared in manuscript.

10

WAR DIARY
~~or~~
INTELLIGENCE ~~SUMMARY~~.
(Erase heading not required.)

Army Form C. 2118.

Place	Date	Hour	Summary of Events and Information	Remarks and references to Appendices
Rue Marle, Armentieres	Nov. 25th/30th		Front Line. Putting in "A" frames, repairing traverses and parapet in Front Line and relaying duck-walks. Repairing fire-bays and revetting in trenches right and left of Salient, relaying duck-walks and building up damaged parados. Installing water storage tank in Front Line. Draining left of Chard's Farm Salient. Concreting around pump in Front Line. Work on construction of New Centre Coy Headquarters in Front Line by Willow Avenue. Constructing concrete Dug-Out for Company Headquarters in Close Supports. Work on construction of Cupola Dug-Outs in Support Line left of Dead Cow Farm, and Support Line left of Wellington Avenue. Construction of Cupola dug-outs in Switch-Line. Draining Company Headquarters in Switch-Line.	

T2134. Wt. W708—776. 500000. 4/15. Sir J. C. & S.

Army Form C. 2118.

Instructions regarding War Diaries and Intelligence Summaries are contained in F. S. Regs., Part II. and the Staff Manual respectively. Title pages will be prepared in manuscript.

WAR DIARY
or
~~INTELLIGENCE SUMMARY.~~
(Erase heading not required.)

Place	Date	Hour	Summary of Events and Information	Remarks and references to Appendices
Rue Marle, Armentieres	Nov 28th/30th		Work on concrete dug-outs at Lille Post.	
			Constructing Light Trench Mortar Emplacement in Park Row, and Trench Mortar Emplacement in left Sub-sector.	
			Draining top and bottom ends of Lille Road.	
			Building kitchen in Centre Sector and making traverse near dug-out Centre Sector.	
			Draining engine room, overhauling and running engine in Nunnery Lane.	
			Draining from Nunnery Lane to Supports.	
			Clearing, draining and repairing 1st Supports, left of Cowgate, also in 1st Supports left of Wine Avenue.	
			Constructing rest rooms for Lille Post, also screens for dumps in Railway Avenue.	
			Constructing drying room at Chapelle-d-Armentieres.	
			Draining, revetting and repairing Wellington Avenue, and relaying duck-walks.	

T2134. Wt. W708—776. 500000. 4/15. Sir J. C. & S.

12

Army Form C. 2118.

Instructions regarding War Diaries and Intelligence Summaries are contained in F. S. Regs., Part II. and the Staff Manual respectively. Title pages will be prepared in manuscript.

WAR DIARY
or
INTELLIGENCE SUMMARY.
(Erase heading not required.)

Place	Date	Hour	Summary of Events and Information	Remarks and references to Appendices
Rue Marle, Armentieres	Nov 26th/30th		Night work, filling in sides of Wellington Av.	
			Draining left of Cowgate.	
			Draining and relaying duck-walks in Cowgate Avenue.	
			Draining, repairing and relaying trench walks in Salop Avenue.	
			Clearing drains in Avondale Avenue and relaying trench walks.	
			Draining and repairing Willow Avenue.	
			Draining Wellington Av., Willow Av., Wine Av., Cowgate Av., Nunnery Lane etc.	
			Draining at Lille Post.	
			[signature] Major R.E.	
			30th November, 1916. O. C. 208th Fld Coy R.E.	

T2134. Wt. W708—776. 500000. 4/15. Sir J. C. & S.

Instructions regarding War Diaries and Intelligence Summaries are contained in F. S. Regs., Part II. and the Staff Manual respectively. Title pages will be prepared in manuscript.

WAR DIARY

~~or~~

~~INTELLIGENCE SUMMARY.~~

(Erase heading not required.)

Army Form C. 2118.

Vol 12

Place	Date	Hour	Summary of Events and Information	Remarks and references to Appendices
			— 208th —	
			Field Company	
			R.E.	
			— December —	
			1916	

T2134. Wt. W708–776. 500000. 4/15. Sir J. C. & S.

1.

Army Form C. 2118.

Instructions regarding War Diaries and Intelligence Summaries are contained in F. S. Regs., Part II. and the Staff Manual respectively. Title pages will be prepared in manuscript.

WAR DIARY
~~or~~
~~INTELLIGENCE SUMMARY.~~
(Erase heading not required.)

Place	Date	Hour	Summary of Events and Information	Remarks and references to Appendices
Rue Marle Armentieres	Decr 1st-8th		Nos. 1, 2 and 4 Sections in billets at Rue Marle, Armentieres, work in trenches. No 3 Section at Erquinghem, working under C. R. E. Mounted sections at Croix-du-Bac. Work done by Nos 1, 2 and 4 Sections:- Constructing cupola dug-outs in Front line, right of Willow Avenue. Remodelling fire-bays and revetting around concreted dug-outs in Front line. Constructing new fire-bay in Salient. Clearing way into Chord-line for proposed dug-outs. Repairing and building up damages to Front line, draining and relaying duck-walks. Work on construction of New Centre Company Headquarters in Front line, by Willow Avenue. Constructing concrete dug-out in Chards Farm Salient.	

T2134. Wt. W708—776. 500000. 4/15. Sir J. C. & S.

2.

Instructions regarding War Diaries and Intelligence Summaries are contained in F. S. Regs., Part II. and the Staff Manual respectively. Title pages will be prepared in manuscript.

WAR DIARY

~~or~~

~~INTELLIGENCE SUMMARY.~~

(Erase heading not required.)

Army Form C. 2118.

Place	Date	Hour	Summary of Events and Information	Remarks and references to Appendices
Rue Marle Armentières	Decr 1st-8th		Repairing fire-bays and revetting in trenches right and left of Salient, refixing duck-walks and building up damaged Parados. Constructing concrete Dug-Outs for Company Headquarters in Close Supports. Work on construction of Cupola Dug-Outs in Support Line left of Dead Cow Farm, and Support Line left of Wellington Avenue. Constructing Cupola dug-outs in Switch-Line. Construction of concrete dug-outs at Lille Post. Clearing site for and constructing new Headquarters left of Cowgate Excavation for concrete Coy. Headquarters in Switch Line. Constructing fire-bay right of Miners Road. do. do. do. Leith Walk. Repairing and heightening parapet close by Coy Headquarters in Switch Line. Fixing fire-step and repairing left of Brick Street. Clearing drain near outfall of Engine, overhauling and running	

3.

Instructions regarding War Diaries and Intelligence Summaries are contained in F. S. Regs., Part II. and the Staff Manual respectively. Title pages will be prepared in manuscript.

WAR DIARY

~~or~~

~~INTELLIGENCE SUMMARY.~~

(Erase heading not required.)

Army Form C. 2118.

Place	Date	Hour	Summary of Events and Information	Remarks and references to Appendices
Rue Marle Armentieres	Dec 1st/8th		engine in Nunnery Lane.	
			Draining and repairing near Farm-le-Biez.	
			Fitting shelves to changing room near Wellington Av. Dump.	
			Installing additional water-tank in Wine Avenue.	
			Relaying trench-walks by Burnt Farm.	
			Draining and relaying duck-walks in Switch-line.	
			Finishing off the construction of kitchen left of Cowgate.	
			Constructing Light Trench Mortar emplacements, at Park Row, in left Sub-Sector, and in Switch-line.	
			Draining top and bottom ends of Lille Road.	
			Draining, revetting and repairing Wellington Avenue and relaying duck-walks.	
			Filling in sides of Wellington Avenue. (Night Work)	
			Draining and relaying duck-walks in Cowgate Avenue.	
			Draining, repairing and relaying trench-walks in Baloo Avenue	
			Clearing drains in Avondale Av. and relaying trench-walks.	

T2134. Wt. W708—776. 500000. 4/15. Sir J. C. & S.

4

Instructions regarding War Diaries and Intelligence Summaries are contained in F. S. Regs., Part II. and the Staff Manual respectively. Title pages will be prepared in manuscript.

WAR DIARY
or
~~INTELLIGENCE SUMMARY.~~
(Erase heading not required.)

Army Form C. 2118.

Place	Date	Hour	Summary of Events and Information	Remarks and references to Appendices
Rue Marle Armentieres	Decr. 1st/8th		Draining Wellington Av., Willow Av.; Cowgate Av., Nunnery Lane etc.	
	9th & 10th		Constructing cupola dug-outs in Front Line, right of Willow Avenue. Clearing way into Chord-Line for proposed dug-outs and relaying trench-walks.	
			Constructing concrete dug out in Chard's Farm Salient.	
			Repairing and building up damages to Front Line, draining and relaying duck-walks.	
			Repairing fire-bays and revetting in trenches right and left of Salient, repairing duck-walks and building up damaged parades.	
			Constructing concrete Dug-outs for Company Headquarters in Close Supports.	
			Work on construction of Cupola Dug-Outs in Support Line left of Dead Cow Farm, and Support Line left of Wellington Avenue. New Cupola Dug-Out in Switch Line right of Wellington Av.	

T2134. Wt. W708—776. 500000. 4/15. Sir J. C. & S.

Army Form C. 2118.

Instructions regarding War Diaries and Intelligence Summaries are contained in F. S. Regs., Part II. and the Staff Manual respectively. Title pages will be prepared in manuscript.

WAR DIARY

~~or~~

~~INTELLIGENCE SUMMARY.~~

(Erase heading not required.)

Place	Date	Hour	Summary of Events and Information	Remarks and references to Appendices
Rue Marle Armentieres	Decr 9th + 10th		Work on concrete dug-outs at Lille Post, and making floors for same.	
			Excavation for concrete bomb-proof Headquarters in Switch-Line.	
			Sand-bagging at Lille Post.	
			Constructing Cupola dug-outs in Switch-Line.	
			Concreting existing and installing additional water-tank near Wine Avenue.	
			Relaying trench-walks by Burnt Farm.	
			Draining, revetting and relaying duck-walks in Switch-Line.	
			Draining, revetting and repairing Wellington Av. and relaying duck-walks	
			Draining, + relaying duck-walks in Cowgate Avenue.	
			Draining right of Wine Avenue.	
			Draining and relaying trench-walks in Avondale Av.	
			Relaying trench-walks and draining Sturt Av.	
			Draining Switch-Line to Support-Line, left of Salop Av.	
			Draining, repairing and relaying trench-walks in Salop Av.	
			Draining Wellington Av. Willow Av., Cowgate Av., Nunnery Lane etc..	

T2134. Wt. W708–776. 500000. 4/15. Sir J. C. & S.

6.

Instructions regarding War Diaries and Intelligence Summaries are contained in F. S. Regs., Part II. and the Staff Manual respectively. Title pages will be prepared in manuscript.

WAR DIARY

~~or~~

~~INTELLIGENCE SUMMARY.~~

(*Erase heading not required.*)

Army Form C. 2118.

Place	Date	Hour	Summary of Events and Information	Remarks and references to Appendices
Armentieres	Decr 11th		This Company being relieved by the 209th Field Coy R.E. at 9 am on the 11th inst, proceeded to billets at Erquinghem factory and there relieved the 2.6 Reserve sections for work as Reserve Field Coy. The 209th Field Coy. R.E. taking over this Company's work in the left Sector, Forward area. (Vide 6 L.I's Operation Order No. 48).	
Erquinghem Factory	Decr 12th to 31st		<u>Construction of Observation Posts</u> at Rendez-vous, Rat Trap, Mosquito Palace, Convent or Ivy Attic, Shrapnel View, Sand-bag Villa, Peach Barn, Madge Cottage, Heavy O.P., The Beacon, Post Office.	
			<u>Constructing Gun Pits and Artillery Dug-outs</u>:-	
			Making four New Gun Pits "A Type" at I, 13, c. 55. 20.	
			do five New Gun Pits and Telephone Dug-Out at I. 1. a. 4. 3.	

7

Army Form C. 2118.

Instructions regarding War Diaries and Intelligence Summaries are contained in F. S. Regs., Part II. and the Staff Manual respectively. Title pages will be prepared in manuscript.

WAR DIARY

or

~~INTELLIGENCE SUMMARY.~~

(Erase heading not required.)

Place	Date	Hour	Summary of Events and Information	Remarks and references to Appendices
Erquinghem Factory	Dec 12th – 31st		Making two new Gun-pits, and strengthening four at I.8.a.8.1.	
			Making new gun-pits at H.29.b.7.8, H.29.b.9.7, H.23.a.cent.,	
			Crombalot and La Vesee.	
			Dug-Outs:-	
			Constructing Concrete Dug-out, 1st Battn (Left Side) Headqrs. Wellington Av.	
			" " + steel " , at Crown Prince House.	
			" " " , Coy Headqrs Dug-Out at H.30.b.55.35.	
			" 2 " "s, Machine Gun Crews at Cowgate Av + H.30.b.95.30.	
			" " First Aid Post Dug-out at White City.	
			" " " " " at Tramline Av.	
			Excavation for " " " " at Unley St.	

8

Army Form C. 2118.

Instructions regarding War Diaries and Intelligence Summaries are contained in F. S. Regs., Part II. and the Staff Manual respectively. Title pages will be prepared in manuscript.

WAR DIARY
~~or~~
~~INTELLIGENCE SUMMARY.~~
(*Erase heading not required.*)

Place	Date	Hour	Summary of Events and Information	Remarks and references to Appendices
Erquinghem	Decr 12th – 31st		Miscellaneous Work:-	
			General Road repairs in Brigade area.	
			Road Drainage at Gris Pot.	
			Trench " at Bois Grenier.	
			Reconstruction & revetting of Right Brigade in Subsidiary Line.	
			" " " of Left " " "	
			Salving revetting Material in Subsidiary Line.	
			Constructing rifle range at Rue Dormoire, Erquinghem	
			" " " " nr Church, do.	
			Repairing barrier on Lille Road.	
			Repairs to well at Lille Post.	
			Repairs to drying room at Crombalot.	
			Constructing S.A. Dug-out at H.9.c.3.1.	
			Installing additional water tank in Front Line, left of Rue-de-Bois.	
			Construction of O.P. exchange at the convent.	

T2131. Wt. W708–776. 500000. 4/15. Sir J. C. & S.

9

Instructions regarding War Diaries and Intelligence Summaries are contained in F. S. Regs., Part II. and the Staff Manual respectively. Title pages will be prepared in manuscript.

WAR DIARY

~~or~~

~~INTELLIGENCE SUMMARY.~~

(*Erase heading not required.*)

Army Form C. 2118.

Place	Date	Hour	Summary of Events and Information	Remarks and references to Appendices
ERQUINGHEM	Dec[r] 22nd		Inspection by the Commander-in-Chief on the Erquinghem – Fort Rompu Road at 12.30 pm on 22nd Dec 1916. March past via Fort Rompu, and return to billets via Bac St Maur, Rue Delpierre, Fort Rompu and Rue-la-Lys. (Vide instructions contained in 34th Div. "Secret" No C.H/384 dated 18-12-16 and 21-12-16).	

H. Hughes
Major R.E.
O.C. 208th Field Coy R.E.

Instructions regarding War Diaries and Intelligence Summaries are contained in F. S. Regs., Part II. and the Staff Manual respectively. Title pages will be prepared in manuscript.

WAR DIARY

~~or~~

~~INTELLIGENCE SUMMARY~~.

(Erase heading not required.)

Army Form C. 2118.

Vol 13

Place	Date	Hour	Summary of Events and Information	Remarks and references to Appendices
			January 1917 208th FIELD COY. R.E.	

T2134. Wt. W708—776. 500000. 4/15. Sir J. C. & S.

Instructions regarding War Diaries and Intelligence Summaries are contained in F. S. Regs., Part II. and the Staff Manual respectively. Title pages will be prepared in manuscript.

WAR DIARY

~~or~~

~~INTELLIGENCE SUMMARY.~~

(Erase heading not required.)

Army Form C. 2118.

Place	Date	Hour	Summary of Events and Information	Remarks and references to Appendices
Erquinghem France.	Jany 1st-26th		Work on the construction of Observation Posts at the following positions, Rendezvous, Mosquito Palace, Convent or Ivy Attic, Shrapnel View, Sandbag Villa, Krump House, Peach Barn, Madge Cottage, Heavy O.P., The Beacon, Spion Kop, Apple House, and Post Office.	
			Construction of Gun Pits + Artillery Dug-Outs at the following battery positions:-	
			B/160 - I.1.a.4.1/2 B/152 - H.23.a.Cent. C/175 - Crombalot	
			D/175 - La Vesee.	
			Constructing splinter-proof dug-outs at Right Battn, Left Brigade Headqrs.	
			Construction of First Aid Posts at White City, Tramline Avenue, Unley Street.	
			Construction of new concrete Company Headquarter dug-outs	

T2134. Wt. W708—776. 500000. 4/15. Sir J. C. & S.

Instructions regarding War Diaries and Intelligence Summaries are contained in F. S. Regs., Part II. and the Staff Manual respectively. Title pages will be prepared in manuscript.

WAR DIARY

~~or~~

~~INTELLIGENCE SUMMARY.~~

(Erase heading not required.)

Army Form C. 2118.

Place	Date	Hour	Summary of Events and Information	Remarks and references to Appendices
Erquinghem, France	Jan[y] 1st-26th		in the Subsidiary Line, right of Cowgate Avenue, left of Wellington Avenue, Shaftesbury Avenue, Tramline Avenue. Construction of Sound Ranging, splinter proof, dug-out in the Subsidiary Line, Wellington Avenue. Carrying out of general road repairs in ~~Brigade~~ Divisional Area, and trench drainage at Bois Grenier. Revetting and reconstruction of the Subsidiary Line, left and right Brigade areas. Construction of Rifle Range, revetting drains at Rue Dormoire. Revetting trenches at the Bayonet Fighting Ground, Erquinghem Church. Construction of Butts at the Rifle Range, Rue Marle. Strengthening roofs & floors of Billets at Rue Delpierre. Repairs to Billets at Rue-des-Acquets. Ballasting & adjusting track of R.A. tramway, Le Verrier. Constructing new gum-boot store & drying room at Rue Allée.	

T2134. Wt. W708—776. 500000. 4/15. Sir J. C. & S.

Instructions regarding War Diaries and Intelligence Summaries are contained in F. S. Regs., Part II. and the Staff Manual respectively. Title pages will be prepared in manuscript.

3/

WAR DIARY

~~or~~

~~INTELLIGENCE SUMMARY.~~

(Erase heading not required.)

Army Form C. 2118.

Place	Date	Hour	Summary of Events and Information	Remarks and references to Appendices
Erquinghem France	Jan 1st-26th		Work on L.A. Exchange at H.9.c.3.1., and O.S. Exchange at the "Convent". Erection of Steel Towers at R.E. Yard. Installing water tanks & repairs to well in Paradise Alley. Repairing bridges in the Subsidiary Line, Haystack Avenue. Draining & relaying trench walks in Lille Rd trench. Constructing stand for tank in Leith Walk. Fitting hasps, hinges & locks to Reserve Water tanks in Subsidiary Line. Repairing doors & skylights of billets at Rue Marle. Carrying into position & fixing three bridges over River Lys. Repairing Magazine (near Bridge) Bac-St-Maur. Wiring approaches to Cowgate, Wine, Haystack, Wellington, Park Row, Tramline, Shaftesbury, Moat Farm and Greatwood Avenues.	

T2134. Wt. W708—776. 500000. 4/15. Sir J. C. & S.

Instructions regarding War Diaries and Intelligence Summaries are contained in F. S. Regs., Part II. and the Staff Manual respectively. Title pages will be prepared in manuscript.

WAR DIARY

~~or~~

~~INTELLIGENCE SUMMARY~~.

(*Erase heading not required.*)

4

Army Form C. 2118.

Place	Date	Hour	Summary of Events and Information	Remarks and references to Appendices
Erquinghem sur la Lys France	26/1/17.	6.30 pm.	Company moved from billets at Erquinghem Factory and marched to Meteren Area. Company less Transport taking following Route. Erquinghem Bridge, Les 3 Tilleuls, Pont de Nieppe, Bailleul, Meteren, Flêtre. Company transport as follows:- Croix du Bac, Steenwerck, La Becque, Noote Boom, Meteren, Flêtre. The whole company being billeted in a large Farm between Flêtre and Caestre on the main road. Arrival at 3.30 am. on the morning of the 27/1/17.	
	28/1/17 to 31/1/17		Fixing and fitting Stoves in billets and offices of Divisional Headquarters at Flêtre.	
			Thawing and repairing, engines, pump, tanks &c at 2 Divisional Baths & Laundries near Meteren (X.20.d.1.8.) on Meteren - Strazeele Rd. also near Meteren (X.9.a.0.7.) Sappers working continuously night and day shifts.	

L J Murphy Capt R.E.
for O.C. 208th Field Coy R.E.

T2134. Wt. W708-776. 500000. 4/15. Sir J. C. & S.

Instructions regarding War Diaries and Intelligence Summaries are contained in F. S. Regs., Part II. and the Staff Manual respectively. Title pages will be prepared in manuscript.

WAR DIARY
or
~~INTELLIGENCE SUMMARY.~~
(Erase heading not required.)

Army Form C. 2118.

Vol 14

Place	Date	Hour	Summary of Events and Information	Remarks and references to Appendices
			208TH FIELD CO. R.E.	
			= February 1917 =	
			= 208th Field Coy R.E. —	

T2134. Wt. W708—776. 500000. 4/15. Sir J. C. & S.

Instructions regarding War Diaries and Intelligence Summaries are contained in F. S. Regs., Part II. and the Staff Manual respectively. Title pages will be prepared in manuscript.

208TH FIELD CO. R. E.

WAR DIARY

~~or~~

~~INTELLIGENCE SUMMARY.~~

(*Erase heading not required.*)

Army Form C. 2118.

1

208TH FIELD CO. R. E.

Place	Date	Hour	Summary of Events and Information	Remarks and references to Appendices
Billets on Main Road Hletre - Caestre	1/2/17 to 3/2/17.		Leaving, repg. and adjusting engines, pump, tanks &c at Divisional Baths and Laundries on Meteren - Strazeele Rd. (X.20. d.1.8.) Sappers working in reliefs night and day. Do do. at Divisional Baths and Laundries near Meteren at (X.9. a.0.7.) Sappers working in reliefs night and day.	
do.	4/2/17 to 13/2/17.		Company Training as follows:- Physical Drill, Section Drill with & without Arms, Company Drill with & without Arms, Firing Exercises, Route Marches Drill with Gas Helmets & Box respirators, Inspections of Kit, Arms, Ammunition &c.	
do.	14/2/17 to 28/2/17		No1. Section, conveyed by Motor Lorries to XVII Corps Headquarters, thence to Hermaville, employed from 15/2/17 to 28/2/17 fitting up New Divisional Headquarters at Hermaville.	
do	14/2/17 to 17/2/17.		Company (less No1. Section) Company Training as above. Physical, Section and Company drill with and without Arms. Route Marches Drill with Gas Helmets & Box Respirators, Inspections of Kits, Arms, Ammunition &c.	

T2134. Wt. W708—776. 500000. 4/15. Sir J. C. & S.

Instructions regarding War Diaries and Intelligence Summaries are contained in F. S. Regs., Part II. and the Staff Manual respectively. Title pages will be prepared in manuscript.

WAR DIARY

or

~~INTELLIGENCE SUMMARY.~~

(*Erase heading not required.*)

2

Army Form C. 2118.

Place	Date	Hour	Summary of Events and Information	Remarks and references to Appendices
Billets on Main Road Stelto-Caestre.	18/2/17.		Company (less 1 section) moved by Route March from Billets to Morbecque. (Le Brearde - Hazebrouck Morbecque - Billets)	
Morbecque.	19/2/17		Company (less 1 Section) moved by Route March from Billets in Morbecque to Molinghem (route - Steenbecque - Boesinghem - Neuffre - Molinghem)	
Molinghem	20/2/17		Company (less 1 Section) moved by Route March to Monneville (route - Molinghem - Mazinghem - St Hilair - Ferfay - Pernes - Monneville).	
Monneville	21/2/17		Company (less 1 Section) moved by Route March from Billets in Monneville to Herlin-le-Vert (route - Monneville - Dieval - La Thieuloye - Monchy-Breton - Chelers - Herlin-le-Vert.) Here the Company rested 2 nights.	
Herlin-le-Vert	23/2/17		Company (less 1 Section) moved by Route March from Billets in Herlin-le-Vert to Hutments at Ecoivres. (route - Herlin-le-Vert - Grevillers - Villers Brulin - Berlette - le Cabaret Blanc - Acq. - Ecoivres).	
Ecoivres Huts.	25/2/17		Establishing Horse Lines - Parking Wagons &c. Dismounted Personnel (less 1 Section) moved to Billets in Arras (Nos. 3, 13 & 19 Rue 29 Juillet) after dusk. Toolcarts and Forage carts parked in the Cavalry Barracks, Quartier Schramm.	

T2134. Wt. W708—776. 500000. 4/15. Sir J. C. & S.

Instructions regarding War Diaries and Intelligence Summaries are contained in F. S. Regs., Part II. and the Staff Manual respectively. Title pages will be prepared in manuscript.

WAR DIARY

~~or~~

~~INTELLIGENCE SUMMARY.~~

(Erase heading not required.)

3

Army Form C. 2118.

Place	Date	Hour	Summary of Events and Information	Remarks and references to Appendices
Arras.	26/2/17 to 28/2/17		Taking over work in Line from 209th Field Coy R.E. in Brigade area. Establishing 2 forward Brigade Dumps. & maintaining same. Cutting new Evacuation Trench from support line, using old communication trenches in parts. Constructing Medium and Heavy T.M. Emplacements at Thelus Avenue, Spook St, Off Monday Avenue, Ghost St. &c.	

L J Murphy Capt RE
for OC 208th Field Coy R.E.

T2134. Wt. W708—776. 500000. 4/15. Sir J. C. & S.

Instructions regarding War Diaries and Intelligence Summaries are contained in F. S. Regs., Part II. and the Staff Manual respectively. Title Pages will be prepared in manuscript.

WAR DIARY

~~or~~

~~INTELLIGENCE SUMMARY~~

(Erase heading not required.)

Army Form C. 2118

208 Fd Coy R.E.

Vol 15

Place	Date	Hour	Summary of Events and Information	Remarks and references to Appendices
			War Diary March 1917	

1875 Wt. W593/826 1,000,000 4/15 J.B.C. & A. A.D.S.S./Forms/C. 2118.

Instructions regarding War Diaries and Intelligence Summaries are contained in F. S. Regs., Part II. and the Staff Manual respectively. Title Pages will be prepared in manuscript.

WAR DIARY

or

~~INTELLIGENCE SUMMARY~~

(Erase heading not required.)

Army Form C. 2118.

1

Place	Date	Hour	Summary of Events and Information	Remarks and references to Appendices
ARRAS.	1/3/17 to		Making and fixing Bunks in Advanced Brigade Headquarters (Half completed then	
„	10/3/17.		work Handed over to 209th Field Coy RE.	
„	do		Altering and rebuilding cookhouses over whole Trench area to take oval dixies, Handed over to 209th Coy RE.	
„	do		Overhauling Water Supply in Dive Trench area.	
„	1/3/17 to		Cutting and constructing new Evacuation Trench, from Lille Road at G.3.d.5.1.	
„	31/3/17		to Laurence Avenue, using part Monday, Tuesday and Wednesday Avenues in parts	
„	do.		Making ramp from Monday Avenue on to Lille Rd, cutting ~~...~~ under Roadway in	
„	do		Wednesday Avenue - Constructing Bridge where road crosses Thursday Avenue.	
„	do.		Clearing repairing & revetting where necessary front system of trenches including	
„	do.		Sunday Avenue, Victoria St, Cannon St, New St, Kitts St, Week End, Spook St, Front Line	
„	do.		from Kitts to New St, from New St to Sunday Avenue, and South to Brigade Boundary.	
„	do		Cutting new Trenches between Week End and Laurence Avenue, between Sunday Avenue and	
„	do		Week End, between Laurence Avenue and Cemetary Alley, between N. of "A" Gap, to new Sunday	
„	do.		Avenue, from Kitts Locality to Kent Locality forward of front line, and South of Kent	
	do.		Locality in front of A Gap.	

1875 Wt. W593/826 1,000,000 4/15 J.B.C. & A. A.D.S.S./Forms/C. 2118.

= Over =

Instructions regarding War Diaries and Intelligence Summaries are contained in F. S. Regs., Part II. and the Staff Manual respectively. Title Pages will be prepared in manuscript.

WAR DIARY
or
~~INTELLIGENCE SUMMARY~~
(Erase heading not required.)

Army Form C. 2118

2/

Place	Date	Hour	Summary of Events and Information	Remarks and references to Appendices
ARRAS.	1/3/17 to 31/3/17		Forming advanced Brigade R.E. Dumps at Laurence Avenue, Battalion Dumps at Kilta St and S work, also 8 dumps in Front Line	
"	do.		Constructing 8 Heavy and 28 Medium Trench Mortar Positions with Ammunition Shelters. 8 Heavy T.M.E's at Thelus Lane (1) Monday Avenue (2) Thelus Redoubt (2) Laurence Avenue (2) Cemetary Alley (1). Mediums at Victoria St (2) Kit St (2) "E" work (2) Laurence Avenue (2) Kilta St (4) Cecil Avenue (4) Father's Footpath (2) Ghost Avenue (2) Spook St (2) "D" work (2) Victoria St Front Line (2) "H" work (2)	
"	do		Making and fixing Screens on Lille Road (1000 yards) making necessary ramps.	
"	do		Monday Avenue, Tramway running to Trench 40 & Missing Link and Cemetary Alley cleared and revetted. Forming and filling "M2" Dump in Monday avenue.	
"	do		Fixing Notice Boards in Monday and Tuesday Avenues.	
"	do		Tuesday Avenue cutting through from Wednesday to Laurence Avenue. Old Tuesday deepened, trench widened in several places, laying duckwalks.	
"	do.		Building and constructing Prisoner's Cage complete, bunks &c fitted to APM's advance Headqrs.	

(over).

1875 Wt. W593/826 1,000,000 4/15 J.B.C. & A. A.D.S.S./Forms/C. 2118.

Instructions regarding War Diaries and Intelligence Summaries are contained in F. S. Regs., Part II. and the Staff Manual respectively. Title Pages will be prepared in manuscript.

WAR DIARY
or
~~INTELLIGENCE SUMMARY~~
(Erase heading not required.)

III

Army Form C. 2118

Place	Date	Hour	Summary of Events and Information	Remarks and references to Appendices
ARRAS	1/3/17 to 31/3/17		Water Supply. Tanks fitted complete at Divisional Baths on piers. Bottle filler fixed	
"	do.		Artillery Roads constructed. Road from Bethune [illegible] Lille Rd complete with bridges	
"	do.		and ramps crossing formed over Tramway.	
"	do		Tuesday Avenue, Digging new trench, clearing old & laying duckwalks.	
"	do.		Secret Routes. Length from Roclincourt to Front Line picketed & white tape laid.	
"	do		Ramps set out and partly cut.	
Ecoivre X Huts	16/3/17		Company transport moved from Ecoivre X Huts, to Maroeuil (L.3.a.) New Horse lines & vehicles parked.	

[signature]
Major RE
OC. 208th Field Coy RE

1875 Wt. W593/826 1,000,000 4/15 J.B.C. & A. A.D.S.S./Forms/C. 2118.

34 Army Form C. 2118

Instructions regarding War Diaries and Intelligence Summaries are contained in F. S. Regs., Part II. and the Staff Manual respectively. Title Pages will be prepared in manuscript.

WAR DIARY

~~or~~

~~INTELLIGENCE SUMMARY~~

(Erase heading not required.)

Original

Vol 16

Place	Date	Hour	Summary of Events and Information	Remarks and references to Appendices
			208th Field Coy RE	208TH FIELD CO. R. E.
			APRIL 1917	

1875 Wt. W593/826 1,000,000 4/15 J.B.C. & A. A.D.S.S./Forms/C. 2118.

Instructions regarding War Diaries and Intelligence Summaries are contained in F. S. Regs., Part II. and the Staff Manual respectively. Title Pages will be prepared in manuscript.

WAR DIARY

~~or~~

~~INTELLIGENCE SUMMARY~~

(Erase heading not required.)

Army Form C. 2118

1

Place	Date	Hour	Summary of Events and Information	Remarks and references to Appendices
ARRAS.	1/5/17 to 4/5/17		Filling "A2" R.E. Dump at G.6.a.2.5. (57 c N.W) with stores at night.	
			Preparing Artillery Forward Route, bridging trenches and ramping tramline crossings etc from Béthune Rd at G.3.c 2.9. to A.28.d.7.1. (57 c N.W)	
			Making and fixing frames for Gas-proof Blankets at Advanced Bde. Hdqrs at Thelus (Redoubt) and Battalion Headquarters in Thelus Redoubt, Kittle St and New St.	
			Preparing 3 Tank Routes, marking out at night with tapes, ramping parapets and parados where necessary.	
			Completing Preparations for Offensive – Assembly Trenches i.e. Front system of Trenches on Divisional front cleared, repaired and revetted where necessary. Tanks and Bottle-filler fixed complete at Spring near Baths, St Catherine. G.15.c.7.7. (57 c N.W.)	
ARRAS.	4/4/17		Company less Mounted Section moves from billets in ARRAS at G.21.d.3.3. to billets at "X" Hutments (F.19.a.6.8) 57 c N.E., Mounted Section remaining at MAROEUIL (L.3.a.4.8.) 57c NE. 102nd Brigade Sapping Coy reported for attachment and duty with Company during offensive. 5 Infantry reported to Company for duty as Stretcher bearers.	
"X" Hutments. F.19.a.6.8.	4/4/17		Reinforcements reported to Company – 4 O.Ranks from Base.	
	5/4/17		Company resting at "X" Hutments, Ecoivres.	
	6/4/17		Trench Notice Boards on main in and out Trenches refixed.	

(over)

1875 Wt. W593/826 1,000,000 4/15 J.B.C. & A. A.D.S.S./Forms/C. 2118.

Instructions regarding War Diaries and Intelligence Summaries are contained in F. S. Regs., Part II. and the Staff Manual respectively. Title Pages will be prepared in manuscript.

WAR DIARY

~~or~~

~~INTELLIGENCE SUMMARY~~

(Erase heading not required.)

2

Army Form C. 2118

Place	Date	Hour	Summary of Events and Information	Remarks and references to Appendices
X Hutments Ecoivres.	7/4/17	–	Company resting in Billets at X Hutments (F.19a.6.8) 51c NE.	
do	8/4/17.	–	On the night of 8/9th April 1917 the Company (dismounted) with attached Sapping	
	"		Coy. moved in Battle Order to their assembly positions in Roclincourt Valley (G 10.a. 3.5) 51 B NW.	
In line Roclincourt	Night		Nos. 1 & 2 Sections with attached Sapping Coy. sections repaired Bailleul Rd.	
Valley.	9/10th.		Nos. 3 & 4. Sections with attached Sapping Coy sections constructed Strong Points C2 & D2	2
	do.		in "Blue Line" C2 (B25 d. 9.9.) & D2 (B.25.c 35.55)	
do.	10/4/17.		Mounted section moved from camp at L 3.a. to G.15 b. 4.3. (51 B NW.)	
do	night 10/11th		Nos. 1 & 2 Sections with attached Sapping Coy Sections repaired and cleared Bailleul Rd.	
	"		Nos 3 & 4. Sections with attached Sapping Coy Sections consolidated "Brown Line" making	
	"		strong points at C3 (B 27.c.5.0.) and D 3 (B.26. c. 9.6.) 51 B. N.W.	
do.	11/4/17.		Nos. 1 & 2 Sections with attached Sapping Company Sections cleared Railway track	
	"		running between points (H.1. b. 9.9.) and (B.26. c. 9.6.) Debris removed to banks of	
			Railway cutting and the track levelled and ballasted.	
			No 3. Section with attached Sapping Section strengthened C 3 Strong Point (B.27.c.5.0.)	
			No 4 Section with attached Sapping Section strengthened D.3. Strong Point. (B.26. c. 9.6.)	
	11/4/17		Casualties (5 O.Ranks wounded – gassed)	
do	13/4/17.		Sapping Company (102nd Brigade) rejoined their Battalions.	

(over)

Instructions regarding War Diaries and Intelligence Summaries are contained in F. S. Regs., Part II. and the Staff Manual respectively. Title Pages will be prepared in manuscript.

WAR DIARY or ~~INTELLIGENCE SUMMARY~~

(Erase heading not required.)

3

Army Form C. 2118

Place	Date	Hour	Summary of Events and Information	Remarks and references to Appendices
Roclincourt Valley G10 a 3 5 (51 b N.W.)	12th and 13th Apl 1917	-	Nos. 1 & 2 Sections cleared GAVRELLER WEG. (German trench) using trench boards from German Dump on Railway.	
	"		No 3. Section working on C3 strong point until completed, Two Machine Gun Emplacements completed and wire strengthened.	
	"		No 4 Section constructing a splinter proof shelter as Battn. Headqrs. behind Brown Line location using cobulas, German timber &c.	
	13/4/17		3 O Ranks reported as Reinforcements from Base.	
do.	14/4/17		Nos 1 & 2 Sections constructing Mortuary 24' x 9' x 7'6" high, Laying duckwalks in GAVRELLER WEG (German trench) Nos 3 & 4 Sections resting.	
	"		Mounted Section carrying stores to R.E. Advanced Dump.	
do.	15/4/17		Relief of Division by 63rd Naval Division This company temporarily attached to CRE 4th Division.	
do	16/4/17		Casualties 1 Officer 1 O Rank (wounded - gassed.)	
do.	16/4/17 to 21/4/17		Company repairing Gavrelle Road to Point du Jour, clearing debris, filling in, widening levelling ballasting and cutting drains - Repairing Bridge at H.8.c.0.0.	
do.	"		Transport employed conveying men to and from work and carting Bricks and Materials needed from Blangy.	
do.	17/4/17		1 Officer 3 O Ranks joined company from Base.	

(over)

1875 Wt. W593/826 1,000,000 4/15 J.B.C. & A. A.D.S.S./Forms/C. 2118.

Instructions regarding War Diaries and Intelligence Summaries are contained in F. S. Regs., Part II. and the Staff Manual respectively. Title Pages will be prepared in manuscript.

WAR DIARY

~~or~~

~~INTELLIGENCE SUMMARY~~

(Erase heading not required.)

4

Army Form C. 2118

Place	Date	Hour	Summary of Events and Information	Remarks and references to Appendices
Roclincourt Valley G.12.a.3.5.	20/4/17	–	Relief of 4th Division by 37th Division, Company under orders of CRE. 37th Division.	
(57 c N.W.) do.	22/4/17	–	Company less Mounted Section, moved from present billets to original No Man's Land G.12.a.3.5. (57 c N.W.) off Bailleul Road, No2 Section moved to billets at H.8.c.0.0. near Railway crossing under orders of CRE, 37th Division.	
	"		Transport lines remaining at G.15.b.4.3.	
G.12.a.3.5.	night 23/24th.		Nos 1.2 & 4 Sections moved up with 9th North Staffs Pioneers for work on consolidating and making fire trench behind new front line	
do.	do.		Two Pontoons with oars only handed over at Railway Bridge at G.14.c.0.3. to CRE, 51st Division for conveying wounded on River Scarpe.	
do.	night 24/25th.		All Sections working on strong points behind our front line. Casualties 3 O.Ranks wounded.	
	do.		34th Division relieved 51st Division in Right Sector of XVII Corps front. Company rejoins Division as Reserve Company.	
do.	25/4/17		Company less Mounted section moves to G.18.c.35.60. in St Laurent Blangy, billeting in old German dugouts. – Advanced Dump at H.13.d.35.25 taken over from 51st Division. Transport used to fill R.E. Dumps. 1 Officer joined Company from Base.	
G.18.c.35.60.	26/4/17.		4 Sections making Overland track for Infantry in Zones from Bailleul Road to Athies H.7.b.9.5. (57 c N.W.) Casualties 1 O.R. (wounded gassed).	

1875 Wt. W593/826 1,000,000 4/15 J.B.C. & A. A.D.S.S./Forms/C. 2118.

Army Form C. 2118

5

Instructions regarding War Diaries and Intelligence Summaries are contained in F. S. Regs., Part II. and the Staff Manual respectively. Title Pages will be prepared in manuscript.

WAR DIARY

~~or~~

~~INTELLIGENCE SUMMARY~~

(Erase heading not required.)

Place	Date	Hour	Summary of Events and Information	Remarks and references to Appendices
St Laurent Blangy G18.c.25.60.	27/4/17	—	4 Sections with 2 Coys 18th Northumberland Fusiliers Pioneers, completed overland track from St Nicholas to Athies.	
do	night 28/29.		Company (4 Sections) stood-to for work on Strong Point, but ~~did~~ could not work on same.	
do.	29/4/17.		4 Sections repairing Road through Fampoux filling shell-holes clearing &c. Casualties 1 O.Rank killed, 3 O.Ranks wounded.	
do.	30/4/17		4 Sections R.E. moved to camp at Transport lines at G.15.b.4.3. (Division relieved) Pontoons taken from River Scarpe, all vehicles packed awaiting further movement order.	

[illegible]
Major R.E.
O.C. 208th Field Coy R.E.

1875 Wt. W593/826 1,000,000 4/15 J.B.C. & A. A.D.S.S./Forms/C. 2118.

Instructions regarding War Diaries and Intelligence Summaries are contained in F. S. Regs., Part II. and the Staff Manual respectively. Title pages will be prepared in manuscript.

WAR DIARY

~~or~~

~~INTELLIGENCE SUMMARY~~.

(Erase heading not required.)

Army Form C. 2118.

Vol 17

Place	Date	Hour	Summary of Events and Information	Remarks and references to Appendices
			208th Field Coy R.E.	
			— MAY. —	

2353 Wt. W2544/1454 700,000 5/15 D. D. & L. A.D.S.S./Forms/C. 2118.

Instructions regarding War Diaries and Intelligence Summaries are contained in F. S. Regs., Part II. and the Staff Manual respectively. Title pages will be prepared in manuscript.

WAR DIARY ~~or~~ ~~INTELLIGENCE SUMMARY.~~

(~~Erase heading not required.~~)

1/

Army Form C. 2118.

Place	Date	Hour	Summary of Events and Information	Remarks and references to Appendices
CAMP at ST NICHOLAS (G.15.b.4.3.)	1/5/17		Camp Fatigues - Company resting awaiting movement order.	Ref MAP. (51 b NW.)
do.	2/5/17		Company moves from Camp at G15.b.4.3. to Rest Billets at BARLY. - mounted section by road - dismounted by Buses.	do.
BARLY	3/5/17		Inspections of Arms, Equipment, Box Respirators Helmets &c. Tool carts over hauled and deficiencies noted - Reinforcements arrived:- 1 Officer, 10 Sappers. from Base.	Sheet Lens 11.
do	4/5/17		Physical, Company and Gas Helmet drills. - Afternoon. sports - Reinforcement 1 O.Rank.	do.
do.	5/5/17		Morning preliminary parade - Afternoon Company inspected by G.O.C. 34th Division	do.
do.	6/5/17		Physical Drill, Company drill, Lecture & demonstration on Bombs.	do.
do.	7/5/17		Company moves by Route March from BARLY to IVERGNY (via Sus. St Leger.)	do.
IVERGNY.	8/5/17		Company moves by Route March from IVERGNY to BOUQUEMAISON. (route - IVERGNY - - LE SOUICH - BOUQUEMAISON.)	do.
BOUQUEMAISON.	9/5/17		Company moves by Route March from BOUQUEMAISON to VACQUERIE. to Rest Billets. Route:- BOUQUEMAISON. - BARLY - MEZEROLLES - LE MEILLARD - BERNAVILLE - VACQUERIE	do. do.
VACQUERIE	10/5/17		Billet Fatigues, Rifle and Squad Drill Reinforcements from Base 4 O.R's.	do.

T2134. Wt. W708—776. 500000. 4/15. Sir J. C. & S.

— over —

Instructions regarding War Diaries and Intelligence Summaries are contained in F. S. Regs., Part II. and the Staff Manual respectively. Title pages will be prepared in manuscript.

WAR DIARY
~~or~~
INTELLIGENCE ~~SUMMARY.~~
(~~Erase heading not required.~~)

II

Army Form C. 2118.

Place	Date	Hour	Summary of Events and Information	Remarks and references to Appendices
VACQUERIE	11/5/17.		No 4 RE Section repairing and reconstructing Rifle Range at MT RENAULT FARM.	LENS 11 Map sheet.
do	12/5/17 to		1 NCO & 3 Men reporting to each Battalion in Brigade (ie 4 NCOs & 12 men) for	
do	–		supervision of construction of assault courses.	
do.	11/5/17		Company parades:– Rifle and Extended Order Drill – Lecture on wiring, Gas Helmet Drill Sports.	do.
do	12/5/17		Company parades:– Physical Drill, Section Drill, Visibility, Weldon Trestle Building,	
do	–		afternoon sports. Reinforcements from Base:– 10 Sappers.	do.
do.	13/5/17		Church Parades, afternoon – baths.	do.
do.	14/5/17		Company Parades: Physical Drill, Extended Order, Gas Helmet Drill & Map Reading. Afternoon Sports. 1 Reinforcement from Base.	do.
do.	15/5/17		Company Parades:– Section Drill, Lectures on Bombs and wiring – afternoon sports	do.
do.	15/5/17		and crickets. 1 Officer instructing platoons of 102nd Infantry Brigade on Rapid wiring, near Rifle Range.	do.
do.	16/5/17		Physical, Section & Extended Order Drill. Musketry Instruction Lecture on Demolitions. Afternoon – Sports. 1 Reinforcement from Base.	do.
do	15/5/17 to 17/5/17		No 3 Section fitting up bunks &c. at 34th Divl Reinforcement Billets	do.
do.	17/5/17		Physical Drill, Musketry Instruction, Knotting and Lashings, Afternoon Sports. Reinforcements from Base:– 3 O Ranks	do.

— over —

T2134. Wt. W708–776. 500000. 4/15. Sir J. C. & S.

Instructions regarding War Diaries and Intelligence Summaries are contained in F. S. Regs., Part II. and the Staff Manual respectively. Title pages will be prepared in manuscript.

WAR DIARY
~~or~~
~~INTELLIGENCE SUMMARY.~~
(Erase heading not required.)

III

Army Form C. 2118.

Place	Date	Hour	Summary of Events and Information	Remarks and references to Appendices
VACQUERIE	18/5/17		Physical Drill – Knotting and Lashings – Lecture on Camp Sanitation – Weldon Trestle Building. Afternoon Sports	SHEET. LENS. 11
do.	19/5/17		Extended Order in Sections, practice in R.E. covering parties to sections at work when on open warfare. Map reading and compass bearing. (Reinforcements 8 O.Ranks)	do.
do	20/5/17		Church Parades – Afternoon Sports and Baths.	do.
do	21/5/17		Physical Drill – Route March and Road Reconnaissance – Afternoon Sports	do.
do.	22/5/17		Rifle Drill, Demonstrations in use of Explosives. do.	do
do.	23/5/17		Company Route March to NAOURS, and return to billets. (1 Reinforcement)	do.
do.	24/5/17		Driving Competitions sports and Tug of war with 209th Field Coy R.E. at CANAPLES.	do.
do.	25/5/17		Pontoon and Trestle Building practice on River at CANAPLES.	do.
do.	26/5/17		Morning – Parades for inspection of kit, equipment, arms, gas helmets & Box respirators in Full Marching Order. Afternoon sports.	do
do.	27th & 28		Camp Fatigues, cleaning and loading wagons, Pontoons &c. Afternoon Sports	do.
do.	29/5/17		Mounted Section of Company moves from billets in VACQUERIE to Billets at COUTERELLE, by march route.	do. do
COUTERELLE	30/5/17		Mounted Section moves from billets at COUTERELLE to camp at ST NICHOLAS by march route. Camp taken over from 93rd Field Coy at G.17.a.7.9.	do. Ref 57 B.NW.

– over –

T2134. Wt. W708–776. 500000. 4/15. Sir J. C. & S.

Army Form C. 2118

Instructions regarding War Diaries and Intelligence Summaries are contained in F. S. Regs., Part II. and the Staff Manual respectively. Title Pages will be prepared in manuscript.

WAR DIARY

or

~~INTELLIGENCE SUMMARY~~

(Erase heading not required.)

Vol 18

Place	Date	Hour	Summary of Events and Information	Remarks and references to Appendices
			208th Field Company R.E. — JUNE. —	

1875 Wt. W593/826 1,000,000 4/15 J.B.C. & A. A.D.S.S./Forms/C. 2118.

Instructions regarding War Diaries and Intelligence Summaries are contained in F. S. Regs., Part II. and the Staff Manual respectively. Title pages will be prepared in manuscript.

WAR DIARY

~~or~~

~~INTELLIGENCE SUMMARY.~~

(~~Erase heading not required.~~)

IIII

Army Form C. 2118.

Place	Date	Hour	Summary of Events and Information	Remarks and references to Appendices
VACQUERIE	31/5/17		34th Division ~~has~~ relieves 17th Division in left sector of XVII Corps Front. 208th Field Coy RE. relieves 93rd Field Coy.	SHEET LENS 11.
			208th Field Coy (less mounted section) marches from VACQUERIE to CANDAS STN. ~~&~~ thence by Rail to ARRAS STN, by route march to dugouts in Railway cutting at H.7 b. 4.7	Trench Map. 57 B. N.W.
Railway Cutting (H.7.b.4.7.)	31/5/17		Sections at work excavating and constructing mined Dugouts for the 50th and 51st Brigades RFA. at the following locations:-	
			2 @ H.10 a. 3.1. – 2 @ H.10 c. 3.9 – 2 @ H.10.c. 5.8. – 2 @ H.10.c. 2.7. (51st Brigade)	Ref Trench Map 57 B NW.
			@ H.10.c. 3.3. – @ H.9. b. 3. 2 – @ H.9 b. 2.4 – @ H.9 d. 4.9. (50th Brigade)	

J N Stephens Major RE.
OC. 208th Field Coy RE.

Instructions regarding War Diaries and Intelligence Summaries are contained in F. S. Regs., Part II. and the Staff Manual respectively. Title pages will be prepared in manuscript.

WAR DIARY
or
~~INTELLIGENCE SUMMARY.~~

(Erase heading not required.)

Army Form C. 2118.

1

Place	Date	Hour	Summary of Events and Information	Remarks and references to Appendices
RAILWAY CUTTING H.7.b.4.7.	1/6/17 to 3/6/17		Company less mounted section in dugouts and shelters at H.7.b.4.7. – Mounted Section in camp at G.17.a.7.9. NOS. 1.3 & 4 Sections excavating and constructing mined dugouts for the 50th and 51st Brigades R.F.A. at the following locations:–	Reference Map sheet 51.B.N.W.
			2 @ H.10.a.3.1. – 2 @ H.10.c.3.9 – 2 @ H.10.c.5.8. – 2 @ H.10.c.2.7. (51st Brigade)	do.
			@ H.10.c.3.3. – @ H.9.b.3.2. – @ H.9.b.2.4. – @ H.9.d.4.9. (50th Brigade)	do.
do	4/6/17.		Company parades for Baths, Inspection of Arms Equipment &c. Practices in laying out Trenches and wiring for Strong Points.	do.
do.	night 1st/2nd		No 2 Section, Digging Trench connecting up TRENT trench with XIII Corps Trench	do.
	nights 2/3rd 3rd/4th 4th/5th		No 2 Section, wiring (Apron Fence) in front of TRENT Trench (H.11.a.) from its junction with "Hudson" Trench to the wire of XIII Corps Trench about H.5.c.9.8.	do
do	night 5/6th.	8 pm	102nd Infantry Brigade attacked and captured Enemy Trenches on western slope of GREENLAND HILL (Ref 1/10,000 Plouvain sheet).	51 B.N.W. and 1/10,000 PLOUVAIN. Sheet.
do	night 5/6th.	9 pm	NOS. 1.3 & 4 Sections with attached Infantry parties assembled in FAMPOUX - GAVRELLE line @ H.11.a. & afterwards moving forward to objectives, No1. Section with attached Infantry Party constructed NO II Strong Point at junction of CHARLIE and COSTA trenches at I.7.b.40.15. but not completed.	do.

– over –

2353 Wt. W2544/1454 700,000 5/15 D. D. & L. A.D.S.S./Forms/C. 2118.

Instructions regarding War Diaries and Intelligence Summaries are contained in F. S. Regs., Part II. and the Staff Manual respectively. Title pages will be prepared in manuscript.

WAR DIARY
or
~~INTELLIGENCE SUMMARY.~~
(Erase heading not required.)

II

Army Form C. 2118.

Place	Date	Hour	Summary of Events and Information	Remarks and references to Appendices
RAILWAY CUTTING. H.7.b.4.7.	night 5/6th (continued)		No3 Section unable to reach NoIII Strong Point in CHARLIE Trench @ I.1.d.75.10. on account of enemy barrage, but assisted Battalion holding new position to consolidate its objective. No4 Section standing by all night unable to reach objective No2 Section standing to in Billets.	Reference Map sheet 51 B N.W. and 1/10,000 PLOUVAIN sheet. do.
do.	night 6th/7th	9pm	All four sections moved up to Assembly positions, Nos 3 & 4 moved to objectives but prevented from completing strong points owing to 2 enemy counter attacks. Sections assisted by carrying up SAA. bombs &c. to the fighting garrisons. Nos 1 & 2 Sections moved to GAVRELLE – FAMPOUX line near "Sunken" Road to hold line as defensive position, and worked until dawn improving and consolidating trench.	do. do. do. do. do.
do.	Night. 7th/8th	9pm	Nos 1.3 & 4 Sections with attached Infantry Parties moved to assembly positions in CABLE Trench, afterwards moving up to objectives. and worked on Strong Points Nos 1 2 & 3. but were hampered by very strong hostile artillery fire. No2 Strong Point completed by No1. Section.	do. do. do. do.
do.	Night 8/9th.	9pm.	Nos 3 & 4 Sections working on Strong Points and completed same. No 3 S.P. @ I.1.d.75.10 and No1. S.P. at junction of CASH and CURLY Trenches at I.7.d.6.5.	do. do

(Casualties 6th 7th & 8th 1 OR Killed 4 OR wounded)

2353 Wt. W2544/1454 700,000 5/15 D. D. & L. A.D.S.S./Forms/C. 2118.

– over –

Army Form C. 2118.

III

Instructions regarding War Diaries and Intelligence Summaries are contained in F. S. Regs., Part II. and the Staff Manual respectively. Title pages will be prepared in manuscript.

WAR DIARY or INTELLIGENCE SUMMARY.

(Erase heading not required.)

Place	Date	Hour	Summary of Events and Information	Remarks and references to Appendices
RAILWAY CUTTING. H.7.b.4.7.	8/6/17 to 20/6/17		All four sections excavating and constructing mined dugouts for the 50th and 51st	Reference Sheet 57.B. N.W.
			Brigades at the following locations:- 2@ H.10.a.31. - 2@ H.10.c.3.9. - 2@ H.10.c.5.8-	
			2@ H10.c.2.7. (51st Brigade) @ H.10.c.3.3. - @ H.9.b.3.2. - @ H.9.b.2.4 - @	do.
			H.9.a.4.9. and H.7.a.7.9. (50th Brigade) and constructing Forward Observation Post @ H.16.b.7.9.	do.
			Mined dugout @ H.3.c.2.4 for 160th Brigade R.F.A.	do.
do.	nights 13th to 18th.		No 2 Section. Deepening TRENT Trench, deepening Existing wire, H.11.a. - Fixing Trench boards	do.
			in TRENT and CABLE Trenches.	do.
do.	21/6/17		34th Divn relieved by 17th Division on nights 20/21st and 21st/22nd. 77th Field Coy	do.
			R.E. takes over work in hand. Company remains in present billets in Railway	do.
			cutting at H.7.b.4.7. and Transport lines remain at G.17.a.7.9. Company takes	do.
			over work on Corps Line (EFFIE Trench) from 93rd Field Coy R.E. at 6am 21st.	do.
			and works under orders of C.E. XVII Corps.	do.
			(Reinforcements 21/6/17 10 O.RANKS)	

(over)

2353 Wt. W2544/1454 700,000 5/15 D. D. & L. A.D.S.S./Forms/C. 2118.

Instructions regarding War Diaries and Intelligence Summaries are contained in F. S. Regs., Part II. and the Staff Manual respectively. Title Pages will be prepared in manuscript.

WAR DIARY

~~or~~

~~INTELLIGENCE SUMMARY~~

(Erase heading not required.)

IIII

Army Form C. 2118

Place	Date	Hour	Summary of Events and Information	Remarks and references to Appendices
RAILWAY CUTTING. H.7.b. 4.7	21/6/17 to 30/6/17		4 Sections working on EFFIE Line, in continuous night and day	SHEET 57. B. N.W.
			shifts with 3/10 th Middlesex as working parties. – Excavating and	do.
			constructing Mined Dugouts for Machine Gunners – Constructing Strong	do.
			Points and wiring whole front of EFFIE Trench.	do.

A H Stephens
Major RE.
OC. 208 th Field Coy R.E.

1875 Wt. W593/826 1,000,000 4/15 J.B.C. & A. A.D.S.S./Forms/C. 2118.

Instructions regarding War Diaries and Intelligence Summaries are contained in F. S. Regs., Part II. and the Staff Manual respectively. Title Pages will be prepared in manuscript.

WAR DIARY
or
INTELLIGENCE SUMMARY
(Erase heading not required.)

Army Form C. 2118

Vol 19

Place	Date	Hour	Summary of Events and Information	Remarks and references to Appendices
			208th Field Coy R.E. — July 1917.	

1875 Wt. W593/826 1,000,000 4/15 J.B.C. & A. A.D.S.S./Forms/C. 2118.

Army Form C. 2118.

WAR DIARY ~~or~~ ~~INTELLIGENCE SUMMARY.~~

(*Erase heading not required.*)

1

Instructions regarding War Diaries and Intelligence Summaries are contained in F. S. Regs., Part II. and the Staff Manual respectively. Title pages will be prepared in manuscript.

Place	Date	Hour	Summary of Events and Information	Remarks and references to Appendices
RAILWAY CUTTING H.7.b.4.7	1/7/17		Company prepared for move, packing &c. Inspection of Arms Equipment Kits &c. Work in Hand handed over to 78th Field Coy R.E.	Reference Map sheet 51 B N.W. Ref. Lens 11.
do	2/7/17		Company moved to HERMAVILLE, and took over Billets evacuated by 18th Northumberland Fusiliers. Mounted Section moved from Camp at G.17.a.7.8. to HERMAVILLE by road. Dismounted Personnel marched from Railway Cutting H.7.b.4.7 to ROND POINT Arras, and embussed there, thence to Camp at HERMAVILLE.	
HERMAVILLE	3/7/17	4/7/17.	Company at rest. Inspections of Arms Ammunition &c. Refitting &c.	do.
do.	5/7/17		(34th Division moved to new area to relieve 4th & 5th Cavalry Divisions) Company marched from Camp at HERMAVILLE and entrained at TINCQUES. Moved by rail to PERONNE, detrained same night and bivouaced at I 28. d. for the night.	do. Ref 62 c FRANCE.
NR. PERONNE	6/7/17		Company marched from PERONNE to Billets at ROISEL at K.16.d.8.8.	do.
ROISEL K.16.d.8.8	7/7/17 and 8/7/17		No1. Section moved to, and constructed billets at, TEMPLEUX L.2.d.5.5.	do
			No3 Section moved to, and constructed billets at HESBECOURT. L.13.c.3.5.	do.
			No4. Section moved to, and constructed billets at JEANCOURT L.26.d.4.7.	do
			Transport Lines H.Q. and Billets for same, also No2 Section established at ROISEL.	do.

— over —

2353 Wt. W2544/1454 700,000 5/15 D. D. & L. A.D.S.S./Forms/C. 2118.

Instructions regarding War Diaries and Intelligence Summaries are contained in F. S. Regs., Part II. and the Staff Manual respectively. Title pages will be prepared in manuscript.

WAR DIARY
or
~~INTELLIGENCE SUMMARY.~~
(Erase heading not required.)

Army Form C. 2118.

2

Place	Date	Hour	Summary of Events and Information	Remarks and references to Appendices
ROISEL. K.16.d.8.8.	9/7/17.		Company relieved 4th Field Squadron in the Left ~~Sub~~ Sector, 34th Divl Front, and took over all work in line as follows:-	Reference 62 c FRANCE.
			No1. Section Billeted at TEMPLEUX work in B3 Subsector, Left. — No3 Section Billeted at HESBECOURT, work in B2 Subsector, Centre — No4 Section billeted at JEANCOURT work in B1. Subsector, Right.	do. do.
ROISEL. K.16.d.8.8.	10th to 24th		3 Sections in Line worked mainly on Intermediate Line, working at night when necessary, as follows:-	do. do.
			B3 Subsector Left. HARGICOURT Trench, comprising a series of 10 Posts, with M.G Emplacements from L.4.b.2.8. on NORTH, to L.10.b.4.3. on the South. Continuous work on whole trench system, deepening, widening, draining, duckwalking and fire stepping trenches.	do. do. do. do.
			B2 Subsector Centre FERVAQUE Trench, a continuous fire Trench with 2 Posts NTS of FERVAQUE Farm. This trench was firestepped for 3/4 of its length from L10.d.3.9 to L.16.c.3.4. Communication Trenches to 2 posts @ L.16.d.4.9. and L.16.c.9.3. partly dug. Continuous work draining duckwalking & firestepping	do. do. do. do.
			B3. Subsector Right. 8 Posts completed, firestepped and made defensible and joined up. No1. 2 & 3 communication trenches constructed from SUNKEN Road. Continuous work on above Intermediate Line, deepening widening draining, duckwalking and firestepping. Field of fire in GRAND PRIEL WOOD cleared	do. do. do.

— over —

2353 Wt. W2544/1454 700,000 5/15 D. D. & L. A.D.S.S./Forms/C. 2118.

Instructions regarding War Diaries and Intelligence Summaries are contained in F. S. Regs., Part II. and the Staff Manual respectively. Title Pages will be prepared in manuscript.

WAR DIARY
~~or~~
~~INTELLIGENCE SUMMARY~~
(Erase heading not required.)

3

Army Form C. 2118

Place	Date	Hour	Summary of Events and Information	Remarks and references to Appendices
ROISEL K16. d 8.8.	10th to 24th incl.		The following work was also carried out :- Observation Posts constructed at Post NO5 L.22. a. 9.2. and at Post No8 L.4.c. 8.8. wiring between posts 9 & 11 in L.6.a. – constructing Shelter at L15 b. 1.3 for Brigade Runners – Also 2 Sappers in each of above subsectors were employed giving technical assistance to Infantry on work in Outposts, East of Intermediate Line.	Reference 62c FRANCE. do. do.
do.	10th to 15th		NO2 Section, was employed working on R.E. Dump MONTIGNY @ K.35.d. 8.6	do.
do.	16th to 20th.		Erecting Divl. Baths at ROISEL K16. c. 7.1. – Fixing and repg. Horse Troughs at HAMELET. – Erecting Baths at HAMELET.	
do	21st to 24th.		NO2 Section ~~...~~ working in B3 Subsector with No1. Section as shewn above.	do.
do.	17th to 20th		4 Sappers employed in line, giving technical assistance to T.M.B's	do.
do.	22/7/17		Casualties. 1 Officer and 1 O.Rank, wounded (Gassed).	
do	25/7/17		Company relieved in Left Sector by 207th Field Coy R.E. Company moved from ROISEL K.16. d. 8.8. to NOBESCOURT WOOD Q.1. a. 8. 8. Nos 3 & 4 Sections moved direct from HESBECOURT and JEANCOURT to NOBESCOURT WOOD. No1 Section moved direct from TEMPLEUX to MONTIGNY DUMP at K 35 d. 8. 6.	do. do do do

— over —

1875 Wt. W593/826 1,000,000 4/15 J.B.C. & A. A.D.S.S./Forms/C. 2118.

Instructions regarding War Diaries and Intelligence Summaries are contained in F. S. Regs., Part II. and the Staff Manual respectively. Title pages will be prepared in manuscript.

WAR DIARY

~~or~~

~~INTELLIGENCE SUMMARY.~~

(*Erase heading not required.*)

4

Army Form C. 2118.

Place	Date	Hour	Summary of Events and Information	Remarks and references to Appendices
NOBESCOURT WOOD. Q.1.a.8.8.	26th to 31/7/17.		Company worked, as Reserve Company, in Back Area as follows:-	Reference 62 C.
			Cleaning wells at BERNES, at Water Points No6 Q.4.c.4.0. & No4 Q4.c.5.2.	FRANCE.
			Constructing Div. Baths at ROISEL K.16.c.7.1. – Repairing	do.
			wells NOS 2, 5 & 8 at VRAIGNES. – Fitting up D.H.Q. at NOBESCOURT	do.
			FARM K.32.d. cent. – Erecting NISSEN Huts in Div. Area – No1 Section	do.
			working on R.E. Dump at MONTIGNY at K.35.d.8.6.	do.

J H Stephens

Major RE

208th Field Coy RE.

Instructions regarding War Diaries and Intelligence Summaries are contained in F. S. Regs., Part II. and the Staff Manual respectively. Title pages will be prepared in manuscript.

WAR DIARY

~~or~~

~~INTELLIGENCE~~ SUMMARY.

(Erase heading not required.)

Army Form C. 2118.

Vol 20

Place	Date	Hour	Summary of Events and Information	Remarks and references to Appendices
			— 208TH FIELD COY. R.E. —	
			AUGUST – 1917.	

A7092 Wt. W128 9/M1293 750,000. 1/17. D. D & L. Ltd. Forms/C2118/14.

Instructions regarding War Diaries and Intelligence Summaries are contained in F. S. Regs., Part II. and the Staff Manual respectively. Title pages will be prepared in manuscript.

WAR DIARY
or
~~INTELLIGENCE SUMMARY.~~
(Erase heading not required.)

Army Form C. 2118.

1

Place	Date	Hour	Summary of Events and Information	Remarks and references to Appendices
NOBESCOURT WOOD Q.1.a.8.8	1/8/17		Company worked as Reserve Company as follows:-	Reference 62c FRANCE
			Divisional Baths constructed at ROISEL K.16.c.7.1. – Fitting up D.H.Q at	do.
			NOBESCOURT FARM. K.32 d. central. – Erected Nissen Huts in Div. area –	do.
			No1. Section employed on R.E. Dump at MONTIGNY. K.35.d.8.6.	do.
do	2/8/17		Company relieved the 209th Field Coy R.E. in the Right Sector of Div.	do.
			Front. Company moved from NOBESCOURT WOOD as follows:-	do.
			No1. & 4 Sections to JEANCOURT L.26 d. 3 3. – No2 Section to VADENCOURT	do.
			R.16.b. 2.2. – No3 Section, Coy H.Q. and Transport to MONTIGNY Dump at	do.
			K.35.b.8.2. (Reinforcements 3/8/17 2 ORs.)	do.
K.35.b.8.2. ~~K.15.b.8.8.~~ (Coy H.Q.)	3/8/17 to 13/8/17		Company working on Right Sector as follows:-	do.
			FORT DYCE (LE VERGUIER) Tunnelling and Making M.G. emplacement, constructing New Fire Trench and New Communication Trench. Draining Trenches and Revetting same. Constructing Mined Dugout.	do. do.
			FORT BELL. (LE VERGUIER) Constructing Mined Dugout, widening and deepening trench Revetting Fire Trench. Constructing Machine Gun Emplacement. Draining Trenches.	do. do.
			FORT GREATHEAD (LE VERGUIER) Constructing New Machine Gun Emplacement, cutting Trench through road, draining Trenches, constructing Mined Dugout, Revetting Trenches.	do.

A7092 Wt. W128 9/M1293 750,000. 1/17. D. D & I. Ltd. Forms/C2118/14.

(over)

Army Form C. 2118.

Instructions regarding War Diaries and Intelligence Summaries are contained in F. S. Regs., Part II. and the Staff Manual respectively. Title pages will be prepared in manuscript.

WAR DIARY
~~or~~
~~INTELLIGENCE SUMMARY.~~
(Erase heading not required.)

2

Place	Date	Hour	Summary of Events and Information	Remarks and references to Appendices
K. 35 b.8.2 Coy HQ	3/8/17 to 13/9/17 (cont)		FORT LEES (LE VERGUIER). Constructing Dugout - Revetting and draining Trench - Making new Fire Trench.	Reference 62 c FRANCE.
			PIEUMAL Trench and PIEUMAL POST. deepening, draining, duckwalking & firestepping from L 28.d 1.9. to L28 d 1.7	do.
			ORCHARD Trench. do. do. from L.34.a.9.8 to L28c.95 25.	do.
			BOB Trench. do. do. from L 34.a.9.6 to L34.a.9.4.	do.
			TAG Trench. do do, strengthening wire {R.4.b.6.7. to Junction of HEN and DEAN Trenches	do
			DEAN Trench. do. do. revetting & wiring. R.4.b.9.5. and R.5.c.7.8	do.
			Sapper assists erection of shelter for M.G Coy at FIR COPSE R.5.a.8.3.	do.
			Camouflaging Road at L.34.a.9.7. - PONTRU and MOREVAL Trenches repairing	do.
			draining deepening and duckwalking - wiring Supporting Point at R.11.a. -	do.
			Constructing Screen from BIHECOURT to Brown Line at R.11.c.	do.
			COOKER'S QUARRY {R.11.c. Constructing mined dugout, Repg Cupola Dugout and flooring 2 Cupolas dugouts.	do
			MUSTARD QUARRY. M.7.b. Constructing Mined Dugout.	do
			PONTRU GARDENS. M.7.d.8.6. Constructing concrete Machine Gun Emplacement.	do.
			Inspecting and overhauling Bridges and Sluices in Right Sector.	do.
	9/8/17 to 13/9/17		No1 Section working on Outposts in Right Sector.	do.

A7092 Wt. W128.9/M1293 750,000. 1/17. D. D & L. Ltd. Forms/C2118/14.

(over)

Instructions regarding War Diaries and Intelligence Summaries are contained in F. S. Regs., Part II. and the Staff Manual respectively. Title pages will be prepared in manuscript.

WAR DIARY

or

~~INTELLIGENCE SUMMARY.~~

(*Erase heading not required.*)

3

Army Form C. 2118.

Place	Date	Hour	Summary of Events and Information	Remarks and references to Appendices
~~35~~ K.E. 6. 8. 2. Coy HQ.	14/8/17		Company relieved by 209th Field Coy RE. in Right Sector of Div. Front. Company	Reference 62 c FRANCE.
			relieves 207th Field Coy RE. in Left Sector of Div. Front and moved as follows:-	do.
			No1 & 2 Sections to Billets at TEMPLEUX L.2.d.5.5 – No3 Section to Billets at HESBECOURT. L.13.c.3.5.	do.
			No4 Section to Billet at JEANCOURT. L.26.d.4.7. HQ and Transport to ROISEL K.16.d.8.8.	do.
ROISEL. K.16. d. 8. 8.	15/8/17 to 25/8/17		Company working continuously as follows:-	do.
			Intermediate Line:- HARGICOURT Trench. Posts Nos 1.2.3.8.9 & 10.	do
			Rep. drains, deepening, duckwalking, revetting and firestepping.	do.
			APPLE TREE Trench. L.28. b. 1. 4. Deepening, widening, draining and duckwalking.	do.
			COTE Trench at junction with FERVAQUE. L.16.a.7.7.	do.
			Deepening, duckwalking and draining. FERVAQUE Trench. L.16.a.5.5. to L.16.c.3.5.	do.
			Draining and duckwalking Trench to FERVAQUE FARM.	do.
			GRAND PRIEL Trench. at L.28.a.9.5., L.22.c.8.3., L.22.c.8.6. and L.22.a.5.2.	do.
			Deepening, widening, firestepping, duckwalking, draining and repairing.	do.
			The following work was also carried out:-	do.
			Culvert 400 yards N.W. of TEMPLEUX completed – Camouflage Screen erected from L.10.a.6.9. to L.10.a.6.6.	do.
			Advanced Bde HQ. L.10.a.4.5. furnished with Bunks and Signal Tables &c. Gas proofing dugout entrances.	do.
			"THE EGG" Battn HQ. L.11.b.5.5. Furnished with Tables – Gas-proofing dugout entrances.	do
			"THE EGG" AID POST. Gas proofing dugout entrances, making and fixing racks for stretchers.	do
			2 Battalion HQ. @ L.5.b.3.1. furnished with Bunks, and Tables for Signallers, gas proofing dugout entrances.	do.

(over).

A7092 Wt. W128.9/M1293 750,000. 1/17. D. D & L. Ltd. Forms/C2118/14.

Instructions regarding War Diaries and Intelligence Summaries are contained in F. S. Regs., Part II. and the Staff Manual respectively. Title Pages will be prepared in manuscript.

WAR DIARY
or
~~INTELLIGENCE SUMMARY~~
(Erase heading not required.)

Army Form C. 2118

4

Place	Date	Hour	Summary of Events and Information	Remarks and references to Appendices
ROISEL. K16.d. 8.8.	15/8/17 to 25/8/17 (cont)		Battalion H.Q. @ L.11.b.1.9 and L.11.a.9.9. Furnishing with Tables, Gas-proofing dugout entrances.	Ref 62c FRANCE.
			AID POST, HARGICOURT erected and completed, furnished with Table and racks for stretchers.	do.
			Entrances fitted and made Gas-proof with Blankets.	do.
			ADVANCED DIVL. HQ. erected at HERVILLY. Nissen huts erected, Armstrong hut re-erected Latrines, cook houses, Engine House, and offices erected and furnished.	do.
			No1. Section employed on Outposts in Right Divl Sector, under orders from G.O.C. 102nd Brigade.	do.
			No3 Section employed on work on COLOGNE Defenses under orders from G.O.C 102nd Brigade.	do.
			4 Sappers attached to H.T.M Battery for technical assistance in constructing emplacements	do.
			in line. (Reinforcements 24th (1 O.R.))	do.
ROISEL K16.d 8.8	25th		Company relieved by 207th Field Coy R.E. in Left Sector and moves to	do.
			NOBESCOURT WOOD Q.1.a. 8.8. (No1. Section remaining in line attached to	do.
			207th Field Coy R.E.)	do.
NOBESCOURT WOOD Q.1.a 8.8	26/8/17 to 28/8/17		Company (less No1. Section) working as Reserve Company: Erecting	do
			and Revetboarding Nissen huts at VENDELLES. 8 O.Rs of No2. Reinforcement Co. R.E.	do.
			at work with Nos. 2 & 4 Sections of this Company on Bde. Lodges,	do
			R.8.b.3.3. No3. Section working on erection of Nissen Huts and	do:
			winter horse standings at NOBESCOURT WOOD. Fitting up cook-house	do.
			(over).	

1875 Wt. W593/826 1,000,000 4/15 J.B.C. & A. A.D.S.S./Forms/C. 2118.

Army Form C. 2118.

Instructions regarding War Diaries and Intelligence Summaries are contained in F. S. Regs., Part II. and the Staff Manual respectively. Title pages will be prepared in manuscript.

WAR DIARY

~~or~~

~~INTELLIGENCE SUMMARY.~~

(Erase heading not required.)

5.

Place	Date	Hour	Summary of Events and Information	Remarks and references to Appendices
NOBESCOURT WOOD. Q.1.a.8.8.	26/8/17 to 28/8/17 (cont)		at D.H.Q. at NOBESCOURT FARM, K.32.g.central. Erected huts at CAULINCOURT. No.1 Section attached to 207th Field Co. R.E. to assist in the preparation of trenches for offensive operations.	Reference 62c FRANCE. do do
do.	29th		Company relieved 209th Field Co. R.E., in Centre & Right Sectors of Divisional front. Company moved from NOBESCOURT WOOD as follows:- Nos. 3 + 4 Sections to JEANCOURT L.26.d.3.3. – No.2 Sectn to VADENCOURT, R.16.b.2.2. – Coy. Hdqrs and Transport to MONTIGNY DUMP at K.35.b.8.2. – No.1 Sectn detached from 207th Fld. Co. R.E., and moved to billets at MONTIGNY DUMP, (K.35.b.8.2).	do do do do do do
K.35.b.8.2. (Coy Hdqrs)	30th to 31/8/17		Work on communication trench from G.7.b.42.45. to POND TRENCH at G.7.b.60.63. Digging trench from NEWPOST No.7. G.7.b.25.30 to road at G.12.c.95.75. (Night 29th-30th Aug. 17.) No.1. Section moved from billets at MONTIGNY DUMP to billets at TEMPLEUX and worked on wiring from G.7.d.15.70. to G.7.d.15.20. No2 Section carried out work as follows:- COOKER'S QUARRY:- Fitting in bomb boxes. – MUSTARD QUARRY:- Making chambers in mined dug-out. COOKER'S TRENCH:- Drainage. PONTRU GARDENS:- Making M.G. Emplacement.	do do do do do do do do

(over).

A7092 Wt. W128 9/M1293 750,000. 1/17. D. D & L. Ltd. Forms/C2118/14.

Army Form C. 2118.

Instructions regarding War Diaries and Intelligence Summaries are contained in F. S. Regs., Part II. and the Staff Manual respectively. Title pages will be prepared in manuscript.

WAR DIARY

~~or~~

~~INTELLIGENCE SUMMARY.~~

(Erase heading not required.)

6.

Place	Date	Hour	Summary of Events and Information	Remarks and references to Appendices
K.35.b.8.2 (Coy Hdqrs)	30/8/17 to 31/8/17 (cont)		Nos 3 & 4 sections also carried out the following:- NEW 6 POST dug and prepared for garrison. Communication trench from NEW 6 to NEW 7 POST dug and communication provided. This line was wired with single apron fence. Wiring carried out in front of communication trench, G.7.b.42.45 to POND TRENCH, G.7.b.60.63. 8 ORs from this company worked on R.E. DUMP, K.35.b.8.2 from 2/8/17 to 31/8/17. 5 ORs were attached to C.E.A. & assisted in the erection of huts in the Divisional area, for them, from 3/8/17 to 31/8/17. [signature] Major RE O.C. 208th Field Coy RE.	Reference 62c FRANCE.

A7092 Wt. W128 9/M1293 750,000. 1/17. D. D & L. Ltd. Forms/C2118/14.

Army Form C. 2118.

Instructions regarding War Diaries and Intelligence Summaries are contained in F. S. Regs., Part II. and the Staff Manual respectively. Title pages will be prepared in manuscript.

WAR DIARY

~~or~~

~~INTELLIGENCE SUMMARY.~~

(Erase heading not required.)

Vol 21

Place	Date	Hour	Summary of Events and Information	Remarks and references to Appendices
			208th Field Coy R.E.	
			September 1917.	

A7092 Wt. W128.9/M1293. 750,000. 1/17. D. D & L. Ltd. Forms/C2118/14.

Army Form C. 2118

Instructions regarding War Diaries and Intelligence Summaries are contained in F. S. Regs., Part II. and the Staff Manual respectively. Title Pages will be prepared in manuscript.

WAR DIARY
~~or~~
~~INTELLIGENCE SUMMARY~~
(Erase heading not required.)

1

Place	Date	Hour	Summary of Events and Information	Remarks and references to Appendices
K35. b 8. 2	1/9/17 to 11/9/17		Company worked in Right Divl Sector as follows:-	Reference 62 c. France.
			COOKERS' Trench - widening, draining, deepening, duckboarding and firestepping.	
			COOKERS QUARRY:- Fixing Gas Curtains and Bomb Boxes, excavating Chamber for same.	do.
			TWIN CRATER:- Making corduroy roadway. - MOREVAL TR: Refitting Gas Blankets to Dugouts.	do.
			MUSTARD QUARRY:- Making chambers in Mined dugout and concreting - PONTRU GARDENS	do.
			Making Concrete Machine Gun Emplacement - BERNES and MONTIGNY Repg Divl: Baths - VADENCOURT	do.
			Erecting Billets - L.b c. 61 Erecting Road Screen - CAULINCOURT Erecting Hutments for R.F.A. -	do.
			K 35. b 8. 2. Coy. Transport Lines erecting winter Horse standings. The following work was carried	do.
			out in conjunction with operations:-	do.
			CLUB Communication Trench completed from POND Trench at G.7 b. 60. 63. to New No7 Post.	do.
			thence to New No6 Post and thence along sunken road to L.12. d 4. 9, wired throughout	do.
			and wire connected up with that at MARTIN post. ONION Lane Trench dug through	do.
			from L.6. d. 6. 2. to POND Trench. A Communication Trench from No4 Post dug Eastwards to	do.
			G.7. d 10. 15, two fire bays constructed to form advanced POST No4, trench continued Eastwards for	do.
			about 140 yards. C.T. dug westward from MARTIN POST to SUNKEN ROAD at L.18. b 45 70.	do
			and joined with MER post. Thence a fire trench dug to No2 Post, and wire complete.	do
			C.T. from MARTIN Post dug for 200 yards due Eastward.	do.

(over)

1875 Wt. W593/826 1,000,000 4/15 J.B.C. & A. A.D.S.S./Forms/C. 2118.

Army Form C. 2118.

Instructions regarding War Diaries and Intelligence Summaries are contained in F. S. Regs., Part II. and the Staff Manual respectively. Title pages will be prepared in manuscript.

WAR DIARY
or
~~INTELLIGENCE SUMMARY.~~

(Erase heading not required.)

II

Place	Date	Hour	Summary of Events and Information	Remarks and references to Appendices
K35. b. 8.2.	12/9/17		Company relieved in Line by 207th Field Coy RE. Coy moves to NOBESCOURT WOOD Q.1 a. 8.8. so worked as Reserve Coy as follows:-	Map Reference 62 C France
Q.1.a. 8.8.	13/9/17 to 17/9/17		Erecting Nissen Huts at BERNES (No2 Hospital Hut, COURT MARTIAL Hut) and at K. 28. b. — Erecting Horse standings for V Battery, RHA — VENDELLES, Erecting Nissen Huts & bomb shelter, bunking adrian Hut — Erecting Adrian Huts and billets for Divl Train at K22. b. — HERVILLY, Erecting Office for 3rd Field Survey Coy RE, bunks in Huts, & Nissen huts for 160th Bde R.F.A. — SMALLFOOT WOOD Camouflaging Huts, — NOBESCOURT WOOD, Erecting Winter Hutments for Reserve Field Coy ie Nissen Huts, adrian Hut, horse-standings &c.	do.
Q.1.a. 8.8.	18/9/17		Company relieves 209th Field Coy RE. in Left Divl. Sector in Line. Company moves from NOBESCOURT Q.1. a. 8.8. to new billets as follows:- H.Q., Transport Lines and No3 Section to ROISEL (K 16. d. 8.8.) No2 Section to Quarry N. of TEMPLEUX (F 27 c r d) Nos 1 & 4 Sections to TEMPLEUX village (L.2 d. 2.1.) Company working in line as	do.
K.6. d. 8.8.	19/9/17 to 26/9/17		follows:- ENFILADE Trench - Deepening and widening laying duckwalks, SUGAR Trench clearing deepening & widening Trench — ONION Deepening & clearing and duckwalking Trench RUBY LANE, deepening & draining trench - MINNOW Trench, duckwalking revetting & fireshipping digging new trench round Manure heap.	do.

(cont.)

A7092 Wt. W12S 9/M1293 750,000. 1/17. D. D & L. Ltd. Forms/C2118/14.

Instructions regarding War Diaries and Intelligence Summaries are contained in F. S. Regs., Part II. and the Staff Manual respectively. Title pages will be prepared in manuscript.

WAR DIARY

or

~~INTELLIGENCE~~ SUMMARY.

(*Erase heading not required.*)

III

Army Form C. 2118.

Place	Date	Hour	Summary of Events and Information	Remarks and references to Appendices
K.16. d. 8.8.	19/9/17 to 26/9/17 (cont.)		BAIT Trench, clearing and revetting, cutting new traverse. _CARBINE Trench digging	Map reference 62 c.
			firebays driving tunnel under 4 cross roads – INDIAN Trench, widening deepening and	France
			duckwalking – FISH LANE, deepening & widening – MALAKOFF Support fixing shelters	do.
			in parapets, cutting firesteps and revetting same and revetting parados. – RIFLE PIT	do.
			Trench, digging trench across road, building sandbag barricade, deepening and widening	do.
			trench, – BOWER LANE widening and deepening trench, – POND Trench, deepening trench – G.1.d. 6.6.	do.
			New trench dug and firestepped, constructing firebays & strongpoint. (this trench joins	do.
			FISH Trench and BAIT Trench) – NEW CUT at junction with SUGAR Trench, clearing	do.
			and deepening. – DIVL. Signal Station HARGICOURT (L.5.c.6.1.) erecting cupola dugout in	do.
			cellar – Dressing Station at TEMPLEUX (L.2.c.8.6.) constructing Dressing Stn using	do.
			arched roof of Stn. and strengthening same. – GUM Boot Store and Drying Room at	do.
			HARGICOURT L.4.d.75.35. constructing same using old houses – Work on Rifle Range at	do.
			HANCOURT, blowing up ground for practices. – WELL at L.10.a 7.6. Repg winding gear.	do.
"	26/9/17		34th Division in line relieved by 24th Division, company relieved in line by	do.
			129th Field Coy R.E., 2 Sections at TEMPLEUX (L.2.d.5.5.) and 1 at TEMPLEUX	do.
			QUARRY (L.4.c.) moved to ROISEL (K.16.d.8.8.).	do.
	1/9/17 to 26/9/17		7 O.R.s employed on R.E. Dump MONTIGNY (K.35.b.8.1)	

(over)

A7092 Wt. W125 9/M1293 750,000. 1/17. D. D & L. Ltd. Forms/C2118/14.

Army Form C. 2118.

Instructions regarding War Diaries and Intelligence Summaries are contained in F. S. Regs., Part II. and the Staff Manual respectively. Title pages will be prepared in manuscript.

~~WAR DIARY~~
~~or~~
INTELLIGENCE SUMMARY.
(*Erase heading not required.*)

IIII

Place	Date	Hour	Summary of Events and Information	Remarks and references to Appendices
K.16. d. 8. 8.	27/9/17 to 30/9/17		Company concentrated at ROISEL K. 16. d. 8. 8, and remaining for work in line as follows:-	Map Reference 62 C France
			Laying out, excavating and digging New Support Line (Fire Trench) between	do.
			TURNIP Trench and VILLERET LANE.	do.
				do.
Casualties :-				
		1/9/17	1 OR. killed.	
			1 OR. wounded.	
		2/9/17	1 Officer killed	
		9/9/17	2 OR's wounded.	

J H Stephens
Major R.E.
Cdg. 208th Field Coy R.E.

A7092 Wt. W128.9/M1293 750,000. 1/17. D. D & L. Ltd. Forms/C2118/14.

Instructions regarding War Diaries and Intelligence Summaries are contained in F. S. Regs., Part II. and the Staff Manual respectively. Title pages will be prepared in manuscript.

WAR DIARY

~~or~~

~~INTELLIGENCE~~ SUMMARY.

(*Erase heading not required.*)

Army Form C. 2118.

Vol 22

Place	Date	Hour	Summary of Events and Information	Remarks and references to Appendices
			208th Field Coy R.E.	
			October 1917	
			VOL XXII	

Instructions regarding War Diaries and Intelligence Summaries are contained in F. S. Regs., Part II. and the Staff Manual respectively. Title pages will be prepared in manuscript.

WAR DIARY or INTELLIGENCE SUMMARY.

(Erase heading not required.)

I

Army Form C. 2118.

Place	Date	Hour	Summary of Events and Information	Remarks and references to Appendices
ROISEL K.16.d.8.8	1/10/17 to 3/10/17	-	Company worked in line as follows:- Laying out, excavating and digging New Support line (Shire Trench) between "Turnip" Trench and VILLERET Lane.	Reference 62c France.
ROISEL K.16.d.8.8	4/10/17		Company moves from Billets at ROISEL to Billets at MONCHIET in VI Corps Area and rejoins Division as follows:- Dismounted personnel by Busses, mounted by March route via LONGAVESNES - NURLU - MANANCOURT - LE TRANSLOY - BAPAUME - BOISLEUX-AU-MONT - MONCHIET.	62c France. LENS 11. AMIENS 17 ST QUENTIN 18.
MONCHIET.	5/10/17 & 6/10/17		Company resting, parades for Inspection of Arms Equipment, Box respirators &c.	LENS. 11
MONCHIET	7/10/17		Division moves from Reserve Area to XIV Corps area 5th Army. Company moves from Billets at MONCHIET and moves to PILGRIM Camp at E.4.c. west of PROYEN as follows:- Marched from MONCHIET to SAULTY Station, there entrained, moved by Rail to PESELHOEK there detrained, marched by road to Billets at PILGRIM Camp.	LENS 11 HAZEBROUCK 5A sheets 27 & 28 France " "
PILGRIM Camp E.4.c	8/10/17		Company moved by night to forward Area to Camp at PARROY FARM. (B.16.c.) to 29th Divl Area as follows:- Dismounted sections marched by road to PROYEN STN, thence by Rail to ELVERDINGHE, thence by road to Camp at PARROY FARM. - mounted sections moved direct by road to PARROY FARM.	Sheets 27 & 28 FRANCE. " " "

A7092 Wt. W128 9/M1293 750,000. 1/17. D. D & L. Ltd. Forms/C2118/14.

— over —

Army Form C. 2118.

WAR DIARY
~~or~~
~~INTELLIGENCE~~ SUMMARY.
(Erase heading not required.)

II

Instructions regarding War Diaries and Intelligence Summaries are contained in F. S. Regs., Part II. and the Staff Manual respectively. Title pages will be prepared in manuscript.

Place	Date	Hour	Summary of Events and Information	Remarks and references to Appendices
PARRDY FARM B.16.c	9/10/17 to 12/10/17		Company employed in reliefs as follows:- Clearing and repairing LANGEMARCK - POELCAPPELLE Road from SCHREIBOOM to V.19.a.5.2. Road was cleared to Stone setts and shell holes filled up with material available on site. Infantry working parties were also employed loading and off-loading wagons and carrying material as far as U.23 central to U.23.b.5.3. Casualties 9th. (1 OR wounded)	FRANCE sheet 28 and BROEMBEEK 1/10,000.
do.	11/10/17 & 12/10/17		TUFTS FARM Road to MARTINS MILL.- Repg road, clearing bad places, filling up holes with hard material; from U.27.c.1.8. to U.27.a.60.25 and from U.27.b.2.5 to U.22.c.07.12. (Casualty 11th 1 OR wounded)	"
do	13/10/17		Company relieved the 9th Field Coy RE in line and moves as follows:- HQ and 4 Sections to dugouts in CANAL BANK at C.19.a.0.3. Transport &c to lines at B.24.c.0.2. 100 Infantry from 102nd Inf. Bde reported to Coy and are permanently attached for work, as carrying parties &c.	"
CANAL BANK C.19.a.0.3.	13/10/17 to 22/10/17		Company ~~is~~ employed on the extension and maintenance of a Trenchboard path known as "TRACK A". The track was duckboarded, partly double-boarded, from CANAL BANK at C.13.a.3.6. to V.13.b.89.90. Notice Boards marked Track "A" were fixed up to V.13.b.89.90. From V.13.b.89.90. ~~to~~ to V.8.c.5.0 the track was taped out.	"

— over —

A7092 Wt. W128 9/M1293 750,000. 1/17. D. D & L. Ltd. Forms/C2118/14.

Instructions regarding War Diaries and Intelligence Summaries are contained in F. S. Regs., Part II. and the Staff Manual respectively. Title pages will be prepared in manuscript.

WAR DIARY

~~or~~

~~INTELLIGENCE SUMMARY.~~

(Erase heading not required.)

III

Army Form C. 2118.

Place	Date	Hour	Summary of Events and Information	Remarks and references to Appendices
CANAL BANK C.19.a.0.3.	13/10/17 to 22/10/17 (cont.)		2 sections were employed by day on the maintenance of the Track in two reliefs of 4 hours each, - the remaining two sections worked at night with infantry parties on the extension of the track. A small party of sappers were employed daily fixing bearers and trench boards laid the previous night. Forward Dumps were established at BROAD ST. Dump at C.8.a.7.5. and WEEDON Dump at V.28.c.5.3. Company transport was employed each night carrying up loads of duckwalks &c to forward dumps. The track, as above, was extended as follows:-	Sheet 28 N.W. BROMBEEK 1/10,000 and SCAAP-BAILIE 1/10,000. " " " "
			From 13th to 18th. to V.13.b.2.2. (Casualties 1 OR. wounded at duty)	"
			19th to V.13.b.3.3. (" 1 OR wounded, 1 OR wounded, gassed)	"
			20th to V.13.b.36.30 (" 2 OR wounded 2 OR wounded gassed at duty)	"
			21st to V.13.b.45.55. (" 1 Officer killed, 1 OR wounded (1 OR. " at duty)	"
			22nd to V.13.b.48.70. (" 1 OR killed 3 OR (wounded) & 1 OR wounded at duty	"
			23rd to V.13.b.85.90. (" NIL.)	"
do	night 21/22nd		Bridges across the STEENBEEK were fixed at V.7.d.70.75 and at V.7.a.90.25	"
do	14/10/17 to 16/10/17		2 Sappers employed fitting up Advanced BHQ (stoves &c) ~~in~~ YPRES CANAL Bank at C.19.a.	"

— over —

A7092 Wt. W12S.9/M1293 750,000. 1/17. D. D & L. Ltd. Forms/C2118/14.

Army Form C. 2118.

Instructions regarding War Diaries and Intelligence Summaries are contained in F. S. Regs., Part II. and the Staff Manual respectively. Title pages will be prepared in manuscript.

WAR DIARY

or

~~INTELLIGENCE SUMMARY.~~

(Erase heading not required.)

IIII

Place	Date	Hour	Summary of Events and Information	Remarks and references to Appendices
CANAL BANK C.19.a.0.3.	23/10/17		34th Division relieved in Line by 50th & 57th Divisions – Coy. relieved by 505th Field Coy R.E. and moved to PROVEN AREA as follows:- Mounted sections direct by road from Camp at B.24.c.0.2. to PILGRIM CAMP (E.4.c.) (27) Dismounted sections and H.Q. marched to ELVERDINGHE Stn, entrained and moved by rail to PROVEN, detrained and marched by road to PILGRIM CAMP (E.4.c) 27.	Sheets 27 & 28 FRANCE. " " " "
PILGRIM CAMP.	24/10/17 to 28/10/17		Company at rest – Inspections of arms, Equipment, Box respirators &c. Parades for Baths at PROVEN.	" "
do.	29/10/17		34th Division moved from XIV Corps Area to VI Corps Area and relieved 51st Division in line. Company marched by road to HOPOUTRE Station (South of POPERINGHE and entrained at 11.25 am, arrived at BOISLEUX-AU-MONT at 7 pm. detrained and marched to ARGYLE CAMP at S.17 central (sheet 51.b S.W.)	HAZEBROUCK 5A. & LENS 11. 51. b. S.W. " "
ARGYLE CAMP. S.17. central	30/10/17		Company relieved 401st Field Coy R.E. (51st Division) in line and moved as follows Nos 2. 3. & 4 Sections to dugouts in SUNKEN ROAD at N.22.d. 8 4. No1 Section to Huts at T.1.c.8 3. – Transport and lines to BOIRY-BECQUERELLE at T.7.b.0.8.	" " "

— over —

A7092 Wt. W128.9/M1293 750,000. 1/17. D. D & L. Ltd. Forms/C2118/14.

Army Form C. 2118.

Instructions regarding War Diaries and Intelligence Summaries are contained in F. S. Regs., Part II. and the Staff Manual respectively. Title pages will be prepared in manuscript.

WAR DIARY
~~or~~
~~INTELLIGENCE~~ SUMMARY.

(Erase heading not required.)

V

Place	Date	Hour	Summary of Events and Information	Remarks and references to Appendices
SUNKEN RD. N.22d 8.4.	31/10/17		Company employed ~~as~~ follows:-	57 c. S.W.
			Revetting Fire bays, making new traverses, firestepping and erecting shelters in the	"
			following posts :- Right Sub-sector - BB, R, O, N, & M. Left Sub sector JJ, KK, LL	"
			M.M, NN and O.O. — Fixing Gas Curtains on dugouts at Regt. aid Post at SHIKAR	"
			AVENUE O.19d.3.8. — Erecting camouflage road screen at N.22.d. — ~~E~~ Making	"
			Entrances and strengthening MARLIERE Caves N.23.b. and bunking same —	"
			Work was also carried out on dugouts (Coy. Billets) at N.22.d.8.4.	"

J H Stephens
Major R.E.
Cd. 208th Field Coy R.E.

A7092 Wt. W128_9/M1293 750,000. 1/17. D. D & L. Ltd. Forms/C2118/14.

Army Form C. 2118.

Vol 23

Instructions regarding War Diaries and Intelligence Summaries are contained in F. S. Regs., Part II. and the Staff Manual respectively. Title pages will be prepared in manuscript.

WAR DIARY

or

~~INTELLIGENCE SUMMARY.~~

(Erase heading not required.)

Place	Date	Hour	Summary of Events and Information	Remarks and references to Appendices
			208th Field Coy R.E.	
			November 1917	

A7092 Wt. W128 9/M1293 750,000. 1/17. D. D & L. Ltd. Forms/C2118/14.

Instructions regarding War Diaries and Intelligence Summaries are contained in F. S. Regs., Part II. and the Staff Manual respectively. Title pages will be prepared in manuscript.

Army Form C. 2118.

WAR DIARY

or

~~INTELLIGENCE SUMMARY.~~

(*Erase heading not required.*)

I

Place	Date	Hour	Summary of Events and Information	Remarks and references to Appendices
T.1.c.8.3.	1/11/17 to 30/11/17		Coy H.Q. remained at T.1.c.8.3. — No2 Section in Huts at T.1.c.8.3 — Nos 1 3 + 4 Sections in shelters and dugouts at SUNKEN RD at N.22.d.8.4. — Transport and lines at BOIRY-BECQUERELLE at T.7.b.0.8. — Attached Infantry at WANCOURT. Company employed continuously in Left Brigade Sector in line and carried out the following work:-	Sheet 57 b. S.W.
	"		Front line — Posts:- O.O. @ O.14.a.75.70 — N.N @ O.14.a.7.6. — M.M. @ O.14.a.7.4. L.L. @ O.14.a.7.3. — K.K. @ O.14.a.7.2 — J.J. @ O.14.a.6.0. — H.H. @ O.14.b.5.9. — G.G. @ O.14.b.6.7. — FF @ O.14.b.3.5. — E.E. @ O.14.b.3.2 — D.D @ O.20.a.4.8. — C.C @ O.20.a.7.5. B.B. @ O.20.a.8.5. — A.A. @ O.20.a.95.45. — R. @ O.20.b.1.3. — P. @ O.20.b.2.1. O. @ O.20.b.3.0 — N @ O.20.d.3.8. — M. @ O.20.d.1.7. — L @ O.20.c.95.50. H. @ O.20.c.8.2 — D @ O.26.a.5.7:- Making and Rifle Racks, S.A.A. and Bomb Boxes &c. in firebays; cutting and making new firebays and traverses; constructing shelters in firebays and traverses; fitting Sump Boxes, clearing berms and parapets, sandbagging elbow rests; deepening, clearing, widening, draining revetting, firestepping + duckwalking constructing overhead traverses.	"

A7092 Wt. W128 9/M1293 750,000. 1/17. D. D & L. Ltd. Forms/C2118/14.

— over —

Instructions regarding War Diaries and Intelligence Summaries are contained in F. S. Regs., Part II. and the Staff Manual respectively. Title pages will be prepared in manuscript.

WAR DIARY
~~or~~
~~INTELLIGENCE SUMMARY.~~ II

(Erase heading not required.)

Army Form C. 2118.

Place	Date	Hour	Summary of Events and Information	Remarks and references to Appendices
T. 1. c. 8. 3.	1/11/17 to 30/11/17 (cont)		Deepening and duckwalking trenches between Posts C.C. & B.B. – Posts B.B. & A.A. and between Posts M. and N.. – Clearing trench from Post H.H. to SOUTHERN AVENUE –	Sheet 57.c. S.W.
			Clearing trench between Posts F.F. and K.K., – Deepening and widening trench between Posts E.E. & F.F., clearing Berms and duckwalking. – BISON RESERVE Trench clearing –	"
			APE SUPPORT, deepening and widening trench –	"
			2 Sappers in charge water supply and Pumps, PANTHER TRENCH.	"
			Converting Gum Boot Store into Recreation Room at N 22. b. – Constructing Gum Boot Store, Right Battalion at entrance SHIKAR AVENUE. – Constructing Gum Boot Store Left Battalion, MARLIERE, bricking up holes in walls, building new end wall, roofing with corrugated iron, fixing racks in drying room.	"
			Constructing H.Q. for 152nd Bde R.A. – Laying and repg duckwalks, repg billets, fixing Electric light engine and dynamo for 102nd Infy Bde H.Q.	"
			RAKE Trench Water Supply :- Excavating recess for tanks, fixing tanks and sandbagging same, constructing chamber for pumps, connecting pipes in trench & cutting road, fitting up and testing ~~the~~ engine.	"

– over –

A7092 Wt. W128 9/M1293 750,000. 1/17. D. D & L. Ltd. Forms/C2118/14.

Army Form C. 2118.

Instructions regarding War Diaries and Intelligence Summaries are contained in F. S. Regs., Part II. and the Staff Manual respectively. Title pages will be prepared in manuscript.

WAR DIARY
or
~~INTELLIGENCE SUMMARY.~~
(Erase heading not required.)

III

Place	Date	Hour	Summary of Events and Information	Remarks and references to Appendices
T.1.c.8.3.	1/4/17 to 30/4/17 (cont)		Footbridge fixed across COJEUL RIVER at O.20.a.25.95.	Sheet. 51 b. SW.
			MARLIERE CAVES. Bunking and strengthening caves, Making entrance to caves, overhead	"
	"		traverse and approach trench from SOUTHERN AVENUE and duckwalking same.	"
	"		Constructing Water Point at WANCOURT.	"
	"		Camouflage Screen between Posts F.F. and D.D. erected complete. – Camouflage Screen	"
	"		between Posts E.E. and D.D. erected completed.	"
	"		Erecting new camouflage screen between Posts D.D. and Z.4, and repg old portion	"
	"		Raising and extending Screens for Road and Artillery at N.23.b, also repg old where	"
	"		damaged.	"
	"		Erecting Camouflage Road Screens at N.18.d. and N.24.b. GUEMAPPE.	"

J.W. Stephens
Major R.E.
O.C. 208th Field Coy R.E.

A7092' Wt. W128 9/M1293. 750,000. 1/17. D. D & L. Ltd. Forms/C2118/14.

Army Form C. 2118.

Instructions regarding War Diaries and Intelligence Summaries are contained in F. S. Regs., Part II. and the Staff Manual respectively. Title pages will be prepared in manuscript.

WAR DIARY

or

~~INTELLIGENCE SUMMARY~~.

(*Erase heading not required.*)

Vol 24

Place	Date	Hour	Summary of Events and Information	Remarks and references to Appendices
			— 208th Field Coy R.E. —	
			— December 1917. —	

A7092). Wt. W12839/M1297 750,000. 1/17. D. D & L., Ltd. Forms/C2118/14.

Instructions regarding War Diaries and Intelligence Summaries are contained in F. S. Regs., Part II. and the Staff Manual respectively. Title pages will be prepared in manuscript.

WAR DIARY

or

~~INTELLIGENCE SUMMARY.~~

(Erase heading not required.)

Army Form C. 2118.

I

Place	Date	Hour	Summary of Events and Information	Remarks and references to Appendices
T.I.c. 8.3.	1/12/17 to 9/12/17		Coy H.Q. remained at T.I.c.8.3. – No2. Section in Huts at T.I.c. 8.3. Nos 1. 3 & 4 sections in shelters	Sheet
			~~and~~ dugouts at SUNKEN Road at N.22.d. 8.4. Transport and lines at BOIRY BEQUERELLE at	57c S.W.
			T.7.b.0.8. – attached Infantry at WANCOURT :- Company employed continuously in Left Brigade	"
			Sector in line and carried out the following work:-	"
			Front line – Posts from O.14.a 75.70 to O.26.a.5.7:- Making and fixing Rifle Racks	"
			SAA and Bomb Boxes &c in firebays, cutting and making new firebays and traverses	"
			constructing shelter in Firebays and traverses; fitting Sump Boxes, clearing berms and	"
			parapets, sandbagging elbow rests; deepening, clearing, widening, draining, revetting,	"
			firestepping + duckwalking, constructing overhead traverses.	"
			Deepening widening and duckwalking the following:-	"
			Trench between EE and FF Posts – Trench between Posts CC and BB – Trench between Posts	"
			BB and AA – Trench between Posts AA and R. – Trench between Post A and Post P. –	"
			Trench between Post O. and N –	"
			GOAT LANE between M.G. 58 and 58(1) Berms cleared, 5 Bays revetted – Constructing	"
			Block Traverse O.14.a.55. — APE SUPPORT Deepened and cleared.	"
			Wiring O.19.a. 4.5. to O.19.a. 9.6. 300 yds double apron fence erected.	"
			Wiring parallel to EGRET Trench S & N. of KESTREL Avenue 225 yds Double double apron entanglement.	"
			—over—	

A7092). Wt. W12839/M1293. 750,000. 1/17. D, D & L., Ltd. Forms/C2118/14.

Instructions regarding War Diaries and Intelligence Summaries are contained in F. S. Regs., Part II. and the Staff Manual respectively. Title pages will be prepared in manuscript.

WAR DIARY

~~or~~

~~INTELLIGENCE SUMMARY.~~

(Erase heading not required.)

II

Army Form C. 2118.

Place	Date	Hour	Summary of Events and Information	Remarks and references to Appendices
T.1.c.8.3.	1/12/17 to 9/12/17 (cont.)		Erecting Artillery Screens for C152 Battery ~~at~~ HENINEL — Erecting road screen N18.d.6.2 through N.24.b.7.8. along GUEMAPPE-CHERISY Rd to EGRET Trench. — Constructing Gun Boot Store Nr SHIKAR AVENUE — Constructing power house for lighting plant MARLIERE CAVES —	Sheet 57. B. S.W. do.
do	10/12/17		Company relieved in Left Sector of Divisional Front by 209th Field Coy RE. Company relieved 209th Field Coy RE. in Reserve, advanced sections Nos 1, 3, and 4 moved from dugouts in SUNKEN ROAD at N.22.d.8.4. to Coy H.Q. at T.1.c.8.3. Attached Infantry moved from WANCOURT to Coy H.Q at T.1.c.8.3.	"
do.	11/12/17 to 26/12/17		Company in reserve concentrated on the following work:- Constructing Refilling point at STONE SIDING, making two corduroy roads and ration sheds. Lock Laundry, ARRAS Road, constructing porch with door fitting up flues, braziers &c. DTMO @ BOIRY BECQUERRELLE, constructing H.Q. and Mess — Erecting hut Adrian for 34th D.A.C. — Reroofing hut of A 261st RFA. — Repg adrian huts for 160th RFA. — Reroofing and repg huts 152nd R.F.A. — Repg Horse standings for 117th R.F.A. Repg Huts and Transport Lines, erecting field ovens repg horse standings at the following:- 103rd Brigade Transport lines, 240th Machine Gun Coy Transport lines, 101st Brigade Transport Lines, 101st Brigade M.G. Coy lines.	"

A7092). Wt. W12839/M1298 750,000. 1/17. D. D & L., Ltd. Forms/C2118/14.

— over —

Instructions regarding War Diaries and Intelligence Summaries are contained in F. S. Regs., Part II. and the Staff Manual respectively. Title pages will be prepared in manuscript.

WAR DIARY

or

~~INTELLIGENCE SUMMARY.~~

(Erase heading not required.)

III

Army Form C. 2118.

Place	Date	Hour	Summary of Events and Information	Remarks and references to Appendices
T.1.c.8.3.	11/12/17 to 26/12/17 (cont)		Building examples of 6 types of revetting for Bomb protection, Lining Nissen Huts and repg same, constructing field ovens &c. at the following Battalion Reserve Camps:- "CARLISLE LINES", "NORTHUMBERLAND LINES" and "DURHAM" Lines.	Sheet 51 b S.W.
			102nd Field Ambulance:- Fitting up Baths, drying rooms &c. alterations to water supply.	"
			"CHEQUERS" Concert Hut, raising roof, refelting room, fitting up additional seating accommodation.	"
			HENIN Camp.- Erecting Nissen Huts, Gum Boot store, Messes &c. – BATHS, BOISLEUX-AU-MONT. fitting up – YMCA. BOISLEUX-AU-MONT. lining inside with felt, reroofing, general fitting up.– Repg pumps at S.11.b.8.5.	"
do.	27/12/17.		Divisional Front held by 3 Brigades in line, right sector becomes centre sector. 208th Field Coy R.E. relieves 207th Field Coy R.E, in new Centre sector. No3 Section with attached Infantry moved from T.1.c. to advanced ~~billets~~ dugouts at CUCKOO Trench. No4 Section with attached Infantry moved from T.1.c to advanced dugouts at HINDENBURG SUPPORT. No1. section remained with attached infantry for work on Intermediate line. No2 Section with attached Infantry continued work on HENIN CAMP.	"
do	28/12/17 to 31/12/17		The following work was carried out:-	"
			R.E. supervision on work in front line – BROWN SUPPORT constructing firebays laying trench walks &c.	"

—over—

A7092). Wt. W12839/M1297. 750,000. 1/17. D. D & L., Ltd. Forms/C2118/14.

Army Form C. 2118.

Instructions regarding War Diaries and Intelligence Summaries are contained in F. S. Regs., Part II, and the Staff Manual respectively. Title pages will be prepared in manuscript.

WAR DIARY

~~or~~

~~INTELLIGENCE SUMMARY.~~

(Erase heading not required.)

IIII

Place	Date	Hour	Summary of Events and Information	Remarks and references to Appendices
T.1.c.8.3.	28/12/17 to 31/12/17 (Cont)		SWIFT SUPPORT:- Revetting 6 firebays, revetting trench. — CONCRETE RES: constructing firebays and	Sheet 57c S.W.
			repg trenchwalks. — CUCKOO RESERVE: constructing 13 new fire bays, levelling parapets, making	″
			firesteps, clearing trench and relaying duckwalks. — MALLARD RESERVE Revetting trench, making firesteps.	″
			Intermediate Line:- Erecting R.A.P. HINDENBURG SUPPORT. — GREY ST, Deepening and laying trench	″
			boards — CABLE trench deepening and clearing — constructing new fire trench from	″
			CABLE to CROW trench — CROW TRENCH, excavating — BOOTHAM trench, making firebays	″
			WATER POINT — HINDENBURG SUPPORT. Erecting heating apparatus to counteract frost. — Fixing gas	″
			blankets in HINDENBURG SUPPORT, SWIFT SUPPORT, and SHAFT TRENCH, Repg steps to dugouts.	″
			N.36.d.8.7. Making trolley for stretcher tramway. — HENIN CAMP Erecting Nissen Huts &c.	″

EWNesham Capt R.E.
o/c 208th Field Coy R.E.

A7092). Wt. W12839/M1293 750,000. 1/17. D. D & L., Ltd. Forms/C2118/14.

Army Form C. 2118.

Instructions regarding War Diaries and Intelligence Summaries are contained in F. S. Regs., Part II. and the Staff Manual respectively. Title pages will be prepared in manuscript.

WAR DIARY

~~or~~

~~INTELLIGENCE SUMMARY.~~

(Erase heading not required.)

Vol 25

Place	Date	Hour	Summary of Events and Information	Remarks and references to Appendices
			208th Field Coy R.E., January 1918.	

A7092). Wt. W12839/M1293 750,000. 1/17. D, D & L., Ltd. Forms/C2118/14.

Instructions regarding War Diaries and Intelligence Summaries are contained in F. S. Regs., Part II. and the Staff Manual respectively. Title pages will be prepared in manuscript.

WAR DIARY
or
~~INTELLIGENCE SUMMARY~~.

(Erase heading not required.)

I

Army Form C. 2118.

Place	Date	Hour	Summary of Events and Information	Remarks and references to Appendices
T.1.c.8 3.	1/1/18		Company H.Q. at T.1.c.8.3. Transport Lines in BOIRY-BEQUERELLE at T.7.b.0.8. Company	Sheet 57b S.W.
			in Centre Sector Divisional front, and working as follows:-	do.
			NOS 3 & 4 Sections with attached Infantry, billeted in dugouts in BOOTHAM Trench and THE	do.
			ROOKERY, attached to Centre Brigade, (102nd Bde) for work in and forward of the RESERVE LINE.	do.
			NOS. 1 & 2 Sections with attached Infantry billeted in huts with Coy HQ. at T.1.c.8.3. working	do.
			under the CRE, 34th Division on the Intermediate Line and on work in Brigade Area.	do.
do	10/1/18		NOS 1 & 2 Sections with attached Infantry relieved NOS 3 & 4 Sections with attached Infantry	do
			each taking over work and billets &c. from opposite sections.	do.
do.	1/1/18 to 27/1/18		The following work was carried out in Brigade Area from 1/1/18 to 27/1/18 inclusive :-	do.
			FRONT LINE:- Post No 2 to PUG AVENUE Marking out line of proposed new trench. - Trench	do.
			between Post 4 and Post 5 cleared & revetted 180x - New cut, clearing trench.	do.
			FRONT LINE and SUPPORT LINE :- 7 Sappers attached to Garrisons for RE. supervising of	do
			firestepping & revetting trenches, fixing SAA. and Bomb cupboards in firebays &c.	do.
			SUPPORT LINE :- SWIFT SUPPORT - Making steps to Dugout (ARGYLE HOUSE).	do.
			RESERVE LINE :- CUCKOO RESERVE Digging and revetting 47 new firebays, draining clearing berms, digging sumps, camouflaging same - 600x of trench clearing, revetting and duckwalked.	do.
			(cont:)	

A7092). Wt. W1289/M1293 750,000. 1/17. D. D & L., Ltd. Forms/C2118/14.

Instructions regarding War Diaries and Intelligence Summaries are contained in F. S. Regs., Part II. and the Staff Manual respectively. Title pages will be prepared in manuscript.

WAR DIARY

~~or~~

~~INTELLIGENCE SUMMARY.~~

(*Erase heading not required.*)

II

Army Form C. 2118.

Place	Date	Hour	Summary of Events and Information	Remarks and references to Appendices
T.1.c.8 3	1/1/18 to 27/1/18 (cont:)		CONCRETE RESERVE. Clearing Trench, draining, revetting and relaying duckwalks.	
			INTERMEDIATE LINE :- HINDENBURG SUPPORT:- Wiring from GREY ST to FOOLEY LANE (Junction	Sheet 57 b. S.W.
			of old German wire) Erecting Double double Apron Fence. — GREY ST Deepening, clearing	do.
			and duckwalking Trench, 3 L Shaped firebays dug and camouflaged. — CABLE TRENCH, 200x	do.
			Trench cleared and duckwalks relaid and repaired, Excavating new Trench between CABLE TRENCH	do.
			and N.35.b.3.3. — CROW TRENCH, 400x Trench cleared, shaped, duckwalks repd and 150x laid.	do.
			New Trench continuation of GREY ST, 150x Trench cleared, shaped, and duckwalks repd. —	do.
			FIRST AVENUE, 800x Trench cleared shaped and duckwalks repaired, 500x berms cleared,	do.
			Bridge repaired over Trench — BOOTHAM TRENCH, Excavating New Trench (near junction of	do.
			Road to FOSTER CUCKOO DUMP) 100x cleared N. of FIRST AVENUE.	do.
			COMMUNICATION TRENCHES :-	
			a Permanent Maintenance Party was employed, the following was also carried out :-	do.
			GREY ST, 560x cleared out and trench shaped up on sides. — FIRST AVENUE, 500x cleared	do.
			out and shaped up on sides — SUSSEX AVENUE, 100x Trench cleared. — FOSTER AVENUE,	do.
			500x Cleared, sides shaped and 200x berm cleared. — AVENUE PASSAGE, clearing	do
			& revetting Trench 120x — SHAWK AVENUE, cutting and revetting firebays, 4 complete.	do.
			SCREENS :- 38 Screens in COJEUL VALLEY, damaged by gale & fire, repaired	do
			Regimental Aid Post constructed in SHAFT TRENCH.	do.

(cont.)

A7092). Wt. W12839/M1293 750,000. 1/17. D. D & L., Ltd. Forms/C2118/14.

Instructions regarding War Diaries and Intelligence Summaries are contained in F. S. Regs., Part II. and the Staff Manual respectively. Title pages will be prepared in manuscript.

WAR DIARY
or
~~INTELLIGENCE SUMMARY.~~
(Erase heading not required.)

III

Army Form C. 2118.

Place	Date	Hour	Summary of Events and Information	Remarks and references to Appendices
T.1.c.8.3.	1/1/18 to 27/1/18 (contd.)		Constructing R.A.P. in FIRST AVENUE with Stretcher Trolley and tramway into dugout. —	Sheet 57b. S.W.
			CONCRETE RES:- Making steps to 2 Entrances to P1. Dugout., Mining P2 Dugout —	do.
			SHAFT TRENCH, Repg Dugout entrance No 102. — SUSSEX AV: 6 bunks fixed in A11. Dugout —	do
			BOOTHAM TRENCH, 41 Bunks fixed in A7. dugout.	do.
			Fixing Anti-gas Blankets with frames complete to dugout entrances over whole Brigade	do.
			Sector, repairing old frames and fixing new blankets where necessary.	do.
			FOSTER CUCKOO DUMP, Water point. 3 Water Tanks repaired, Digging Trench for water	do.
			Tanks and installing same. — PELICAN DUMP, Water point, 3 Water Tanks repaired	do
			Recess for tanks dug and revetted, 6 Tanks fixed in Recess, Splinter proof roof constructed.	do.
			FOSTER AVENUE, GUM BOOT STORE, Trench to Entrance cleared & revetted, gallery roof repaired.	do.
			2 Sappers in SHAFT TRENCH i/c of Electric Light supply for HINDENBURG TUNNEL.	do.
			Reserve Section worked as follows:- Erecting Camp, Nissen huts &c at HENIN. —	do.
			102nd Bde Q.M. Stores ARRAS RD. (M. 23 d.) 4 Nissen huts erected, lined complete, Blanket	do
			stores roofed in — 4 Sappers were attached D.A.C. lines for supervision of hutting —	do.
			2 Sappers attached 104th F.A. for hutting —	do

(over)

A7092). Wt. W12839/M1293 750,000. 1/17. D. D & L., Ltd. Forms/C2118/14.

Instructions regarding War Diaries and Intelligence Summaries are contained in F. S. Regs., Part II. and the Staff Manual respectively. Title pages will be prepared in manuscript.

WAR DIARY
or
~~INTELLIGENCE SUMMARY.~~

(Erase heading not required.)

IIII

Army Form C. 2118.

Place	Date	Hour	Summary of Events and Information	Remarks and references to Appendices
T.1.C. 8.3.	1/1/18 to 27/1/18 (cont.)		150 German shells destroyed (certified unfit to travel) at Divl. Salvage Dump, BOISLEUX-ST-	Sheet 51 b. S.W.
			MARC. — Revetting round HQ. huts completed for Bomb protection. — 2 Sappers in charge of	do.
			Sawmill near Coy HQ. — Notice Boards and SAA & Bomb Box Recesses for firebays made at Coy H.Q.	do.
			HENINEL SWITCH, Set out with tapes, defining firebays.	do.
do.	28/1/18.		34th Division relieved in line by 3rd Division, and moved to Corps Reserve Area.	51 b. S.W. and 57c N.W.
			208th Field Coy R.E. relieved by 56th Field Coy R.E. and moved by route march to MORY	do.
			(MORY – FAVREUIL Road, B. 28. a. 4. 6) Attached Infantry rejoined Battalions 27th inst.	do
MORY. (B. 28. a. 4. 6)	29/1/18 to 31/1/18.		Company resting, prior to work to be commenced on 2/2/18 on HENINEL SWITCH.	do.
			Inspections of kits, arms, ammunition, gas helmets and Box respirators.	do.
			Parades :- Gas helmet and Box respirator drill, section drill with and without arms &c.	do.
			Baths. — Officers and details reconnoitred new line and arranged for forward	do.
			dumps, materials &c.	do.
			(Casualties — NIL. —)	

[illegible]
Major R.E.
O.C. 208th Field Coy R.E.

A7092). Wt. W12839/M1293. 750,000. 1/17. D, D & L., Ltd. Forms/C2118/14.

Army Form C. 2118.

Instructions regarding War Diaries and Intelligence Summaries are contained in F. S. Regs., Part II. and the Staff Manual respectively. Title pages will be prepared in manuscript.

WAR DIARY

or

~~INTELLIGENCE SUMMARY.~~

(Erase heading not required.)

Vol. 26

Place	Date	Hour	Summary of Events and Information	Remarks and references to Appendices
			208th Field Coy RE. February 1918.	

A7092). Wt. W12839/M1293 750,000. 1/17. D, D & L., Ltd. Forms/C2118/14.

Instructions regarding War Diaries and Intelligence Summaries are contained in F. S. Regs., Part II. and the Staff Manual respectively. Title pages will be prepared in manuscript.

WAR DIARY or ~~INTELLIGENCE SUMMARY.~~

(Erase heading not required.)

I

Army Form C. 2118.

Place	Date	Hour	Summary of Events and Information	Remarks and references to Appendices
MORY. B.28.a 4 6	1/2/18	-	4 Dismounted Sections moved from camp at MORY to HENIN CAMP. Coy H.Q. and Transport remained at MORY B.28.a. 4.6.	Sheets 51 B S.W. + 57 c N. do.
HENIN CAMP	2/2/18 to 8/2/18	-	4 Dismounted Sections worked at night as follows:- Digging HENINEL SWITCH Defence line from N.22a. to N.29.d., wiring same with double apron fence making use of old German wire in parts, strengthening with apron fences back and front. Digging 300 yds BROWN LINE between C12 and C13 in N.34.d.	do. do. do. do.
HENIN CAMP & MORY. B28.a.4.6.	9/2/18.		34th Division relieved in Corps Reserve by 59th Division. 208th Field Coy RE moved from HENIN CAMP and MORY (B.28.a.4.6) to billets at HENDECOURT-LES-RANSART Camp (X.17.a.)	do + 51.c. do.
HENDECOURT LES-RANSART	10/2/18.		Company moved by March Route to billets at BAVINCOURT (HQ at P.34.d.8 1)	do.
BAVINCOURT.	11/2/18		Company moved by March Route to billets at VILLERS-SIR-SIMON (1.4.b.)	do.
VILLERS-SIR SIMON.	-	-	34th Division in rest in LE CAUROY training area, 208th Field Coy training as follows:-	do.
do.	12/2/18	-	Inspections of arms, equipment and kit.	do.
do.	13/2/18	-	Morning:- Physical Training, Musketry. Afternoon:- Sports.	do.
do.	14/2/18	-	Morning:- Physical Training, Gas Drill, Squad Drill, Pontoon Drill, Trestle Bridging. afternoon Musketry.	do
do.	15/2/18	-	Morning:- Physical Training, Route March in Battle Order.	do

A7092). Wt. W12839/M1293. 750,000. 1/17. D. D & L., Ltd. Forms/C2118/14.

—Over—

Army Form C. 2118.

WAR DIARY

or

~~INTELLIGENCE SUMMARY.~~

(Erase heading not required.)

II

Instructions regarding War Diaries and Intelligence Summaries are contained in F. S. Regs., Part II. and the Staff Manual respectively. Title pages will be prepared in manuscript.

Place	Date	Hour	Summary of Events and Information	Remarks and references to Appendices
VILLERS-SIR-SIMON.	16/2/18	-	Morning:- Physical Training, Drill with Arms, Section & Company Drill. Afternoon Construction of M.G.E's.	51. C.
"	17/2/18.	-	Fatigues, Sports and Baths. (Sunday)	do.
"	18/2/18	-	Morning:- Physical Training, Section Drill, Company Drill, Afternoon:- Ceremonial Drill.	do.
"	19/2/18	-	Inspection at DOFFINE FARM. by G.O.C. 34th Division.	do.
"	20/2/18	-	Morning:- Physical Training, Pontooning. Afternoon:- Trestle Bridging.	do.
"	21/2/18	-	Morning:- Physical Training, Trestle Bridging. Afternoon:- Sports.	do.
"	22/2/18	-	Morning:- Physical Training, Pontoon & Trestle Bridging. Afternoon:- Sports.	do.
"	23/2/18	-	Practice Bridging over river at N.1.a.2.3. N. of REBREUVIETTE.	do
"	24/2/18	-	(Sunday) Fatigues, Sports & Baths.	do
"	25/2/18	-	Physical Training, Strong Point Scheme. Afternoon:- Revetments. (Capt J Russell arrived to command Company)	do
"	26/2/18		Coy was inspected by VI Corps Commander forming part of 102 Inf Bde Group.	
HUMBERCAMP	27/2/18.		Marched from VILLERS-SIR-SIMON to HUMBERCAMP	
HAMELINCOURT	28/2/18.		Marched from HUMBERCAMP to HAMELINCOURT	

James Russell Major R.E.
OC 208 Field Coy R.E.

A7092). Wt. W12839/M1293 750,000. 1/17. D. D & L., Ltd. Forms/C2118/14.

34th Divisional Engineers

WAR DIARY

208th FIELD COMPANY R. E.

MARCH 1918

34

Army Form C. 2118.

Instructions regarding War Diaries and Intelligence Summaries are contained in F. S. Regs., Part II. and the Staff Manual respectively. Title pages will be prepared in manuscript.

WAR DIARY
~~or~~
~~INTELLIGENCE~~ SUMMARY.

(*Erase heading not required.*)

Vol 27

Place	Date	Hour	Summary of Events and Information	Remarks and references to Appendices
			208th Field Coy R.E. — March 1918. —	

D. D. & L., London, E.C.
(A8001) Wt. W1771/M2031 750,000 5/17 Sch. 52 Forms/C2118/14

Instructions regarding War Diaries and Intelligence Summaries are contained in F. S. Regs., Part II. and the Staff Manual respectively. Title pages will be prepared in manuscript.

WAR DIARY
or
INTELLIGENCE SUMMARY.
(Erase heading not required.)

208 Field Coy R.E.

Army Form C. 2118.

Place	Date	Hour	Summary of Events and Information	Remarks and references to Appendices
HAMELINCOURT.	1st March 1918.		Coy resting. Orders received that Coy will relieve 470 Field Coy 59th Div in St LEDGER on 2nd inst. and will work on right sector of 34th Div with the 102 Inf Bde. Cold. Snow.	
St LEDGER.	2nd "		HQ one section & Transport proceeded to St LEDGER – 3 sections to dugouts in U19.a. Sheet 57B.S.W. 2nd Lt HIBBERT proceeded on leave to England. Snow	
"	3rd "		100 Infantry from 102 Bde joined Coy for attachment. Work was started on digging TIGER. TRENCH U26 b.65 to junction with St RAY. RESERVE U13d65 ~~also~~ with infantry party of 400 men. – trench was divided into series of posts each to be defended by one platoon.	
"	4th "		An additional 100 infantry worked on TIGER Trench as day party. Work was started on steel shelter accommodation for Reserve Bn in Sunken Road and Railway Cutting U25 a and b – one Section and 50 infantry employed. Copy of weekly works report to 6am 4th inst attached.	
"	5th "		A reconnaissance was made of the HINDENBURG TUNNEL running under the front line with view to making "Cubby Holes" in each entrance for front line garrison.	
"	6th "		Work on TIGER TRENCH by night party extremely slow. Also difficulty being	

A7092). Wt. W12839/M1293 750,000. 1/17. D. D & L., Ltd. Forms/C2118/14.

Instructions regarding War Diaries and Intelligence Summaries are contained in F. S. Regs., Part II. and the Staff Manual respectively. Title pages will be prepared in manuscript.

WAR DIARY
or
~~INTELLIGENCE SUMMARY.~~
(Erase heading not required.)

Army Form C. 2118.

208 Field Coy RE

Place	Date	Hour	Summary of Events and Information	Remarks and references to Appendices
St LEDGER	6th March 1918		experienced in getting Shelters etc for Reserve Bn accommodation.	R
"	7th	"	Brigade relief 103 relieving 102 Inf Bde. No infantry parties available. Sappers and attached infantry continued work on Tiger Trench and Shelters in BUNHILL ROW. Brigade area was extended on the left to FACTORY AVENUE.	R
"	8th	"	CE VI Corps & CRE visited Bde Sector. Party of 400 Infantry resumed work on TIGER TRENCH with Section III. Section III relieved Section IV and proceeded from St LEDGER to forward RE Billets. 25% of attached infantry were withdrawn to St LEDGER.	R
"	9th	"	Day parties continued work as usual on TIGER TRENCH and BUNHILL ROW. The Section in rest at St LEDGER commenced preparation for demolition of 10 large trees immediately S. of St LEDGER apparently used as ranging marks for enemy artillery	R

A7092). Wt. W12839/M1293 750,000. 1/17. D. D & L., Ltd. Forms/C2118/14.

Instructions regarding War Diaries and Intelligence Summaries are contained in F. S. Regs., Part II. and the Staff Manual respectively. Title pages will be prepared in manuscript.

WAR DIARY
or
INTELLIGENCE SUMMARY.
(Erase heading not required.)

Army Form C. 2118.

208 Field Coy RE

Place	Date	Hour	Summary of Events and Information	Remarks and references to Appendices
St LEDGER.	10th March 1918		All night working parties on TIGER TRENCH were changed to day parties commencing work at 6 am. — the trench now affording sufficient cover for this purpose. The digging of platoon posts was completed, and the trench in a good state of defence. Work was started on an Intelligence O.P. in Queens Lane. About 5 pm CRE called and stated that the enemy were expected to attack on the morning of the 13th inst, and that the following work was to be carried out (1) Front line to be filled with barbed wire leaving gaps for patrols. (2) HINDENBURG TUNNELS running under the front line of the left Bn front Right Brigade to be prepared for demolition at points where 3 subways leading from CTs between front and support lines met the tunnel, and Officers detailed to fire the charges on the Enemy being seen in possession of the front line. (3) Preparations for the demolition of the 10 trees at St LEDGER. — (1) (2) and (3) to be complete on 12th inst Very fine weather	

A7092). Wt. W12839/M1293 750,000. 1/17. D. D & L., Ltd. Forms/C2118/14.

Instructions regarding War Diaries and Intelligence Summaries are contained in F. S. Regs., Part II. and the Staff Manual respectively. Title pages will be prepared in manuscript.

WAR DIARY
or
INTELLIGENCE SUMMARY.
(*Erase heading not required.*)

Army Form C. 2118.

208 Field Coy R.E.

Place	Date	Hour	Summary of Events and Information	Remarks and references to Appendices
St LEDGER	11th March 1918		Work concentrated on demolitions and defences of TIGER TRENCH. Wiring of Front line was cancelled. Instructions received that the company would move to BOYELLES on receipt of code word "BATTLE". Copy of weekly works report attached.	F. R.
"	12th		Preparation for demolition of lines at St LEDGER and the blowing in of the HINDENBURG TUNNEL completed. In addition pumping station at St LEDGER was prepared for demolition. Further instructions were received that the company and attached infantry would concentrate at St LEDGER — move to commence at 6 pm. and to remain in a state of readiness to move at ½ hours notice. Capt Chalmers, 2/Lt Morris, 2/Lt Gray with 8 men remained at forward billets to fire tunnel charges. 3 ORs. remained at ECOUST Dump to destroy dump if necessary. St LEDGER was heavily shelled for 10 minutes about 5 pm — no casualties. Lt FOWLER returned from leave.	F. R.
"	13th		All quiet	F. R.

A7092). Wt. W12839/M1297 750,000. 1/17. D. D & L., Ltd. Forms/C2118/14.

Instructions regarding War Diaries and Intelligence Summaries are contained in F. S. Regs., Part II. and the Staff Manual respectively. Title pages will be prepared in manuscript.

WAR DIARY
or
~~INTELLIGENCE SUMMARY.~~
(Erase heading not required.)

Army Form C. 2118.

208 Field Coy RE

Place	Date	Hour	Summary of Events and Information	Remarks and references to Appendices
St LEDGER.	14th March 1918.		One section worked on TIGER TRENCH with Infantry party of 400 men. One section on Battn accommodation in BUNHILL Row. Remaining sections at Coy HQ. Sections I II & III with 50 attached infantry moved to Advanced RE Billets in Quarry U.19.a. at 6pm to stay also 20 attached infantry to ECOUST RE Dump. Capt Chalmers returned to Coy HQ as leads for the Centre and North charges in tunnel now led to one point and could be fired by the same officer. Fine W.	
BOYELLES.	15th		At 12.30 am code word BATTLE was received. Coy Transport moved immediately to HAMELINCOURT. The Sections at Forward RE Billets were withdrawn with the exception of 2/Lt Morris 2/Lt Clark and 8 Sappers. Coy HQ and all Sappers marched to BOYELLES. Attached infantry concentrated at St LEDGER HILL and reported for duty to 102 Inf Bde. 3 Sappers were left in charge of ECOUST DUMP. The whole Coy was employed digging a cable trench from Left to Right Bde HQ from 7pm to midnight. Fine W.	

A7092). Wt. W12839/M1293 750,000. 1/17. D. D & L., Ltd. Forms/C2118/14.

Instructions regarding War Diaries and Intelligence Summaries are contained in F. S. Regs., Part II. and the Staff Manual respectively. Title pages will be prepared in manuscript.

WAR DIARY
~~or~~
~~INTELLIGENCE SUMMARY.~~
(Erase heading not required.)

Army Form C. 2118.

208 Field Coy RE

Place	Date	Hour	Summary of Events and Information	Remarks and references to Appendices
BOYELLES	16th March 1918		Coy was employed digging a cable trench similar to night of 15th	Fine K
"	17th	"	One section was employed on demolition of large tree stumps to prepare for an RFA Battery position and the preparation for demolition of 6 large trees interfering with gunners near St LEGER. Remainder of the Coy was employed on the cable trench as before	Fine K
"	18th	"	Work as on 17th. ~~The~~ The stumps in Battery position were all cleared. Copy of weekly works report attached. 2/Lt HIBBERT returned from leave.	Fine K
"	19th	"	Work as on 18th. In addition work was restarted on OP in Queens Lane for Intelligence. Heavy Rain all day.	K.
"	20th	"	Preparation for demolition of trees at St LEGER completed. Arrangements made that 107 Bde should take forward trench boards for TIGER TRENCH badly required. Coy employed as on 19th. 2/Lt Clark proceeded on leave.	Rain K.

A7092). Wt. W12839/M1293 750,000. 1/17. D. D & L., Ltd. Forms/C2118/14.

Instructions regarding War Diaries and Intelligence Summaries are contained in F. S. Regs., Part II. and the Staff Manual respectively. Title pages will be prepared in manuscript.

WAR DIARY
or
~~INTELLIGENCE SUMMARY.~~
(Erase heading not required.)

Army Form C. 2118.

208 Field Coy RE.

Place	Date	Hour	Summary of Events and Information	Remarks and references to Appendices
BOYELLES	21st March 1918.		Enemy bombardment commenced at 5am – enemy attacks developed during the day. Relief for work on OP in Queens Lane failed to get through enemy barrage and returned. At noon Coy. received orders to standby. at 4.45pm 2/Lt Gray returned to Coy HQ and reported that he had successfully fired the charges in the HINDENBURG TUNNEL at junction with MARS LANE SUBWAY, after the enemy had occupied our front line. At 5.45pm 2/Lt Morris returned to Coy HQ and reported that he had successfully fired the charges in the HINDENBURG TUNNEL at its junctions with BOW LANE and JUNO LANE. and that the enemy occupied the front line of the 102 Inf Bde Sector about 3pm. Also that he had given instructions for the firing of GUINNESS DUMP at ECOUST and had seen this dump burning as the enemy entered the village. L/Cp Ward and 2 Sappers in charge of the dump failed to return also Cpl Irving detailed for duty with 2/Lt Morris on destruction of the HINDENBURG TUNNEL. 2/Lt Morris and 2/Lt Gray were both slightly gassed And 2/Lt Morris slightly wounded.	

D. D. & L., London, E.C. (A8001) Wt. W1771/M2031 750,000 5/17 Sch. 52 Forms/C2118/14

Instructions regarding War Diaries and Intelligence Summaries are contained in F. S. Regs., Part II. and the Staff Manual respectively. Title pages will be prepared in manuscript.

WAR DIARY
or
~~INTELLIGENCE SUMMARY.~~
(Erase heading not required.)

Army Form C. 2118.

208 Field Coy RE

Place	Date	Hour	Summary of Events and Information	Remarks and references to Appendices
BOYELLES	21st March (Continued)		At 6pm the Coy proceeded to and occupied the Army Line immediately W of St LEDGER. The night was quiet. Fim R.	
HAMELINCOURT	22nd March		About 1am Coy marched to ERVILLERS and occupied old German Trenches defending the village. Enemy commenced shelling about 4pm – becoming intense between 6pm and 7pm, & attacks developing from the direction of MORY. On receipt of orders the Coy was withdrawn about 10pm and marched to ARMAGH CAMP HAMELINCOURT. 3 men on patrol missing. Fim R.	
BOIRY St RICTRUDE	23rd March		Coy joined its transport lines at BOIRY St RICTRUDE. Fim R.	
"	24th	"	Transport moved to HENDECOURT. Coy was employed on putting trenches immediately E of FICHEUX in a state of defence. Fim R.	
BLAIRVILLE	25th	"	Coy dug 250 yds new trench immediately E of FICHEUX. Sappers moved from BOIRY St RICTRUDE to Camp at BLAIRVILLE. Transport moved to new camp between BLAIRVILLE and BRETENCOURT. Fim R.	

D. D. & L., London, E.C. (A8001) Wt. W1771/M2031 750,000 5/17 Sch. 52 Forms/C2118/14

Instructions regarding War Diaries and Intelligence Summaries are contained in F. S. Regs., Part II. and the Staff Manual respectively. Title pages will be prepared in manuscript.

WAR DIARY
or
INTELLIGENCE SUMMARY.
(Erase heading not required.)

Army Form C. 2118.

208 Field Coy R.E.

Place	Date	Hour	Summary of Events and Information	Remarks and references to Appendices
BRETENCOURT	26th March 1918		Sappers and transport concentrated at BRETENCOURT during early hours of the morning. Coy continued work at night on old trenches E of FICHEUX.	Fine R.
"	27th	March	Coy was employed on putting in a state of defence old German Front line prior to the Somme Battle E of BRETENCOURT.	Fine R.
"	28th	"	Coy marched to VILLERS. S^R SIMON.	Very wet during afternoon R.
"	29th	"	Coy marched to AUCHEL.	Very wet morning R.
"	30th	"	Coy marched to VIEUX. BERQUIN.	Very wet all day R.
"	31st	"	Coy marched to PONT. DE NIEPPE and took over billets and work of 123 Field Coy R.E. 38th Div.	Fine R.

James Russell Major R.E.
OC 208 Field Coy R.E.

D. D. & L., London, E.C.
(A8001) Wt. W1771/M2031 750,000 5/17 Sch. 52 Forms/C2118/14

34th Divisional Engineers

WAR
DIARY

208th FIELD COMPANY R. E.

APRIL 1 9 1 8

Wad of maps in separate file

Vol 28

WAR DIARY

APRIL 1918

208TH FIELD COY R.E

Army Form C. 2118.

Instructions regarding War Diaries and Intelligence Summaries are contained in F. S. Regs., Part II. and the Staff Manual respectively. Title pages will be prepared in manuscript.

WAR DIARY
or
~~INTELLIGENCE SUMMARY.~~
(*Erase heading not required.*)

208 Field Coy RE.

Place	Date	Hour	Summary of Events and Information	Remarks and references to Appendices
PONT DE NIEPPE.	1st April 1918.		Coy rested. Officers reconnoitred line	R.
"	2nd		Work started on concrete MG Emplacements and Shelters for gun crews at LILLE GUARDIAN, at H12.6.75 and at H18b.35.35. Also on preparation for demolition of 6 bridges over the RIVER LYS at B24c08, C19c.77 C19c60 C25a.9.0. C25d.3.9 and C26a.2.2, and on completion of two emergency barrel pier bridges at B18c.9.3 and B18d.27 with marked tracks leading to and from them. Reference map attached.	R.
"	3rd	"	Work as on 2nd inst. Party from Section III commenced preparations for blowing of Tank Trap CRATERS in No mans land across roads at I5c.11. and I5a.5.5	R.
"	4th		Work as on 3rd inst. Site reconnoitred, plans and estimate of materials and time of construction made for a reinforced concrete Div. ~~HQ~~ Battle HQ. near STEENWERCK. 100 Infantry from 102 Inf Bde reported for attachment as Sappers mates.	R.

D. D. & L., London, E.C.
(A8001) Wt. W1771/M2031 750,000 5/17 Sch. 52 Forms/C2118/14

Instructions regarding War Diaries and Intelligence Summaries are contained in F. S. Regs., Part II. and the Staff Manual respectively. Title pages will be prepared in manuscript.

WAR DIARY
or
~~INTELLIGENCE SUMMARY.~~
(Erase heading not required.)

Army Form C. 2118.

208 Field Coy RE

Place	Date	Hour	Summary of Events and Information	Remarks and references to Appendices
PONT DE NIEPPE	5th APRIL 1918		Tank Crater blown during night 4/5th at I 5 c. 1.1. Crater was 16 ft wide 10 ft deep and filled with water immediately – charge 100 lbs ammonal. Party unable to blow crater at I 5 a 5 5 owing to covering party going astray in the dark. Copy of weekly works report attached.	K
"	6th	"	Intermediate Zone trenches were reconnoitred in Square H12 and H18 and arrangements made to employ 600 men from Bde in Reserve commencing night 7th/8th. Effort made to blow tank crater at I 5 a 5.5 during night 5/6th failed owing to charges getting wet	K
"	7th	"	Battn Commanders Lucans Bde were shown work to be carried out on Intermediate ZONE TRENCHES.	K
"	8th		Little work was done by the 600 men infantry party from 16th Royal Scots during the night owing to heavy gas shell bombardment and men were withdrawn after one hours work. Preparation for demolition of bridges as detailed	
"	9th		in diary of 2nd inst, also repair of the 2 barrel pier bridges with tracks to and from them completed. Tank Trap Crater at I 5 a 5 5 was successfully blown during night 7/8 – dimensions and charge similar to the one at I 5 c. 1.1.	K

D. D. & L., London, E.C. (A8001) Wt. W1771/M2031 750,000 5/17 Sch. 52 Forms/C2118/14

Instructions regarding War Diaries and Intelligence Summaries are contained in F. S. Regs., Part II. and the Staff Manual respectively. Title pages will be prepared in manuscript.

WAR DIARY
or
~~INTELLIGENCE SUMMARY.~~
(Erase heading not required.)

208 Field Coy R.E.

Army Form C. 2118.

Place	Date	Hour	Summary of Events and Information	Remarks and references to Appendices
PONT DE NIEPPE	9th April 1918.		Good work was done by party of 450 men from 15th Royal Scots on Intermediate Zone Trenches during night 8/9th. Enemy commenced heavy bombardment at 5am. All working parties were held back until shelling should decrease. Instructions received at 9am to cancel all working parties and the company to stand by for orders. At 9.30am instructions received to detonate all charges in bridges, also that the company would be responsible for the demolition of bridge at C19 c 8.4. Parties were sent out to stand by all bridges with instructions not to blow them until the enemy was in the act of crossing them. The 2 emergency barrel pier bridges were brought into position. Transport moved during night to PONT DE PIERRE. Enemy attack south of the Divisional front apparently successful.	
"	10th	"	2/Lt. CLARK was wounded about 10am. 2/Lt MORRIS wounded about 1pm and Sgt MACKAY killed. About 1pm instructions recd from 102 Inf Bde that ARMENTIERES would be evacuated — evacuation to commence at 3pm. At 3pm 102 Bde issued orders that all bridges across the RIVER LYS	

D. D. & L., London, E.C.
(A8031) Wt. W1771/M2031 750,000 5/17 Sch. 52 Forms/C2118/14

Instructions regarding War Diaries and Intelligence Summaries are contained in F. S. Regs., Part II. and the Staff Manual respectively. Title pages will be prepared in manuscript.

WAR DIARY
or
~~INTELLIGENCE SUMMARY.~~
(Erase heading not required.)

208 Field Coy R.E.

Army Form C. 2118.

Place	Date	Hour	Summary of Events and Information	Remarks and references to Appendices
PONT DE NIEPPE	10th APRIL 1918 Continued		East of PONT de NIEPPE BRIDGE were to be immediately destroyed. ~~This was completed by 3.45pm~~ The 6 for which this company was responsible were destroyed by 3.45pm demolition being complete in each case. The work was carried out under great difficulties as four of the bridges were under constant shell fire and the other two under M.G. Fire. On completion 3½ Sections under 2/Lt HIBBERT were sent to join wagon lines at PONT DE PIERRE whilst one half section under Lt FOWLER remained to destroy PONT DE NIEPPE BRIDGE when evacuation completed. About 6.30pm 102 Inf Bde reported evacuation of Bde complete. Enemy drove in bridge head party at Jute Factory bridge about 6.45pm. This party retired and blew up bridge, and also destroyed the emergency barrel pier bridge between PONT DE NIEPPE and Jute Factory bridges. PONT DE NIEPPE was now the only bridge across the RIVER LYS remaining. As the enemy was only shelling slightly, and his advance along the	

D. D. & L., London, E.C. (A8001) Wt. W1771/M2031 750,000 5/17 Sch. 52 Forms/C2118/14

Army Form C. 2118.

Instructions regarding War Diaries and Intelligence Summaries are contained in F. S. Regs., Part II. and the Staff Manual respectively. Title pages will be prepared in manuscript.

WAR DIARY
or
~~INTELLIGENCE SUMMARY.~~
(Erase heading not required.)

208 Field Coy RE

Place	Date	Hour	Summary of Events and Information	Remarks and references to Appendices
PONT DE NIEPPE	10th APRIL 1918 Continued		RIVER LYS. from the Jute Factory was slow, it was decided not to destroy the PONT DE NIEPPE bridge until the last moment in order to save as many stragglers and wounded men as possible. From 6.45 to 7.15 pm no one crossed the bridge. About 7.20 pm a column of men suddenly appeared marching from ARMENTIERES which turned out to be the 103 Inf Bde. This Bde had failed to cross the river on its own front at ERQUINGHAM and was obliged to come right round through ARMENTIERES. A platoon was obtained from the leading Battn to deploy along the River bank S. towards the Jute Factory and to stop advance of the enemy until the Bde was safely across the Bridge. A message was also sent to the 102 Bde to hold the flank N of PONT DE NIEPPE between the River and the line the Division was falling back onto, as the enemy was machine gunning from this direction, apparently about the bend of the River, and by advancing S along W bank of the River would cut off the whole party. By 8 pm the whole Bde was safely across bridge. Between 8 pm	

D. D. & L., London, E.C. (A8001) Wt. W1771/M2031 750,000 5/17 Sch. 52 Forms/C2118/14

Instructions regarding War Diaries and Intelligence Summaries are contained in F. S. Regs., Part II. and the Staff Manual respectively. Title pages will be prepared in manuscript.

WAR DIARY
or
~~INTELLIGENCE~~ SUMMARY.
(*Erase heading not required.*)

Army Form C. 2118.

208 Field Coy RE

Place	Date	Hour	Summary of Events and Information	Remarks and references to Appendices
PONT DE NIEPPE	10th April 1918 Continued		until 9.30 pm no one passed over the Bridge, and, as enemy was directing MG Fire from either flank and commencing to shell PONT DE NIEPPE it was decided to destroy the bridge. Bridge head party was withdrawn and bridge blown at 9.40 pm. On examination of demolition which was complete (2856 lbs guncotton being used) 4 men were discovered in the water on the enemy side of River. These men were rescued with difficulty by means of planks and a raft. A party of 7 RAMC and 1 stretcher case was apparently on the bridge when the explosion took place and 4 were killed. This party had gone back into ARMENTIERES to bring out a wounded man. Every precaution had been taken to ensure no men being on the bridge, but ten minutes had elapsed after withdrawal of Bridge head party and patrols until the explosion, in order to allow party to get clear. Demolition Party marched to OUTERSTEEN arriving there about 3am on 11th inst. 2/Lt HIBBERT was unable to reach PONT DE PIERRE owing to enemy occupation of STEENWERCK, and proceeded to NEUVE EGLISE with	

(A8001) Wt. W1771/M2031 750,000 5/17 Sch. 52 Forms/C2118/14
D. D. & L., London, E.C.

Instructions regarding War Diaries and Intelligence Summaries are contained in F. S. Regs., Part II. and the Staff Manual respectively. Title pages will be prepared in manuscript.

WAR DIARY
or
INTELLIGENCE SUMMARY.
(*Erase heading not required.*)

208 Field Coy R.E.

Army Form C. 2118.

Place	Date	Hour	Summary of Events and Information	Remarks and references to Appendices
OUTERSTEEN	10th April 1918 continued		1½ Sections. His other 2 Sections were cut off and were used by Staff Captain 102 Inf Bde in a local counter attack near ~~[illegible]~~ NIEPPE. The objective was taken, with the loss of 3 men wounded. Transport moved from PONT DE PIERRE to OUTERSTEEN. Transport Casualties 1 OR killed 2 horses 4 mules killed.	R
"	11th	–	2/Lt HIBBERT with 1½ Sections and Lt FOWLER with ½ Section joined wagon lines. Remaining two sections remained at disposal of 102 Inf Bde. At 3pm available Sappers were ordered to man line of Railway immediately S of OUTERSTEEN forming part of a composite force under MAJOR TROWBRIDGE Brigade Major 102 Inf Bde. Transport moved to STRAZEELE. 50 men 22nd N. Fusiliers were attached to this company about 11pm to assist in the defence of the right flank held by this company. The night was quiet.	
RAVELSBURG.	12th	–	As no attack developed, Major TROWBRIDGE's force was withdrawn at 9am and marched to 102 Inf Bde HQ near junction of NEUVE EGLISE and BAILLEUL – ARMENTIERES ROAD	R

D. D. & L., London, E.C. (A8001) Wt. W1771/M2031 750,000 5/17 Sch. 52 Forms/C2118/14

Instructions regarding War Diaries and Intelligence Summaries are contained in F. S. Regs., Part II. and the Staff Manual respectively. Title pages will be prepared in manuscript.

WAR DIARY
or
INTELLIGENCE SUMMARY.
(*Erase heading not required.*)

Army Form C. 2118.

208 Field Coy R.E.

Place	Date	Hour	Summary of Events and Information	Remarks and references to Appendices
RAVELSBURG.	12TH APRIL 1918 continued		All attached infantry were returned to their Battns. At 11pm Company marched to RAVELSBURG to organise line to be taken up by 34th Div should a withdrawl become necessary, as reports were received that the enemy were in BAILLEUL and had taken NEUVE EGLISE. Transport moved to PRADELLES.	
HILLE	13th APRIL.		Line of posts organised as shown in attached map from MONT DE LILLE to CRUCIFIX CORNER and manned by a Bn of MIDDLESEX Regt on the right and by 103 Inf Bde on left, in touch with 100th Bde. Casualties 3 men killed 3 wounded and Lt FOWLER wounded. OC proceeded to DHQ at MONT NOIR and obtained permission to utilize all available sappers of the division for organising and digging successive lines of defence. Company moved from RAVELSBURG to HILLE on DRANOUTRE - BAILLEUL ROAD. Transport moved to BOESCHEPE.	

D. D. & L., London, E.C.
(A8001) Wt. W1771/M2031 750,000 5/17 Sch. 52 Forms/C2118/14

Army Form C. 2118.

Instructions regarding War Diaries and Intelligence Summaries are contained in F. S. Regs., Part II. and the Staff Manual respectively. Title pages will be prepared in manuscript.

WAR DIARY
or
INTELLIGENCE SUMMARY.
(*Erase heading not required.*)

208 Field Coy RE.

Place	Date	Hour	Summary of Events and Information	Remarks and references to Appendices
CROIX DE POPERINGHE	14th APRIL 1918.		A defensive line behind crest of hill from RAVELSBURG to wood in valley in S12d was dug in a series of posts and manned by a Bn of NORFOLK Regt. A third defensive line was reconnoitred along forward slope of crest commencing on the left at trenches dug and manned by Brig. Gen. WYATTS FORCE in Square S6 to Square S8 immediately N of BAILLEUL. 102 Inf Bde dug a portion of this line from forked roads at S3d 2.7 to S8.b.5.5. This line denied the enemy the valley immediately E of BAILLEUL and the high ground immediately N of BAILLEUL. It was arranged with Bdes to complete this line on 15th inst. 209 Field Coy RE joined 208 Field Coy RE to assist on the work. Company moved to Croix de POPERINGHE.	
FARM R24 a 0.5	15th APRIL		The Division was relieved by the 59th Div during the night 15/16th. On proceeding to work 103, 74, 101, 147 Bdes were found to be digging in on line indicated on map from S10b.3.8 to X12a 0.4. On the left the line was as reconnoitred yesterday, — on the right a new line was being dug	

D. D. & L., London, E.C.
(A8001) Wt. W1771/M2031 750,000 5/17 Sch. 52 Forms/C2118/14

Instructions regarding War Diaries and Intelligence Summaries are contained in F. S. Regs., Part II. and the Staff Manual respectively. Title pages will be prepared in manuscript.

WAR DIARY
or
INTELLIGENCE SUMMARY.
(*Erase heading not required.*)

Army Form C. 2118.

208 Field Coy RE

Place	Date	Hour	Summary of Events and Information	Remarks and references to Appendices
FARM R24a.0.5.	15th APRIL 1918. Continued		instead of the continuation of the line dug yesterday by 102 Inf Bde, and which this Bde was now improving. The new line being dug allowed the enemy the crest of the hill immediately N of BAILLEUL ASYLUM. ~~Asylum~~. One party taped out the new line of trenches on right and assisted Bde digging. OC went round line with CRE and suggested that line dug by 102 Inf/Bde should be continued to join new line at S1d.6.1 During the afternoon enemy attacked the 59th Div. 34th Div were informed that 59th Div would come back through them, and that line now held by 34th Div would form the front line and be held by them. OC assisted 102 Bde to link up line dug by 74th Bde on right and 103 Inf/Bde on left. 102 Bde issued orders that line dug yesterday was to be occupied as soon as 59th Div Pioneer Battn, who were holding it, was withdrawn. ~~[illegible]~~ 102 Inf Bde was withdrawn before this took place — 103rd and 74th Bdes linking up. The trench dug yesterday by 102 Bde was left unoccupied and passed into enemy hands giving them the high ground immediately NE of Bailleul Asylum. Coy moved about 11pm to farm at R24a.	

D. D. & L., London, E.C.
(A8001) Wt. W1771/M2031 750,000 5/17 Sch. 52 Forms/C2118/14

Instructions regarding War Diaries and Intelligence Summaries are contained in F. S. Regs., Part II. and the Staff Manual respectively. Title pages will be prepared in manuscript.

WAR DIARY
or
INTELLIGENCE SUMMARY.
(Erase heading not required.)

208 Field Coy RE

Army Form C. 2118.

Place	Date	Hour	Summary of Events and Information	Remarks and references to Appendices
FARM H24.a.05	16th April 1918		Company with 310 Infantry Carrying party from 88th, 101st and 102nd Inf Bdes wired appx 2300 yds of Support Line (ie 1st ARMY LINE) linking up all existing belts of wire and forming a complete belt between the Divisional Boundaries. Work commenced at dusk – shelling on right only.	R
~~Farm~~ BOESCHEPE	17th	"	Company shelled out of billets about 10 am and moved to farm at R.10 d 7.0 near BOESCHEPE. During night 17th/18th Company improved wire erected on previous night for a length of 900 yards and erected 500 yds new entanglement on SW slope of hill at MEULEHOUCK in S2.a. 500 yds of trench was spitlocked on left flank of hill at MEULEHOUCK linking up existing posts. No infantry parties were available. Very heavy shelling during the day. The night was comparatively quiet. Transport moved from BOESCHEPE to ABEELE	
"	18th	"	Switch Line from Right Flank Defences of the MEULEHOUCK to join 2nd ARMY LINE about M26.d.7.9 behind crest of hill and passing immediately N of CROIX DE POPERINGHE was sited and 180 yds on	R

D. D. & L., London, E.C. (A8001) Wt. W1771/M2031 750,000 5/17 Sch. 52 Forms/C2118/14

Instructions regarding War Diaries and Intelligence Summaries are contained in F. S. Regs., Part II. and the Staff Manual respectively. Title pages will be prepared in manuscript.

WAR DIARY
or
~~INTELLIGENCE SUMMARY.~~
(*Erase heading not required.*)

208 Field Coy RE

Army Form C. 2118.

Place	Date	Hour	Summary of Events and Information	Remarks and references to Appendices
BOESCHEPE	18th April 1918 continued		N side of MEULEHOUCK dug. A small party was employed on keeping road open for wheeled traffic at junction of 5 roads ¾ mile NW of ST JANS CAPEL. Numerous shell holes filled and fallen trees cleared. No infantry parties were available.	
"	19th	–	Defences of the MEULE HOUCK on right flank were improved by linking up existing posts. Appx 200 yds trench dug. No infantry parties available. 2/Lt J F STATON RE joined as reinforcement.	
"	20th	–	Company was relieved by 28/54th Field Coy RE 133 French Division and joined Transport Lines at ABEELE. Work was handed over as follows. (1) Completing and wiring outpost line to the defences of the MEULE HOUCK from S.2 a.9.3 parallel to road to road junction S.2 c.2.9 thence NW along W side of road to junction with 1st ARMY LINE at S.16. 85. 40. (2) Continuation of switch line between defences of the MEULE HOUCK	

D. D. & L., London, E.C. (A8001) Wt. W1771/M2031 750,000 5/17 Sch. 52 Forms/C2118/14

WAR DIARY
or
INTELLIGENCE SUMMARY.
(Erase heading not required.)

Army Form C. 2118.

Instructions regarding War Diaries and Intelligence Summaries are contained in F. S. Regs., Part II. and the Staff Manual respectively. Title pages will be prepared in manuscript.

208 Field Coy R.E.

Place	Date	Hour	Summary of Events and Information	Remarks and references to Appendices
BOESCHEPE	20th APRIL 1918 continued		and 2nd ARMY LINE running NE from end of continuous trench at S2a 28 along 55 contour line, thence linking with posts running NE and passing immediately N of CROIX DE POPERINGHE & join 2nd ARMY LINE about M26 d.7.9. (3) Maintenance party to keep road open for wheeled traffic at 6 road junction 3/4 mile NW of St JANS CAPEL	R
ABEELE	21st April		Coy resting at ABEELE	
St JANSTER BIEZEN	22		Coy moved to camp 3/4 mile NW of St JANSTER BIEZEN	R
"	23rd	"	Coy resting. Coy was inspected by GOC 34th Div and congratulated on work and fighting performed between 9th and 20th inst	R

D. D. & L., London, E.C. (A8001) Wt. W1771/M2031 750,000 5/17 Sch. 52 Forms/C2118/14

Instructions regarding War Diaries and Intelligence Summaries are contained in F. S. Regs., Part II. and the Staff Manual respectively. Title pages will be prepared in manuscript.

WAR DIARY
or
~~INTELLIGENCE SUMMARY.~~
(Erase heading not required.)

Army Form C. 2118.

208 Field Coy R.E.

Place	Date	Hour	Summary of Events and Information	Remarks and references to Appendices
St JANSTER BIEZEN.	24th APRIL 1918.		Company resting. Officers reconnoitred and taped line of trenches one mile S.E. of POPERINGHE between POPERINGHE - RENINGHELST and POPERINGHE - BUSSEBOOM ROADS. 2nd Lt C. BOWES R.E. joined as reinforcement. K.	
"	25th	"	Coy. dug line taped yesterday with working party of 450 Inf from 102 Inf Bde. 2Lt GRAY admitted to hospital suffering from gas poisoning. At 5 pm orders received to stand to and move under orders of 102 Bde. At 10 P.M. OC proceeded to HQRE. and received instructions to relieve all Field Coys of 25th Div working on the POPERINGHE SYSTEM of TRENCHES one mile NE of POPERINGHE and between the POPERINGHE - ELVERDINGHE and POPERINGHE - WOESTEN ROADS. 102 Inf Bde would occupy this line and furnish working parties. K.	
PESELHOEK.	26th.		Coy relieved Field Coys 25th Div and moved to PESELHOEK. Transport remained at St JANSTER BIEZEN. Arrival of Bde in works delayed owing to shelling of POPERINGHE. Little work done. Bde moved 3 times during the day. K.	

D. D. & L., London, E.C.
(A8004) Wt. W1771/M2031 750,000 5/17 Sch. 52 Forms/C2118/14

Instructions regarding War Diaries and Intelligence Summaries are contained in F. S. Regs., Part II. and the Staff Manual respectively. Title pages will be prepared in manuscript.

WAR DIARY
or
~~INTELLIGENCE SUMMARY.~~

(*Erase heading not required.*)

Army Form C. 2118.

208 Field Coy RE

Place	Date	Hour	Summary of Events and Information	Remarks and references to Appendices
PESELHOEK	27th APRIL 1918		Switch line between BRANDHOEK – OUDERDOM and POPERINGHE SYSTEMS reconnoitred and portion 1100 yds long immediately N of RENINGHELST dug by 1 Section RE and a Bn 59th Div. 3 Sections worked with 102 Inf Bde on POPERINGHE SYSTEM between POPERINGHE – RENINGHELST and POPERINGHE – YPRES ROADS.	K.
"	28th "		Portion of BRANDHOEK – OUDERDOM SYSTEM between POPERINGHE – YPRES ROAD and the RIVER DRINGONBEEK taken over by 102 Inf Bde reconnoitred and work arranged for following day. Coy employed on digging and wiring the POPERINGHE SYSTEM between 102 Bde boundaries. Shelling interfered with work on left.	K.
"	29th "		2 Sections worked on the BRANDHOEK SYSTEM with 2 Bns 102 Inf Bde. 2 Sections on the Poperinghe System with 1 Bn 102 Inf Bde and 1 Coy 18 N.F. PIONEER Battn attached to 102 Inf Bde. Heavy enemy shelling retarded work on the BRANDHOEK SYSTEM. 1 NCO & 18 Sappers & 2 drivers arrived as reinforcements.	K.

D. D. & L., London, E.C.
(A8031) Wt. W1771/M2031 750,000 5/17 Sch. 52 Forms/C2118/14

Army Form C. 2118.

Instructions regarding War Diaries and Intelligence Summaries are contained in F. S. Regs., Part II. and the Staff Manual respectively. Title pages will be prepared in manuscript.

WAR DIARY
or
~~INTELLIGENCE SUMMARY.~~

(Erase heading not required.)

208 Field Coy R.E.

Place	Date	Hour	Summary of Events and Information	Remarks and references to Appendices
PESELHOEK	30th April 1918.		Work as on 29th inst. Good progress made. Enemy quiet. Fine	
			Casualties during April Personnel { 4 Officers wounded. 1 Sergt. Killed. 4 Sappers " 17 Sappers Wounded.	
			Animals { 4 Officers riders killed 1 ——— wounded. 9 mules killed.	
			James Russell Major R.E. OC 208 Field Coy R.E.	

D. D. & L., London, E.C.
(A8001) Wt. W1771/M2031 750,000 5/17 Sch. 52 Forms/C2118/14

34th Divisional Engineers

M A P S to accompany

208th FIELD COMPANY R. E.

WAR DIARY FOR

APRIL 1 9 1 8

1/20,000

BELGIUM AND PART OF FRANCE. EDITION

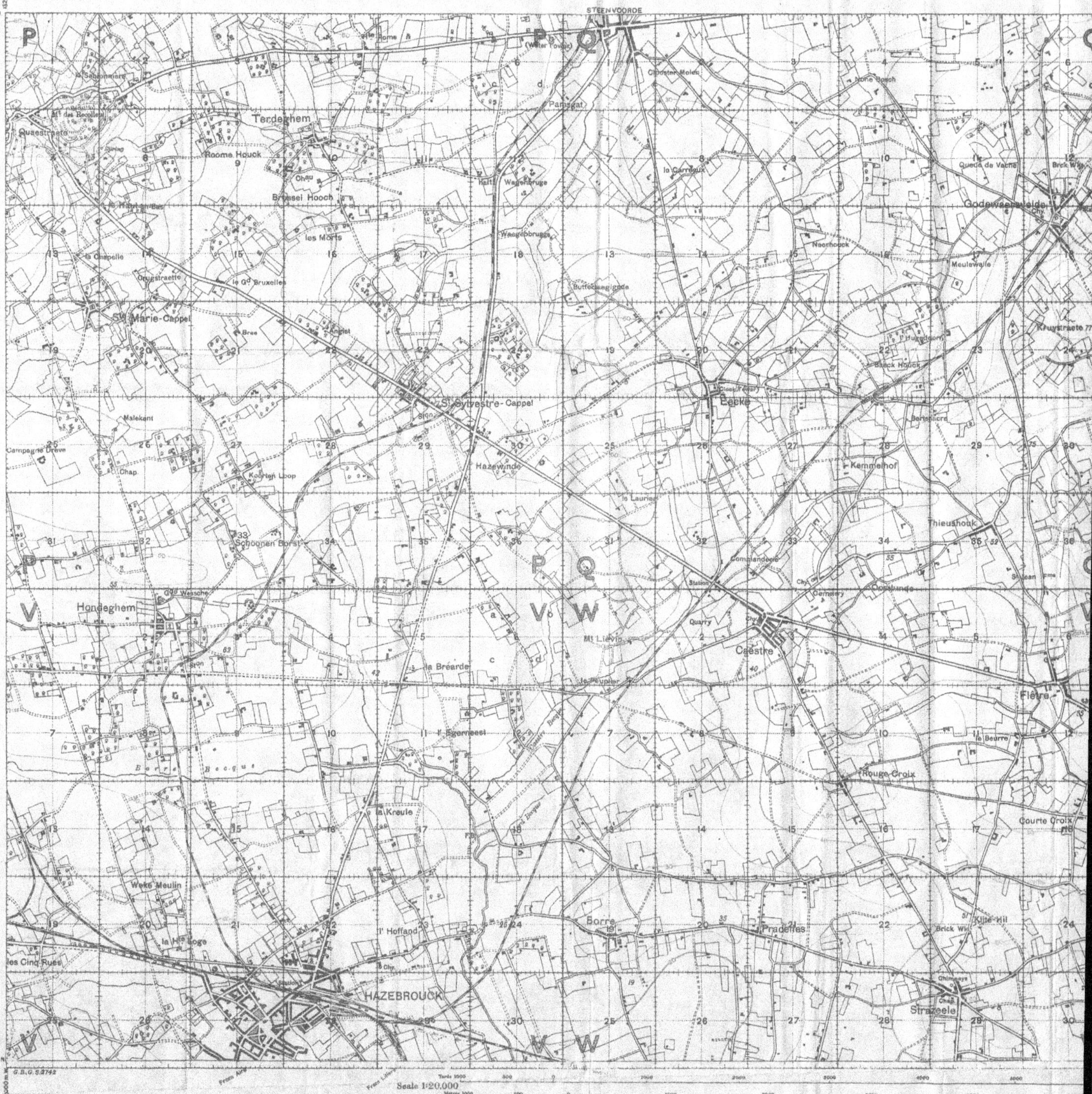

BELGIUM AND PART OF FRANCE. EDITION 3 SHEET 27 S.E.

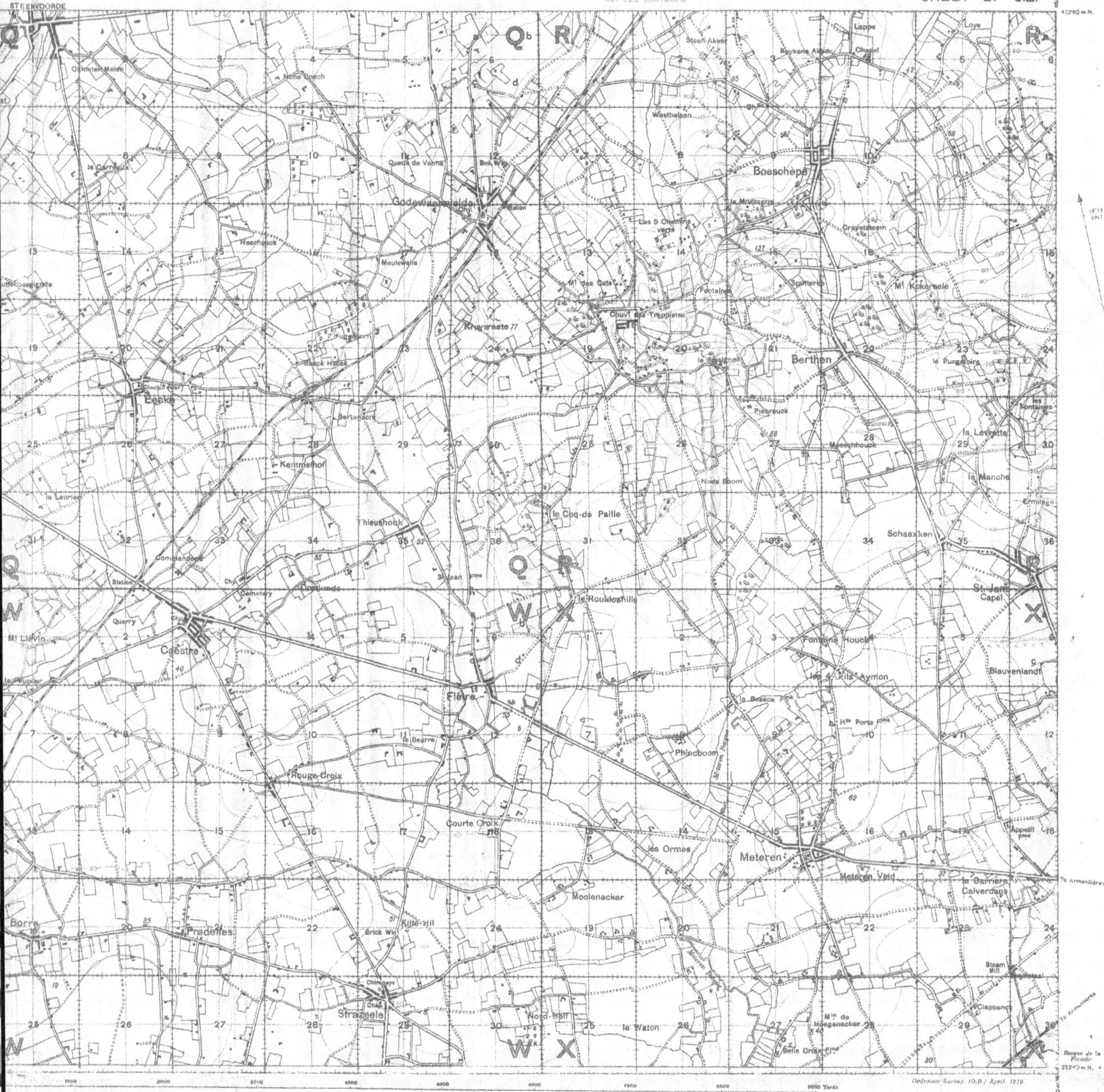

1 / 20,000

BELGIUM AND PART OF FRANCE

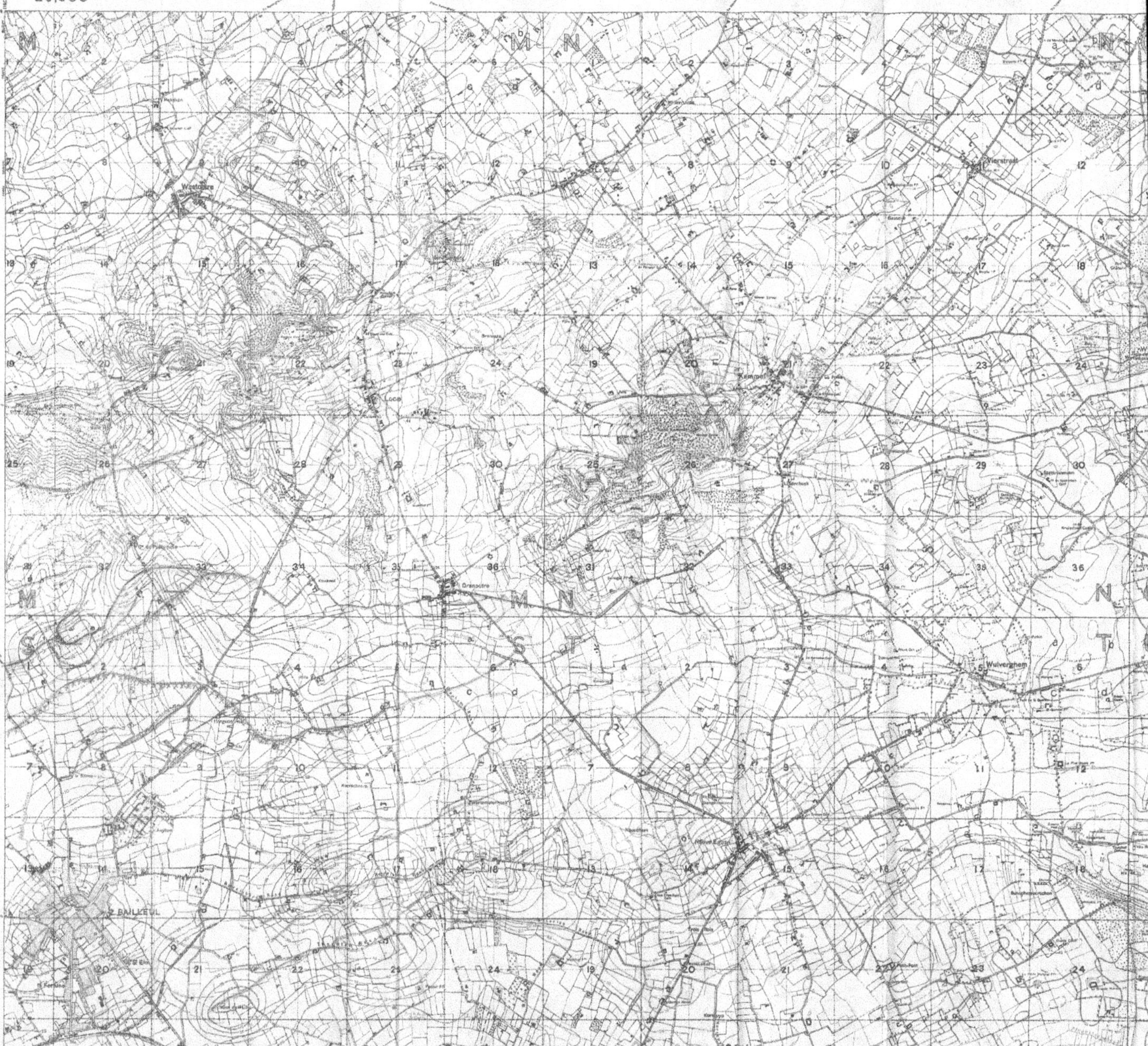

G.S G.S. 2742.

REFERENCE.

Enemy Trenches { Any trench apparently organised for fire; Other Trenches (Important ones are shown by thick line. Old or disused by dotted line.)

British Trenches

Wire Entanglement or Other Obstacle

Enemy's Tracks

Buried Pipeline or Cable

Airline

Supply Dumps

Ammunition "

Earthworks

Dug-outs

Huts

Works reinforced by concrete

Gun Emplacements

Machine Gun "

Trench Mortar "

A. A. Gun "

Observation Posts

Listening Posts

Mine Craters

" Fortified

Organised Shell Holes

Hedge, Fence or Ditch

Ditch with Permanent Water

Conspicuous Points (Position of point in centre of circle. Dot shows that point is trigonometrically fixed). Church, Wind Mill, Any trig. point.

Houses: Standing, Ruined. Shrine +

Railways { Permanent { Normal Gauge, Double; " " Single; Light } Temporary { Trench Tramways; Metre Gauge Railways }

NOTE.—The fact that an obstacle is not represented on the map does not necessarily mean that there is none there. It is often impossible to distinguish obstacles or to identify their character. It may be assumed that there are obstacles in front of all fire trenches (shown by thick line).

INSTRUCTIONS AS TO THE USE OF THE SQUARES.

1. The large rectangles on the map, lettered M, N, O, etc., are divided into squares of 1,000 yards side, which are numbered 1, 2, 3, etc. Each of these squares is sub-divided into four minor squares of 500 yards side. These minor squares are considered as lettered a, b, c, d. (See Square No. 6 in each rectangle).

A point may thus be described as lying within Square B.8, M.5.b, etc.

2. To locate a point within a small square, consider the sides divided into tenths, and define the point by taking so many tenths from W. to E. along Southern side, and so many from S. to N. along Western side; the S.W. corner always being taken as origin, and the distance along the Southern side being always given by the first figure. Thus the point Z would be 63; i.e. 6 divisions East and 3 divisions North from origin.

3. When more accurate definition is wanted (on the 1:20,000 or 1:10,000 scales) use exactly the same method, but divide sides into 100 parts and use four figures instead of two. Thus 0647 denotes 06 parts East and 47 parts North of origin (see point X). Point Y is 8503.

4. Use 0 but not 10; use either two or four figures; do not use fractions ($8\frac{1}{4}$, $4\frac{1}{2}$, etc).

CONTOUR INTERVAL 5 METRES.

Scale 1:20,000

Yards 1000 500 0 1000 2000 3000

Metres 1000 500 0 1000 2000 3000

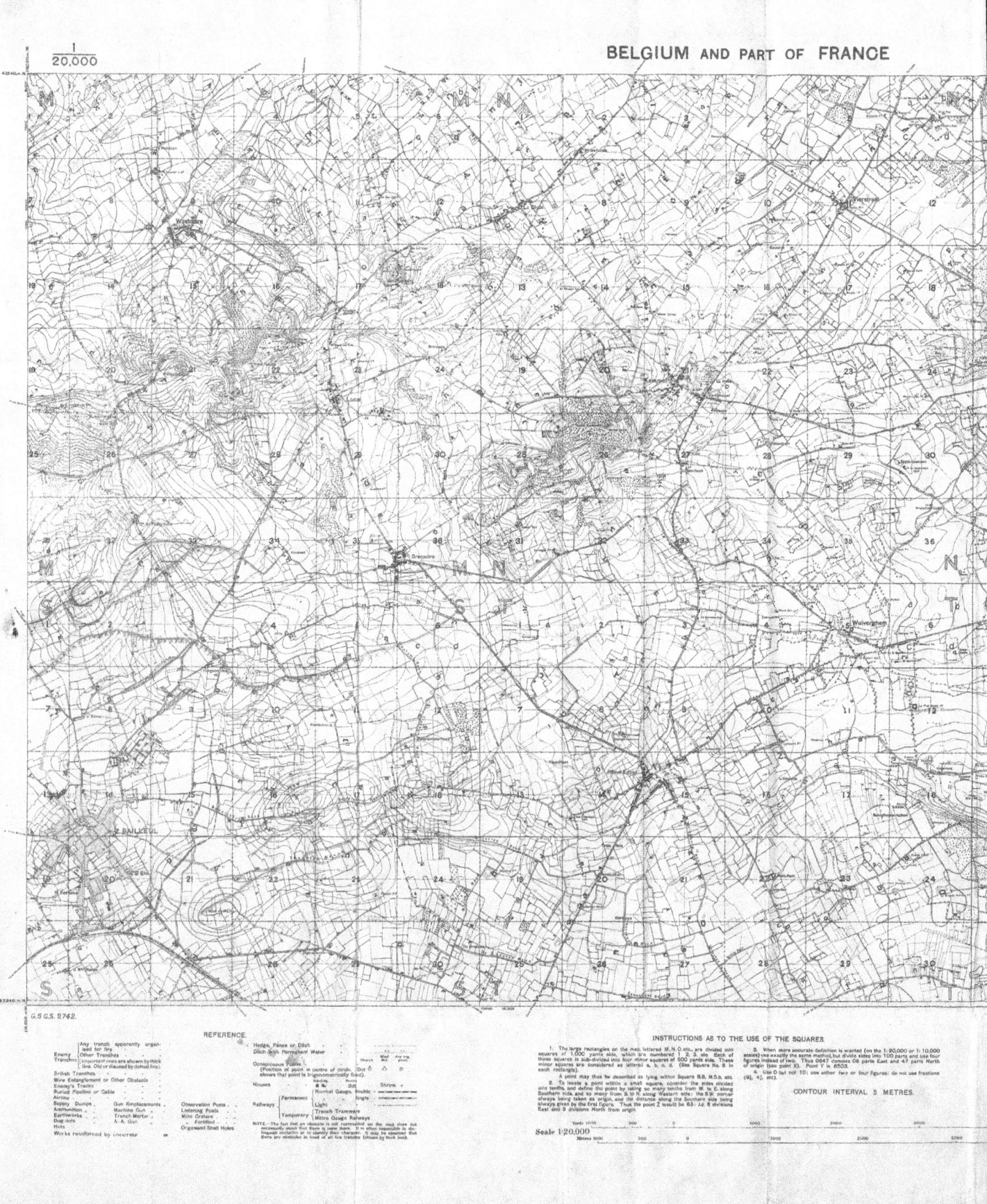

BELGIUM AND PART OF FRANCE

EDITION 6

SHEET. 28. S.W.

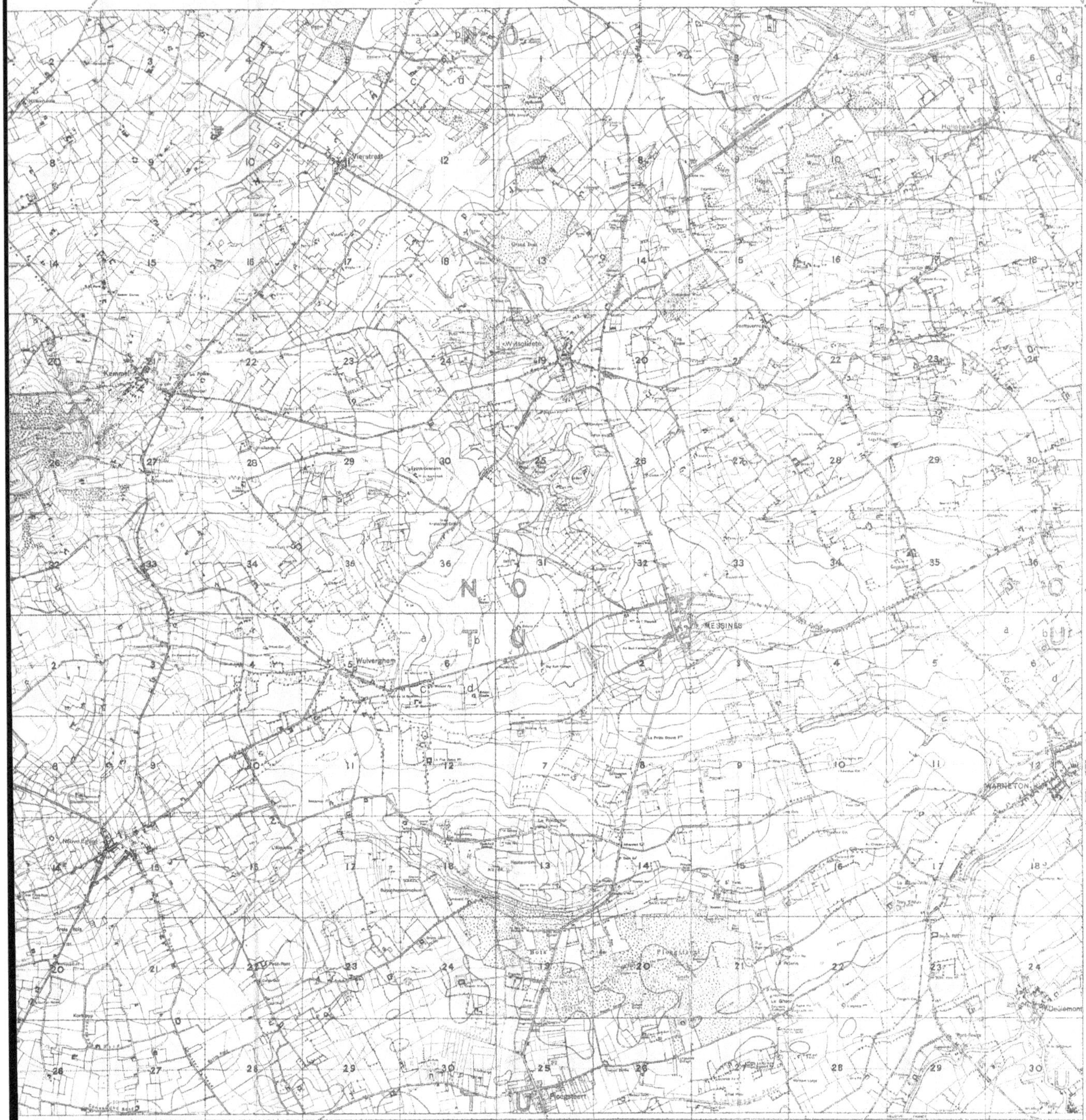

Ordnance Survey, December 1917.

INDEX TO ADJOINING SHEETS

27 N.E.	28 N.W.	28 N.E.
27 S.E.	28 S.W.	28 S.E.
36 N.E.	36 N.W.	36 N.E.

COMPILATION DIAGRAM

10,000 TRENCH MAPS

12°23' 1917

Magnetic

Grid North

On squared maps all bearings should be given with reference to the vertical grid lines, which are parallel to the East and West edges of the sheet. Bearings should always be reckoned clockwise from 0° to 360°.

Grid bearings are less than compass bearings, the difference being called the deviation of the compass. To find out what this deviation is, take a compass bearing to a distant point, and measure on the map the grid bearing to that point. The difference between the two bearings is the deviation of that compass from Grid North. To obtain the grid bearing of any point this deviation must be subtracted from the compass bearing (adding 360° to the latter if necessary).

On this sheet the mean deviation of a normal compass is 12° 23'; but to obtain accurate results the exact deviation of each compass should be tested as described above, and this test should be repeated in each locality.

ALL HEIGHTS IN METRES

INSTRUCTIONS AS TO THE USE OF THE SQUARES.

large rectangles on the map, lettered M. N. O. etc., are divided into 1,000 yards side, which are numbered 1, 2, 3, etc. Each of s is sub-divided into four minor squares of 500 yards side. These es are considered as lettered a, b, c, d. (See Square No. 6 in gle).

oint may thus be described as lying within Square B.6, M.5.b, etc. ocate a point within a small square, consider the sides divided nd define the point by taking so many tenths from W. to E. along e, and so many from S. to N. along Western side; the S.W. corner taken as origin, and the distance along the Southern side being by the first figure. Thus the point Z would be 63; i.e. 6 divisions divisions North from origin.

3. When more accurate definition is wanted (on the 1:20,000 or 1:10,000 scales) use exactly the same method, but divide sides into 100 parts and use four figures instead of two. Thus 0847 denotes 08 parts East and 47 parts North of origin (see point X). Point Y is 6503.

4. Use 0 but not 10; use either two or four figures: do not use fractions (8½, 4¼, etc).

DIAGRAM

CONTOUR INTERVAL 5 METRES.

TABLE FOR CONVERTING METRES TO FEET

Metres	0	1	2	3	4	5	6	7	8	9
0	0	3·3	6·6	9·8	13·1	16·4	19·7	23·0	26·2	29·5
10	32·8	36·1	39·4	42·6	45·9	49·2	52·5	55·8	59·0	62·3
20	65·6	68·9	72·2	75·4	78·7	82·0	85·3	88·6	91·8	95·1
30	98·4	101·7	105·0	108·2	111·5	114·8	118·1	121·4	124·6	127·9
40	131·2	134·5	137·8	141·0	144·3	147·6	150·9	154·1	157·4	160·7
50	164·0	167·3	170·6	173·8	177·1	180·4	183·7	187·0	190·2	193·5
60	196·8	200·1	203·4	206·6	209·9	213·2	216·5	219·8	223·0	226·3
70	229·6	232·9	236·2	239·4	242·7	246·0	249·3	252·6	255·8	259·1
80	262·4	265·7	269·0	272·2	275·5	278·8	282·1	285·4	288·6	291·9
90	295·2	298·5	301·8	305·0	308·3	311·6	314·9	318·1	321·4	324·7
100	328·0	331·3	334·6	337·8	341·1	344·4	347·7	351·0	354·2	357·5

Yards 1000 500 0 1000 2000 3000 4000 5000 6000 7000 8000 9000 Yards

…0,000

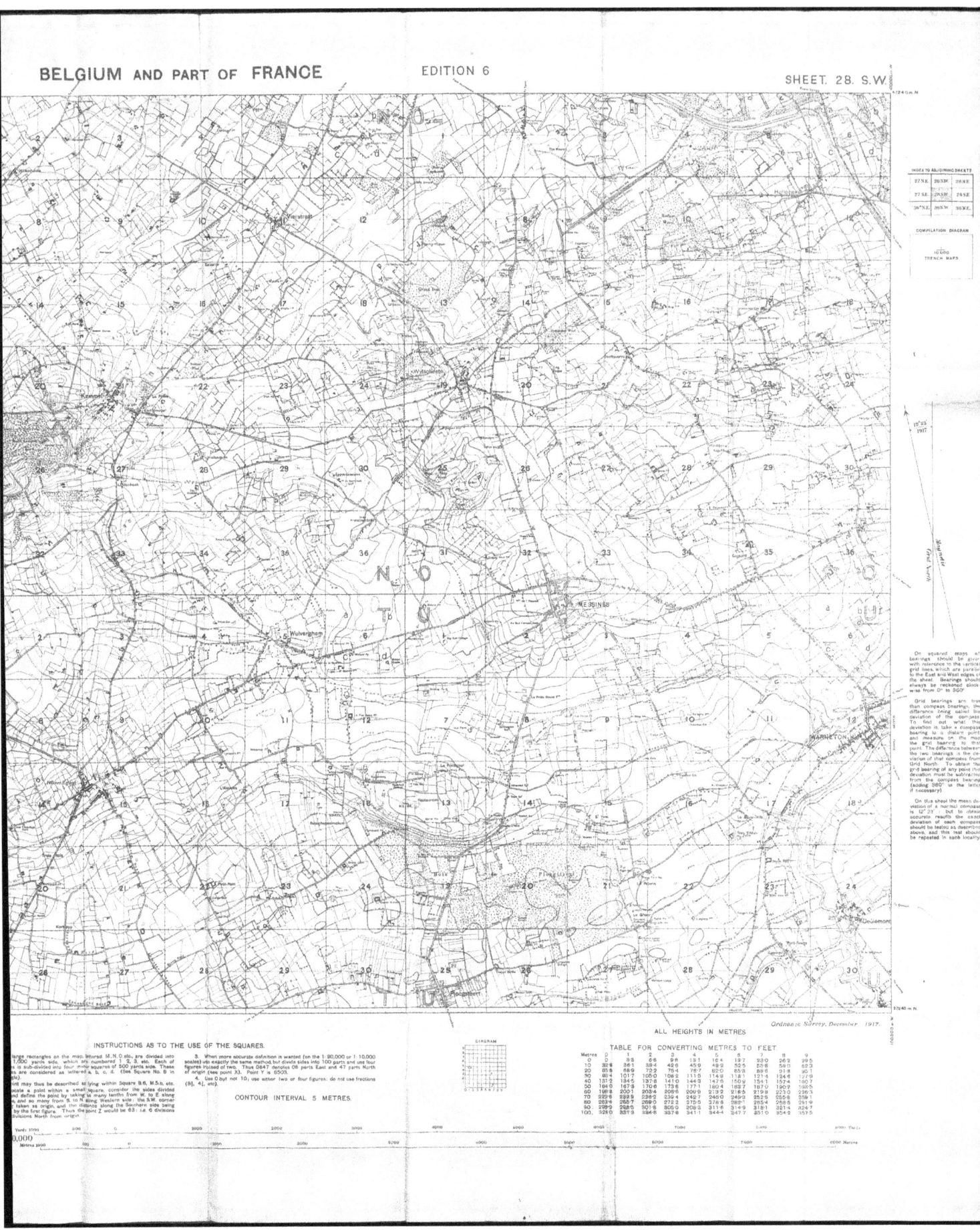

Metres 1000 500 0 1000 2000 3000 4000 5000 6000 7000 8000 Metres

208th Field Co RE

BRIDGE I   C 25.a 9.0.

HEAVY STEEL GIRDER BRIDGE SUPPORTED ON STONE PIERS.

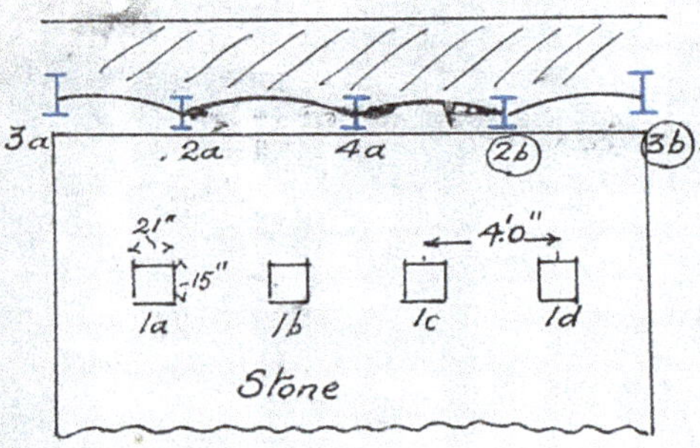

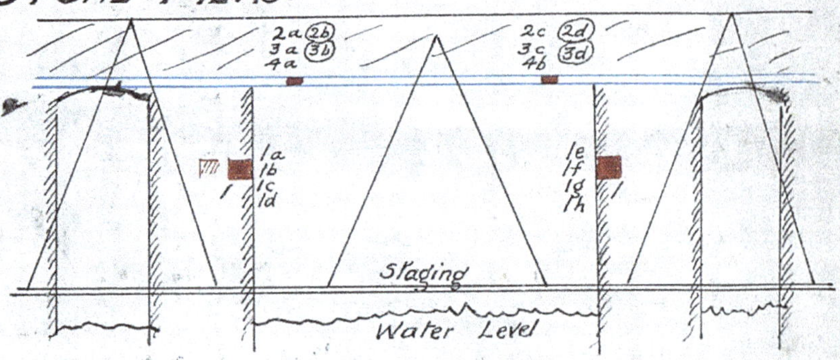

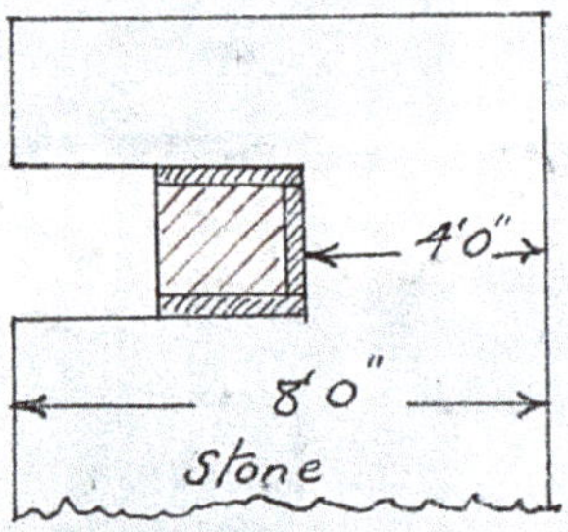

Charges Nos 1a, 1b, 1c, 1d, | 1e, 1f, 1g, 1h.

Each charge 108 lbs. gun-cotton with 2 Primers.

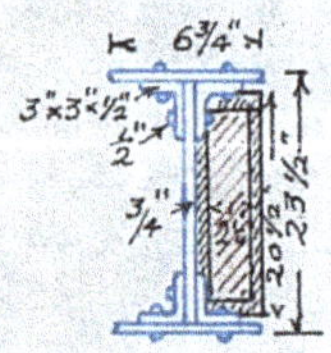

Inner Girders.

Charges Nos 2a. (2b) | 2c. (2d)

Each charge 25 lbs. gun-cotton with 1 Primer.

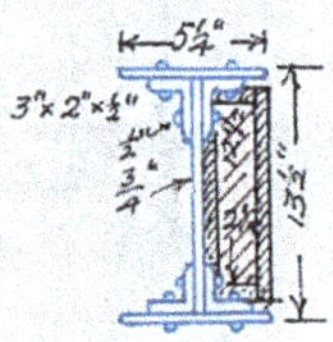

Outer Girders.

Charges Nos. 3a (3b) | 3c. (3d)

Each charge 12 lbs. gun-cotton with 1 primer.

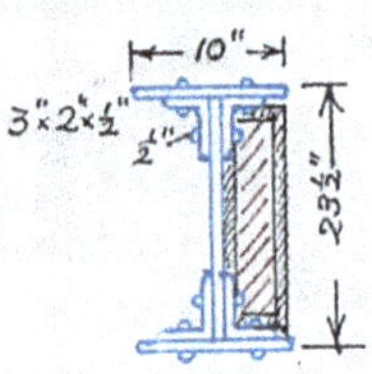

Central Girder

Charges Nos 4a. 4b.

Each charge 25 lbs. gun-cotton With 1 Primer

TABLE OF CHARGES

Charge No	Amt. of G.C.	Primers and Detonators	Remarks.
1a, 1b, 1c, 1d	Each 108 lbs	2 Each	Fired electrically with 400 Yards of insulating cable, and 1 Exploder.
1e, 1f, 1g, 1h.	Each 108 "	2 "	
2a, (2b) 2c, (2d)	25 lbs each	1 "	
3a, (3b) 3c, (3d)	12 lbs. each	1 "	Exploder in Magazine.
4a, 4b	25 lbs each	1 "	
Total	1062 lbs.	26	

Steel ———
Wood Framing & Tamping ———
Gun Cotton Charges ———

NOTE. Numbers enclosed with a circle refer to charges on other side of Bridge.

"J" BRIDGE C 25 d 3.9.

(15)

LATTICE R.S.J. BRIDGE FOR INFANTRY IN FOURS.

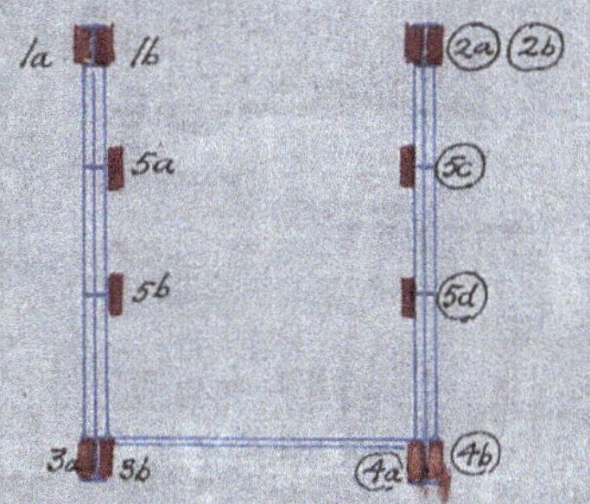

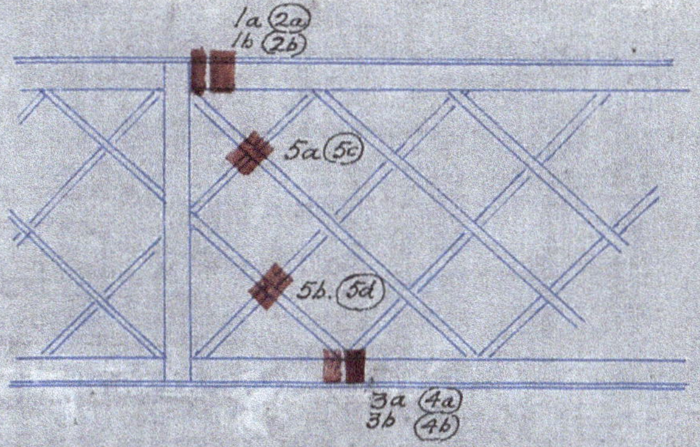

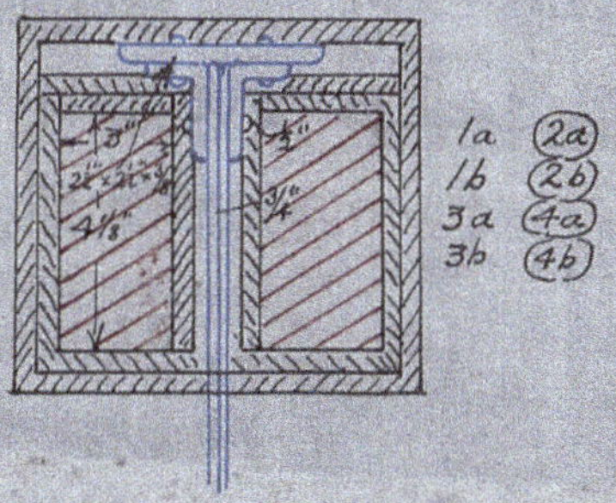

Charges Nos. 1a 1b 3a 3b | (2a) (2b) (4a) (4b)

Each charge 3 lbs. gun-cotton with 1 primer.

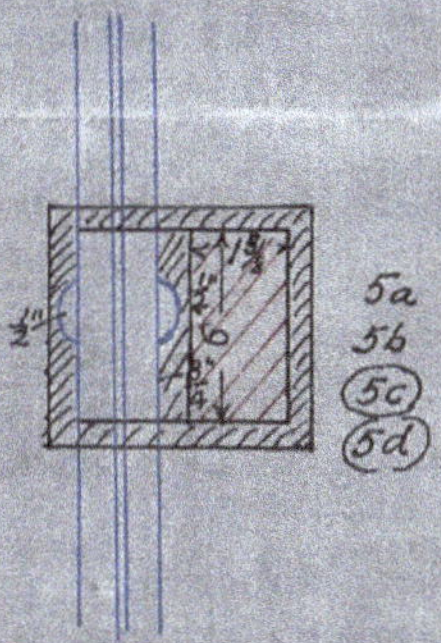

Charges Nos. 5a 5b | (5c) (5d)

Each charge 1 lb. gun cotton with 1 primer.

TABLE OF CHARGES.

Charge No.	Amt. of G.C.	Primers and Detonators	Remarks
1a (2a) 1b. (2b) 3a 3b (4a) (4b)	3 lbs. each	1 each.	Fired electrically with 60 Yards of insulating cable, and 1 Exploder.
5a 5b (5c) (5d)	1 lbs. each	1 each	
Total	28 lbs	12	

Steel.
Wood Framing & Tamping
Gun Cotton Charges.

NOTE. Numbers enclosed with a circle refer to charges on other side of Bridge.

Exploder in Magazine.

"K" BRIDGE. C 26 a. 2.2.

HEAVY STEEL LATTICE GIRDER SWING BRIDGE SUPPORTED ON STONE COLUMN AT CENTRE. (THREE LATTICE GIRDERS)

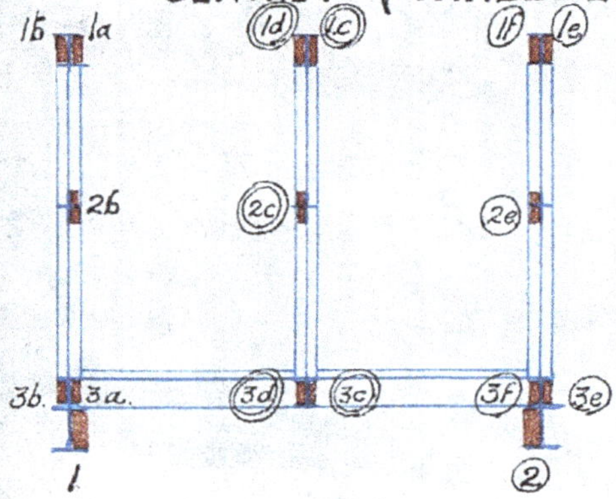

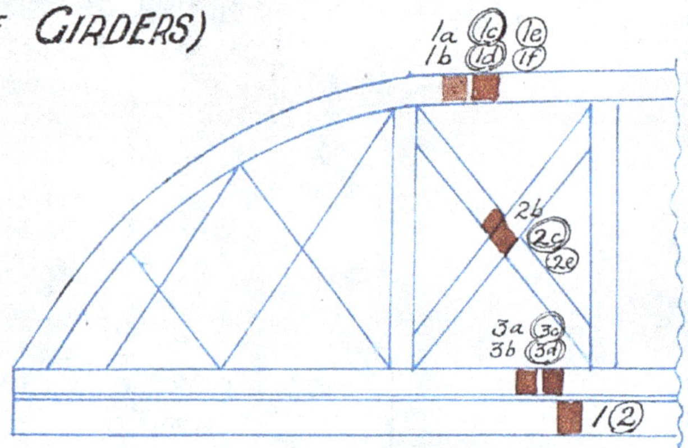

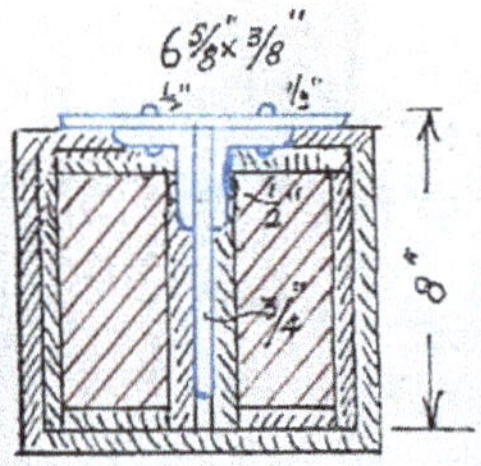

Charges Nos. 1a, 1b, (1c), (1d), (1e), (1f) | 3a, 3b, (3c), (3d), (3e), (3f)

Each charge 8 lbs. gun cotton with 1 Primer.

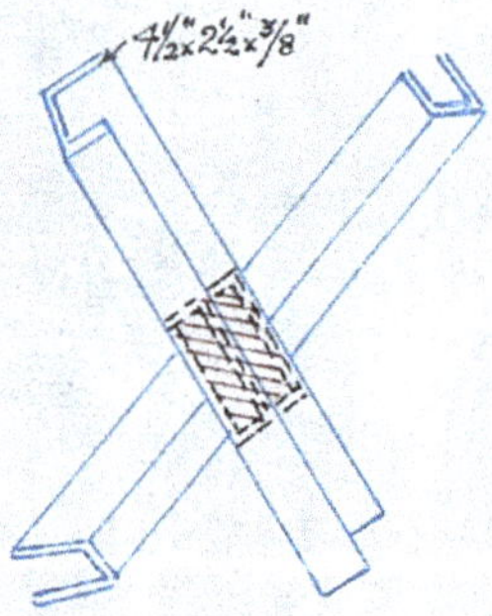

Charges Nos 2b, (2c), (2e)

Each charge 7 lbs. guncotton with 1 Primer.

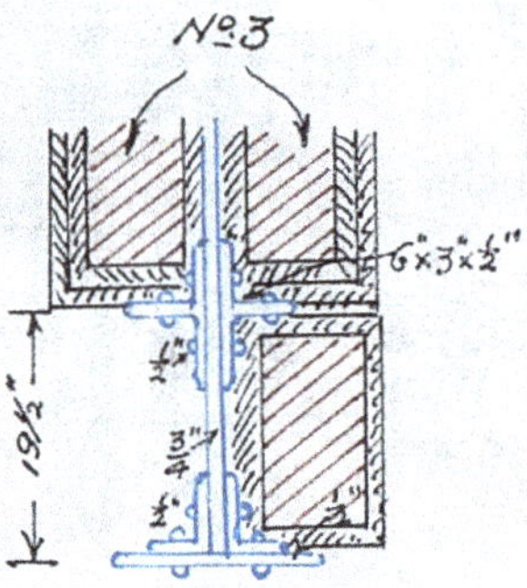

Charges Nos. 1, (2)

Each charge 25 lbs. gun cotton with 2 Primers.

Steel
Wood Framing & Tamping
Gun-cotton Charges.

NOTE. Numbers enclosed with a circle refer to charges on other side of Bridge. Double circles refer to charges in Centre of Bridge.

TABLE OF CHARGES.

Charge No.	Amt. of G.C.	Primers and Detonators.	Remarks.
1a.b. 3a.b. 1e.f. 3e.f. (1c)(d) (3c)(d)	8 lbs. each	1 Each	Fired electrically with 100yds. of Insulating cable, and 1 Exploder.
2b, (2c) (2e)	7 lbs "	1 "	
1. (2)	25 lbs "	2 "	
Total	167 lbs.	19.	

Exploder in Magazine.

Pont de Nieppe

No. 7 Stone Bridge. B24 c0.8.

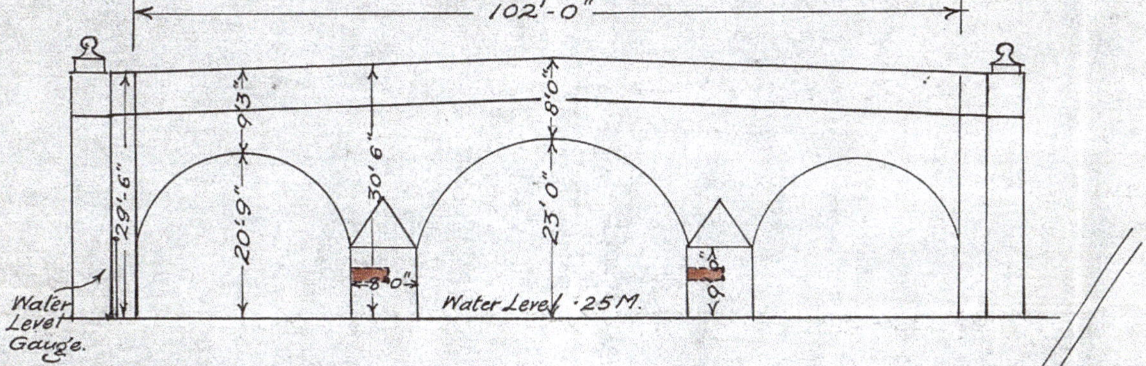

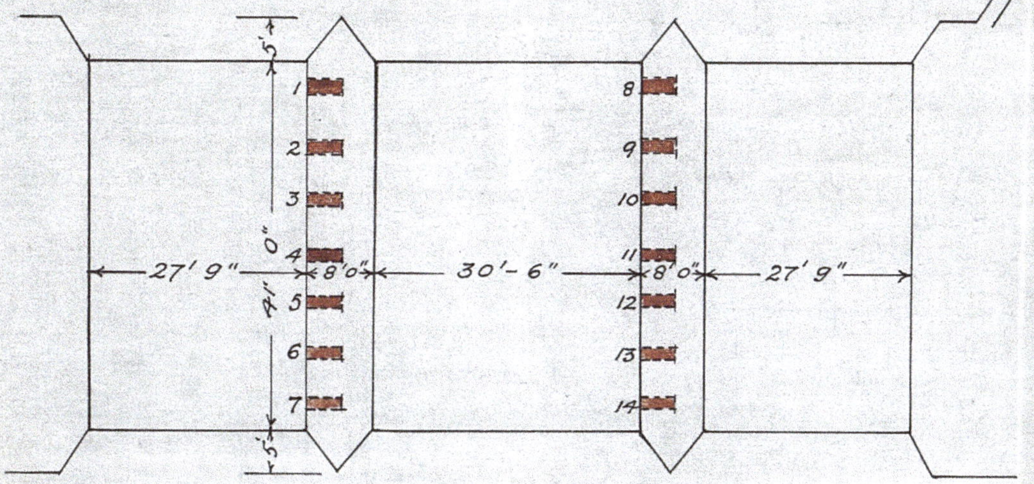

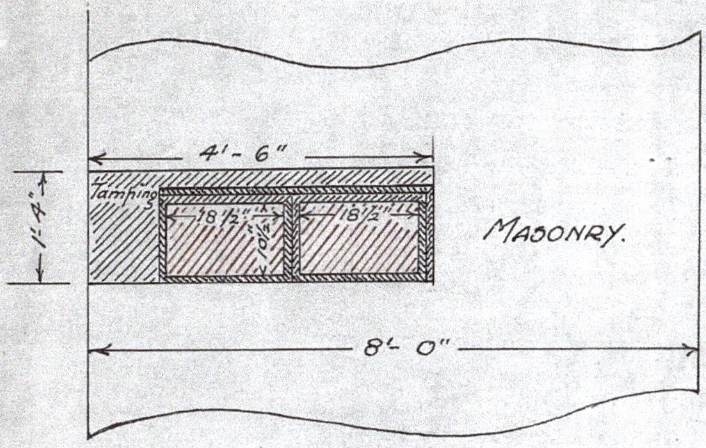

Charges. Nos 1·2·3·4·5·6·7·8·9·10·11·12·13·14· Seven holes in each pier. 14 similar charges. Each hole containing 2 boxes of 102 lbs guncotton each box.

Each Charge
204 lbs Guncotton
with 1. Primer.

Wood Framing & Tamping
Gun Cotton Charges.

TABLE OF CHARGES.

Charge No.	Amount of Guncotton	No. of Primers & Detonators	Remarks
1·2·3·4·5·6·7	Each 204 lbs	Each 1	Fired Electrically with 1 coil of Insulating Cable & 1 Exploder
8·9·10·11· 12·13·14·	Each 204 lbs	Each 1	
Total.	2856 lbs	" 14	

Exploder in Magazine.

"H" BRIDGE C25. a. 6.9.

HEAVY IRON GIRDER ELEVATING BRIDGE.

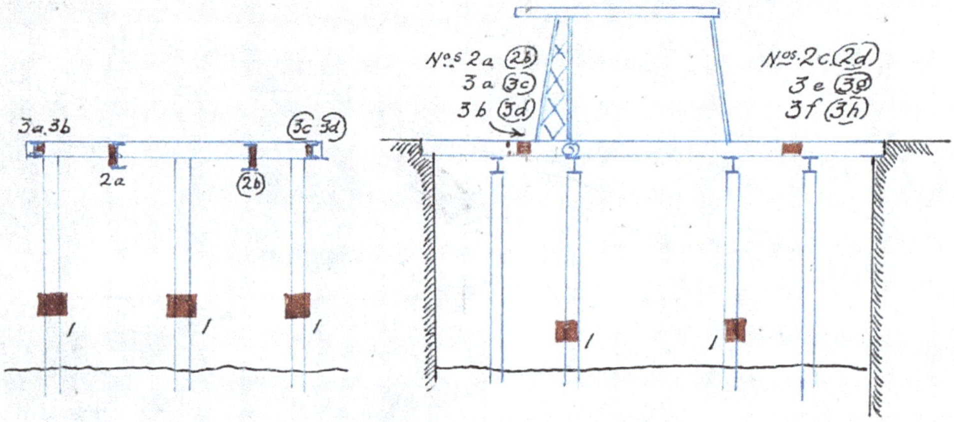

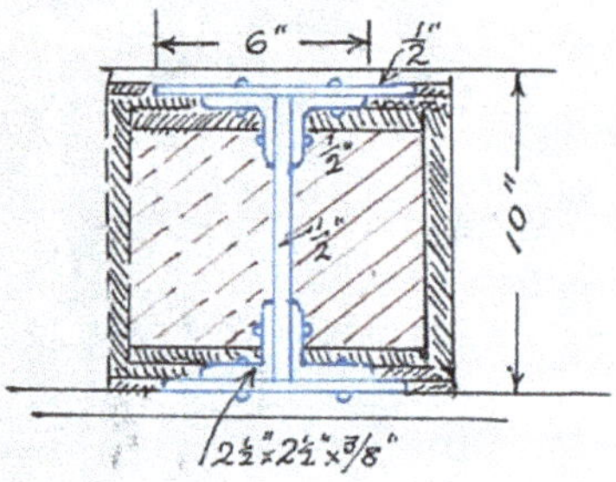

Charges No 3a, 3e.
3b, 3f.
(3c), (3g)
(3d) (3h)

8 Charges 6 lbs. each with 1 primer.

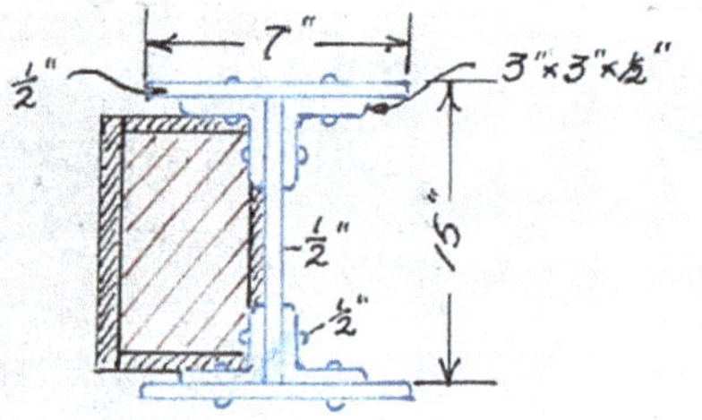

Charges No 2a.
(2b)
2c.
(2d)

4 Charges 16 lbs. each with 1 primer.

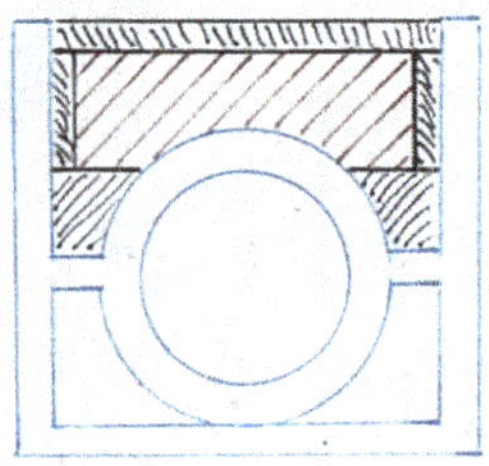

CHARGES No 1

Six Charges, 10 lbs. each, with 1 Primer.

TABLE OF CHARGES.

Charge No	Amt. of G.C.	Primers and Detonators	Remarks.
1.	10 lbs.	1	Six Similar Charges
2	16 "	1	4 Similar Charges Nos 2a, 2b, 2c, 2d.
3.	6 "	1	8 Similar Charges Nos 3a, 3b, 3c, 3d, 3e, 3f, 3g, 3h.
Total	172 lbs	18	200 Yards insulating Wire. 1 Exploder. Fired electrically

Steel.
Wood Framing & Tamping
Gun Cotton Charges

NOTE. Numbers enclosed with a circle refer to charges on other side of Bridge.

Exploder in Magazine.

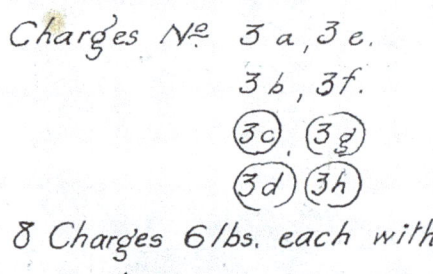

No 10 BRIDGE. C·19 c 7·7·

STEEL FOOT BRIDGE. INFANTRY IN FILE.

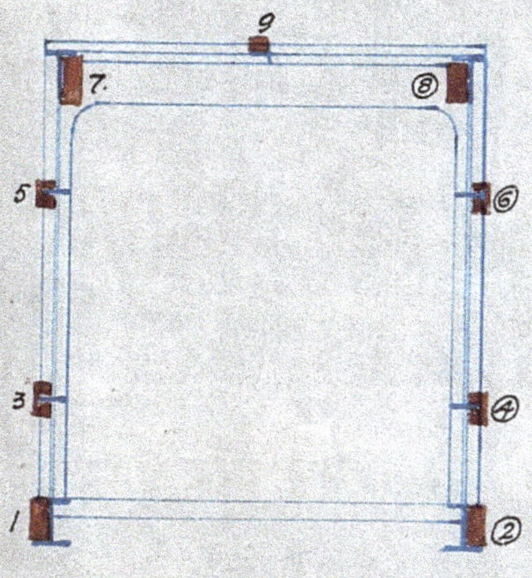

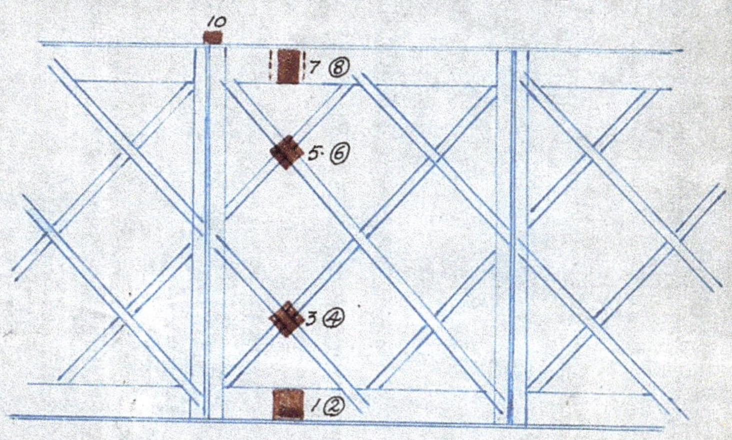

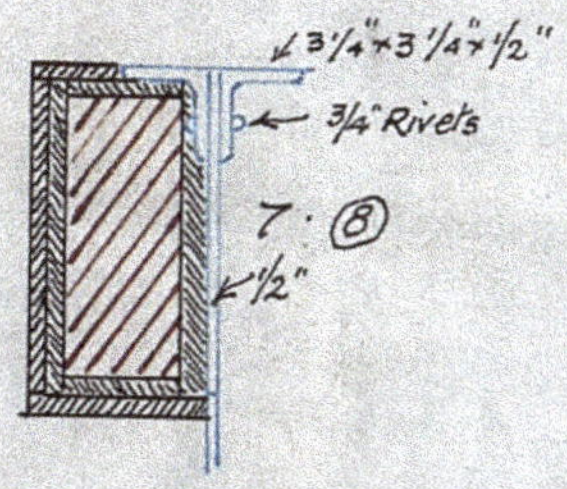

Charges Nos 7 ⑧
Each charge 12 lbs Guncotton
with 3 primers.

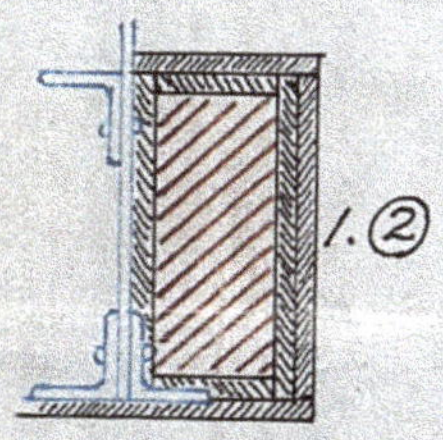

Charges Nos 1. ②
Each charge 32 lbs Guncotton.
with 3 primers.

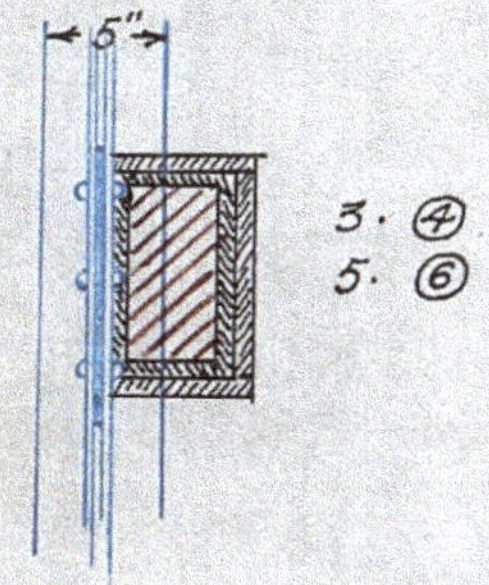

Charges Nos 3 ④ 5 ⑥
Each charge 6 lbs Guncotton
with 2 primers.

Charge No 9
4 lbs Guncotton & 1 primer.

Charge No 10
39 lbs Guncotton & 1 primer.

Steel. ———
Wood Framing & Tamping ———
Gun cotton charges. ———

NOTE· Numbers enclosed with a circle refer to charges on other side of Bridge.

TABLE OF CHARGES.

Charge No	Amt. of G.C.	Primers & Detonators	Remarks.
1. ②	Each 32 lbs	Each 3	Fired electrically with coil of insulating cable and Exploder.
3. ④ 5. ⑥	Each 6 lbs	Each 2	
7. ⑧	Each 12 lbs	Each 3.	
9	4 lbs	1	
10	39 lbs	2	
Total	155 lbs	23	

Exploder in Magazine.

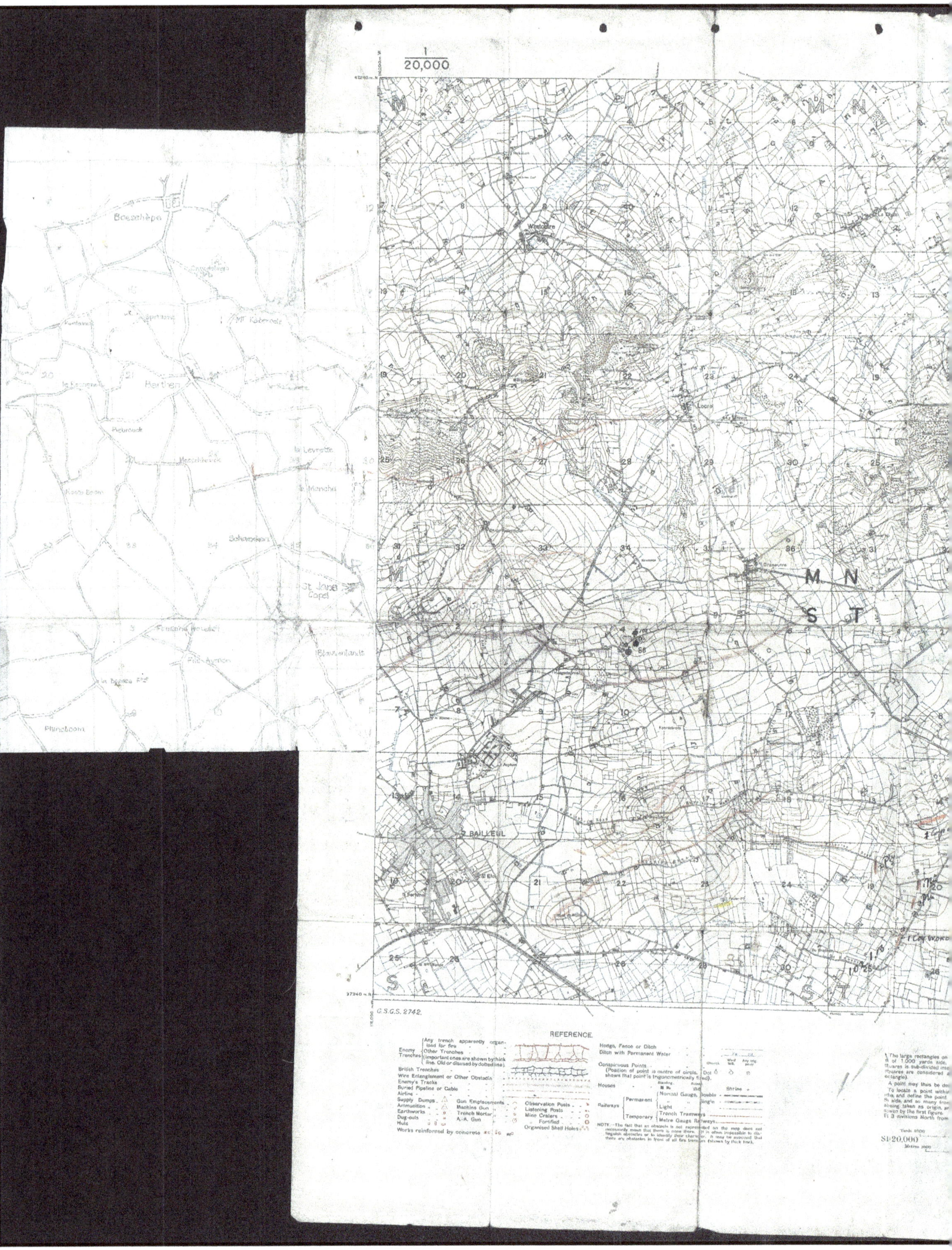

1/20,000
Westoutre
Locre
BAILLEUL
Boeschèpe
Berthen
Meesekbrook
la Levrette
Schaexken
St Jans Capel
Fontaine Houck
Blauwenhuis
Plingeboom
M N
S T
G.S.G.S. 2742.
REFERENCE.
Enemy Trenches
Any trench apparently organised for fire
Other Trenches
British Trenches
Wire Entanglement or Other Obstacle
Enemy's Tracks
Buried Pipeline or Cable
Airline
Supply Dumps
Ammunition
Earthworks
Dug-outs
Huts
Gun Emplacements
Machine Gun
Trench Mortar
A.-A. Gun
Observation Posts
Listening Posts
Mine Craters
Fortified
Organised Shell Holes
Works reinforced by concrete
Hedge, Fence or Ditch
Ditch with Permanent Water
Conspicuous Points
Houses
Railways
Permanent
Temporary
Normal Gauge
Light
Trench Tramways
Metre Gauge Railways
1:20,000

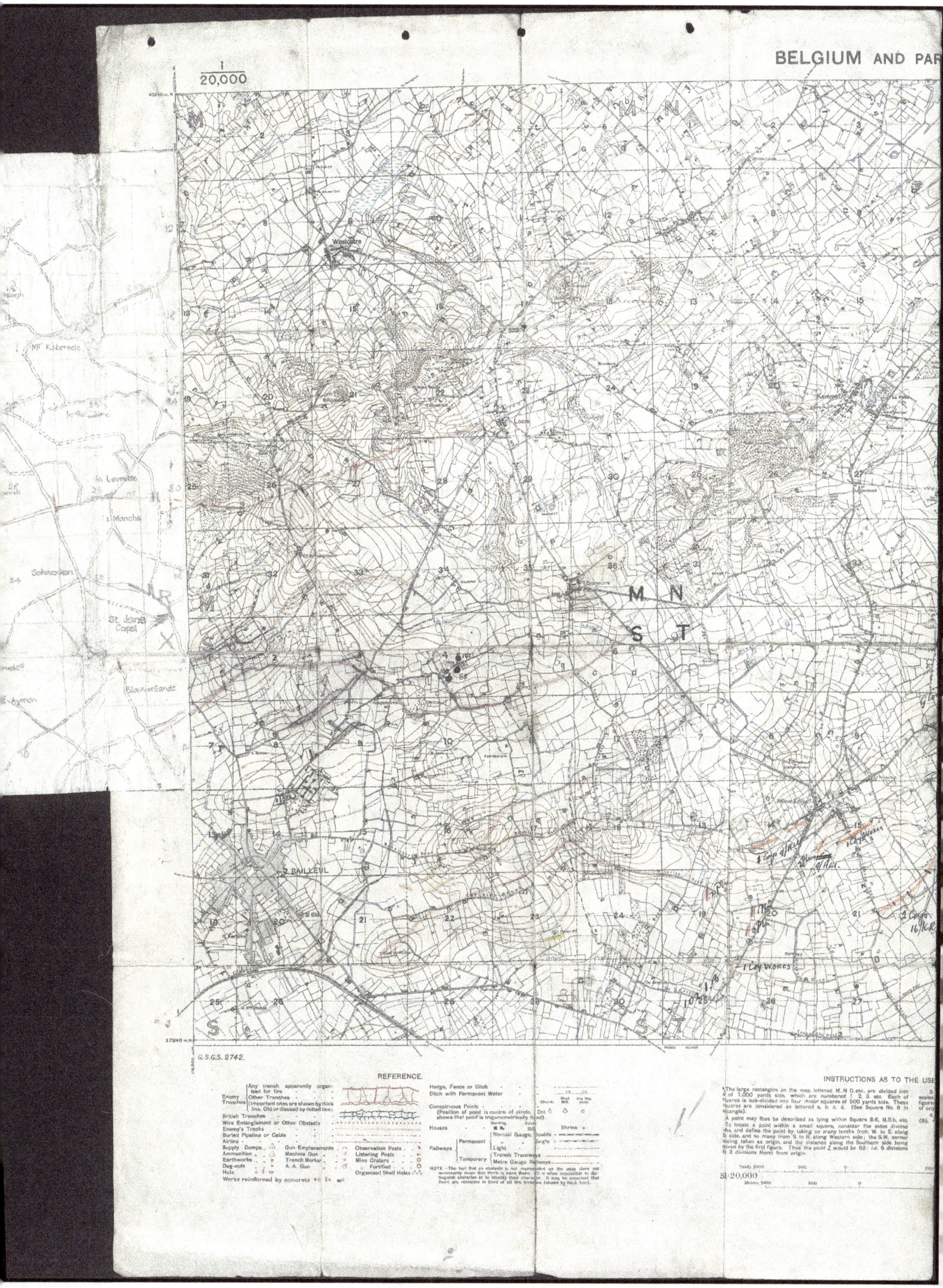
BELGIUM AND PAR
1
20,000
M N
S T
Westoutre
Locre
Dranoutre
Kemmel
BAILLEUL
St Jans Capel
Blauwersande
G.S.G.S. 2742.
REFERENCE.
INSTRUCTIONS AS TO THE USE

Nacelle -	Ferry.
Orme - -	Elm.
Orphelinat	Orphanage.
Oseraies -	Osier-beds.
Ouvrage - -	Fort.
Ouvrages hydrauliques	Water works.
Papeterie -	Paper-mill.
Parc - -	Park, yard.
„ aérostatique-	Aviation ground.
„ à charbon -	Coal yard.
„ à pétrole -	Petrol store.
Passage à niveau P.N.	Level-crossing.
Passerelle, Pas[lle]	Foot-bridge.
Pepinière - -	Nursery-garden.
Peuplier - -	Poplar tree.
Phare -	Light-house.
Pilier, Pil[r] - -	Post.
Plaine d'exercice-	Drill grouud.
Pompe - -	Pump.
Ponceau - -	Culvert.
Pont - -	Bridge.
„ levis - -	Drawbridge.
Poste / Station } de garde-côte	Coast-guard station.
Poteau P[au] -	Post.
Poterie	Pottery.
Poudrière, Poud[re] / Magasin à poudre }	Powder magazine.
Prise d'eau	Water supply.
Puits	Pit-head, Shaft, Well.
„ artésien -	Artesian well.
„ d'aérage / „ ventilateur }	Ventilating shaft.
„ de sondage -	Boring.
Quai - -	Quay, Platform.
„ aux bestiaux -	Cattle platform.
„ aux / „ des } marchandises	Goods platform.
Raccordement -	Junction.
Raffinerie - -	Refinery.
„ de sucre	Sugar refinery.
Râperie - -	Beet-root factory.

Remblai - -	Embankment.
Remise (des / aux) Machines -	Engine-shed.
Réservoir, Rés[r] -	Reservoir.
Route cavalière -	Bridle road.
Rubanerie - -	Ribbon Factory.
Ruine / Ruines / En ruine / Ruiné - e } -	Ruin.
Sablière - -	Sand-pit.
Sablonnière, Sablon[re]	„
Sapin - -	Fir tree.
Saule - -	Willow tree.
Saunerie - -	Salt-works.
Scierie, Sc[ie] -	Saw-mill.
Sondage - -	Boring.
Source - -	Spring.
Sucrerie, Suc[ie] -	Sugar factory.
Tannerie - -	Tannery.
Tir à la cible -	Rifle range.
Tissage - -	Weaving mill.
Tôlerie - -	Rolling mill
Tombeau - -	Tomb.
Tour - - -	Tower.
Tourbière -	Peat-bog, Peat-bed.
Tourelle - -	Small tower.
Tuilerie - -	Tile works.
Usine à gaz - -	Gas works.
„ électrique / „ d'électricité }	Electricity works.
„ métallurgique	Metal works.
„ à agglomérés -	Briquette factory.
Verrerie, Verr[ie] -	Glass works.
Viaduc - -	Viaduct.
Vivier - -	Fish Pond.
Voie de chargement - / „ „ déchargement / „ „ d'évitement - / „ „ formation - / „ „ manœuvre - }	Siding.
Zinguerie - -	Zinc works.

TRENCH MAP.

FRANCE.

SHEET 28 S.W.

EDITION 6. A.

INDEX TO ADJOINING SHEETS.

SCALE 1/20,000.

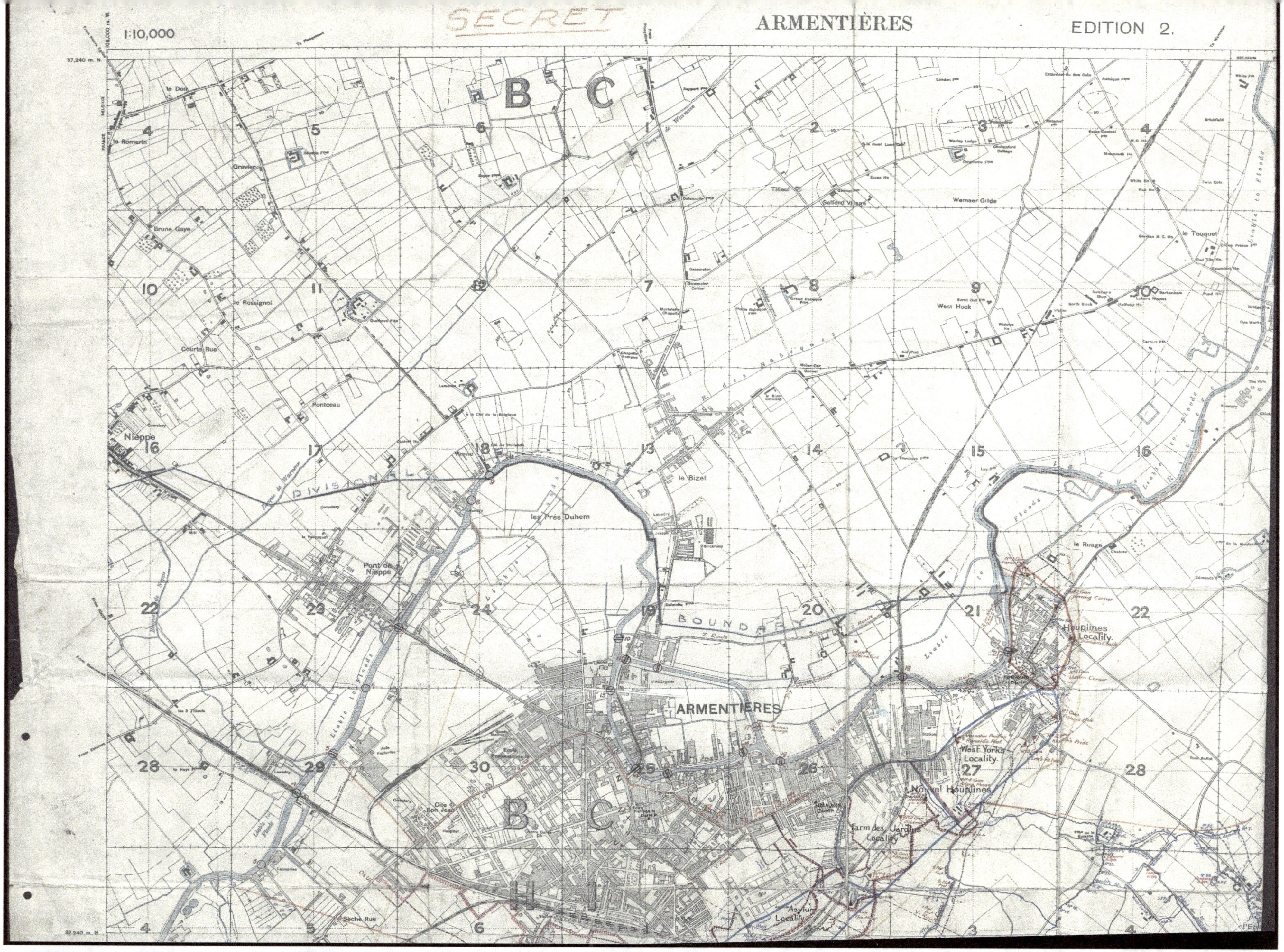

SECRET
ARMENTIÈRES
EDITION 2.
1:10,000
B C
ARMENTIÈRES
Houplines Locality.
West Yorks Locality.
Nouvel Houplines
Farm des Jardins Locality
Asylum Locality
Pont de Nieppe
Nieppe
les Prés Duhem
le Bizet
le Ruage
le Touquet
West Hock
Wemaer Gilde
Tilleul
Salford Village
le Rossignol
Courte Rue
Pontceau
Brune Gaye
Gravier
le Romarin
le Doo
Cite Bon Jean
Sèche Rue
BOUNDARY
DIVISIONAL

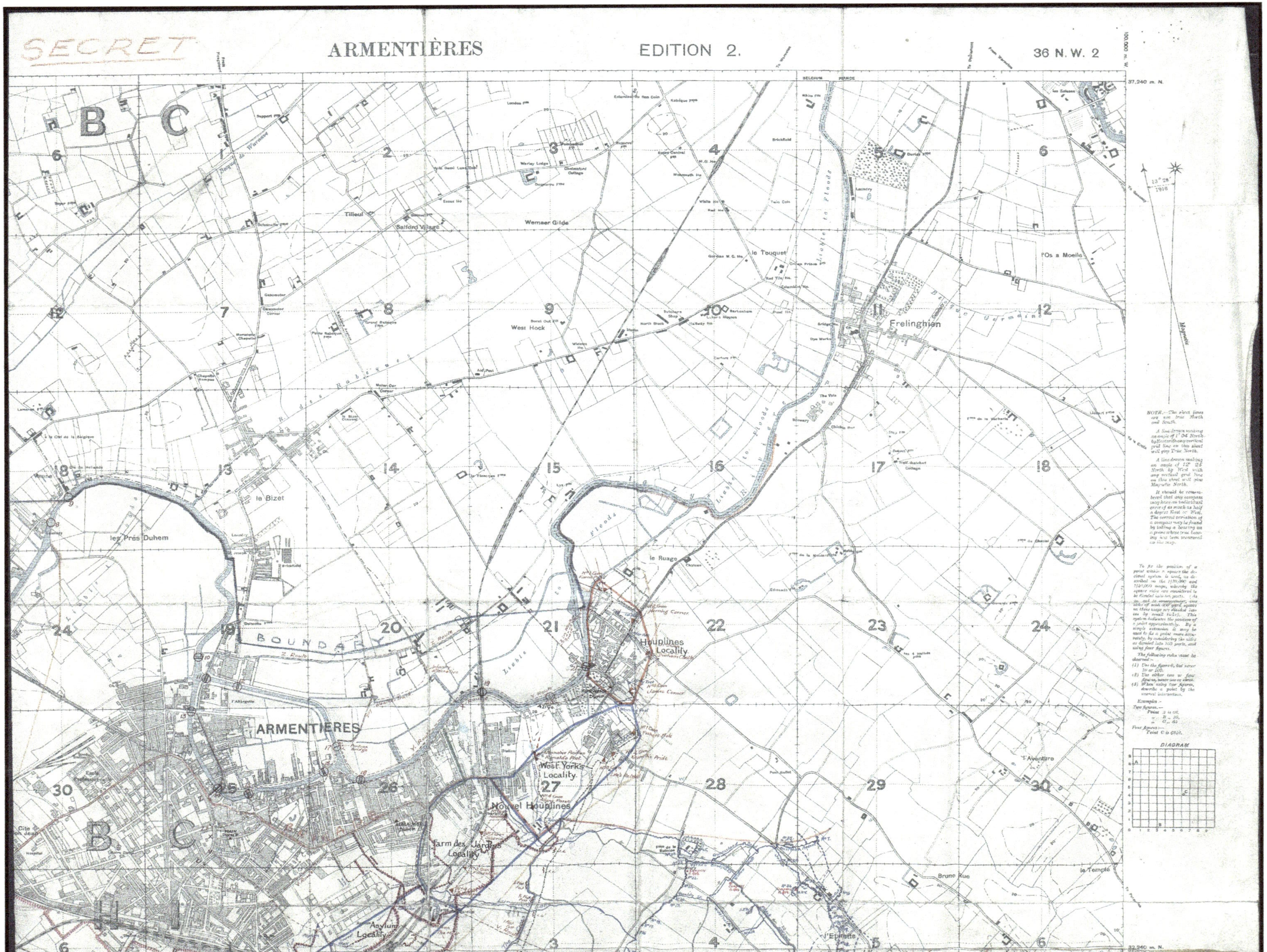
SECRET
ARMENTIÈRES
EDITION 2.
36 N.W. 2
BELGIUM
FRANCE
Frelinghien
le Touquet
Wemaer Gilde
West Hock
Tilleul
Salford Village
le Bizet
les Prés Duhem
le Ruage
Houplines Locality
ARMENTIÈRES
West Yorks Locality
Nouvel Houplines
Farm des Jardins Locality
Asylum Locality
BOUNDARY
Brune Rue
le Temple
l'Aventuro
l'Epinette
l'Os a Moelle
Magnetic
DIAGRAM

ARMENTIERES
Houplines Locality
West Yorks Locality
Nouvel Houplines
Farm des Jardins Locality
Asylum Locality
Erquinghem-Lys
Rue Marle
Sèche Rue
la Chapelle d'Armentieres
Rue Allée
Rue Fleurie
Bois-Grenier
Gris Pot
Wez Macquart
BOUNDARY
DIVISIONAL

ARMENTIERES
Houplines Locality
West Yorks Locality
Nouvel Houplines
Farm des Jardins Locality
Asylum Locality
Rue Marle
la Chapelle d'Armentières
Rue Allée
Rue Fleurie
l'Epinette
Wez Macquart
Premesques
Ruelle de la Nois
le Temple
Bruno Rue
l'Aventure
BOUNDARY
DIAGRAM
Central Ave
Rue du Bois
Half Way House
Brickfield
To Lille

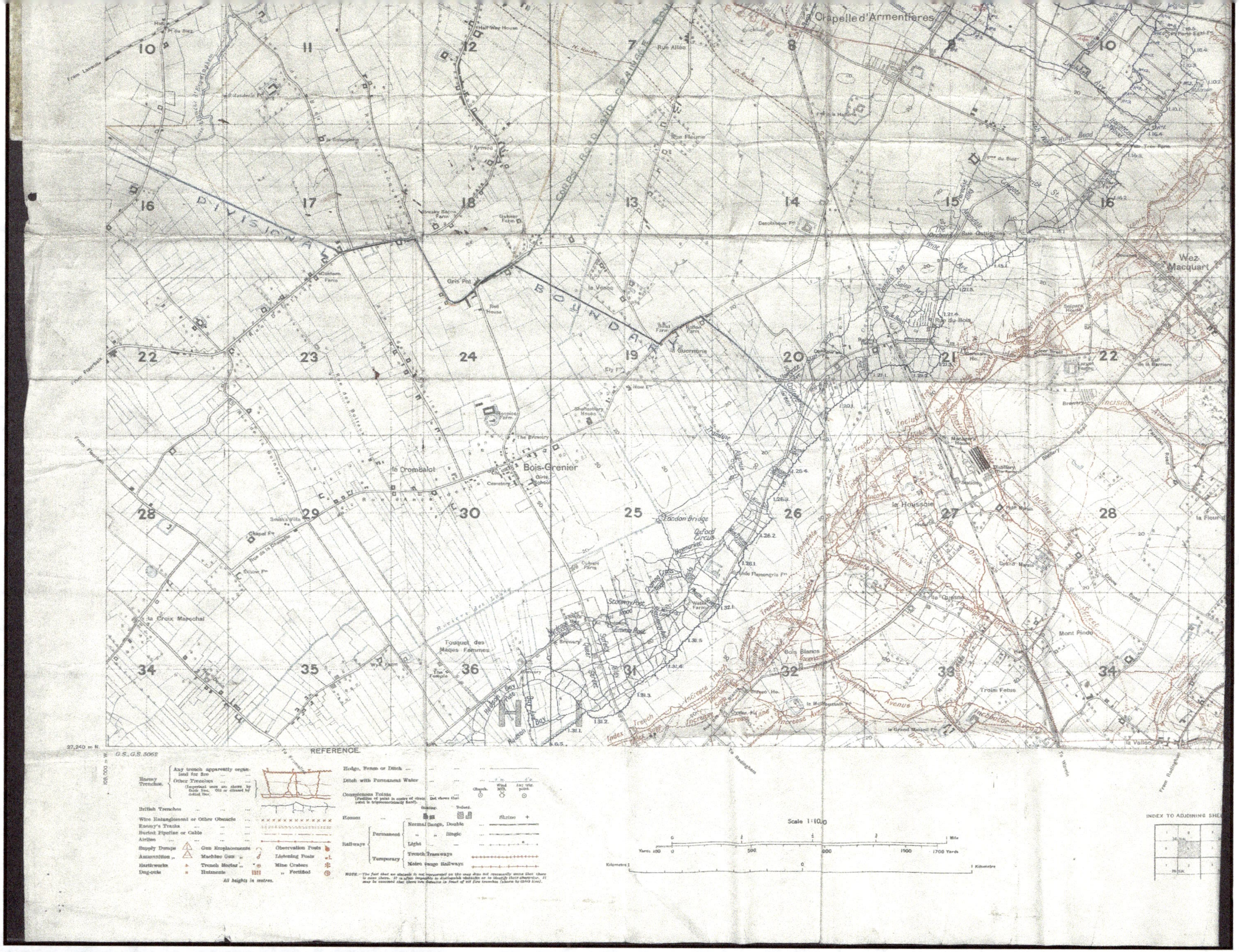
la Chapelle d'Armentières
Wez Macquart
Bois-Grenier
le Crombalot
la Houssoie
Bois Blancs
Mont Pindu
Trois Fetus
la Croix Marechal
Touquet des Mages Femmes
DIVISIONAL BOUNDARY
REFERENCE
Scale 1:10,000
INDEX TO ADJOINING SHE
All heights in metres.

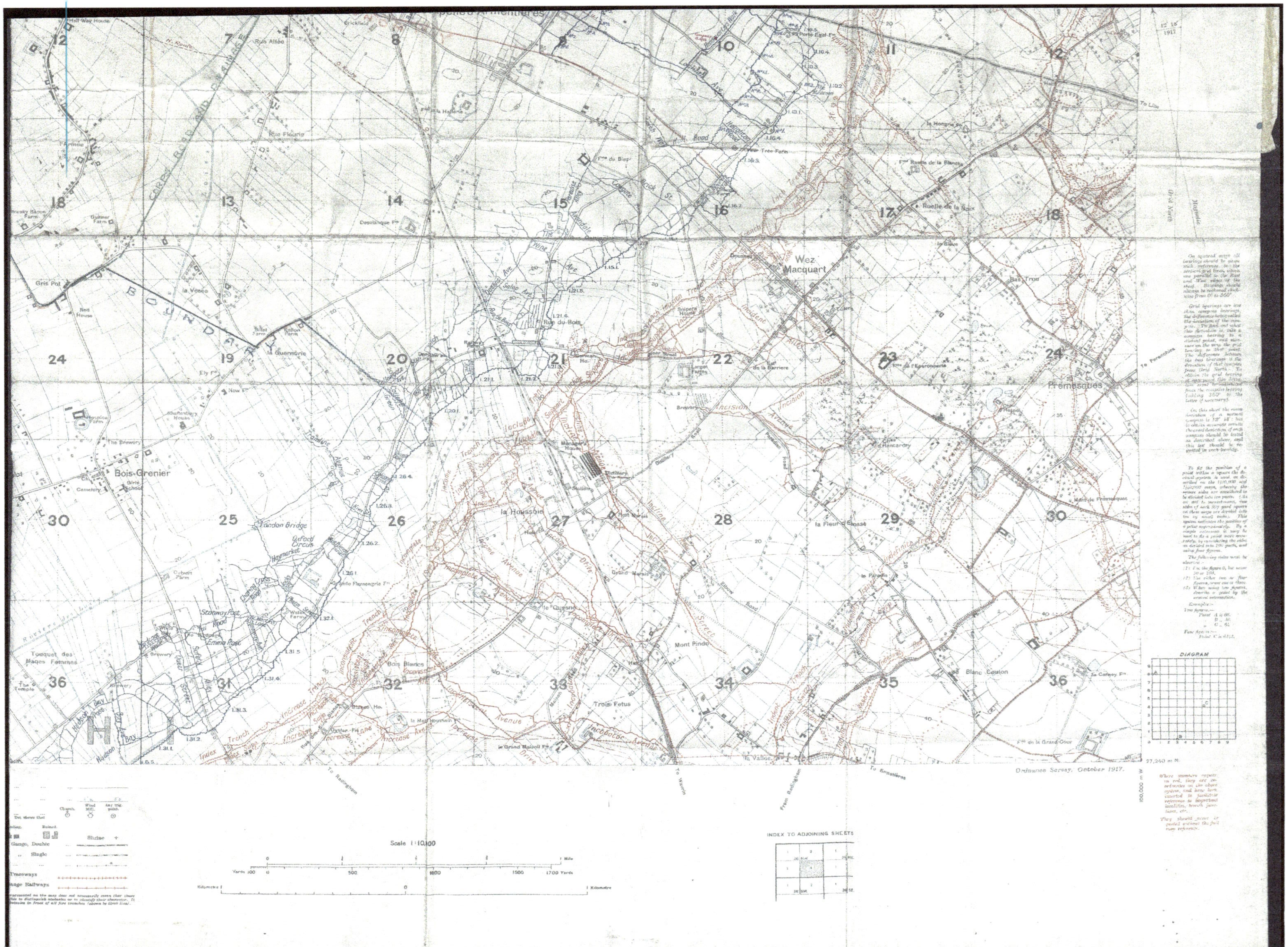
Wez Macquart
Bois-Grenier
Prémesques
la Houssoie
Mont Pindo
Trois Fetus
Blanc Coulon
la Fleur d'Écosse
Bois Blancs
Touquet des Mages Fermes
Ordnance Survey, October 1917.
DIAGRAM
INDEX TO ADJOINING SHEETS
Scale 1:10,000
To Lille
To Wavrin
To Radinghem
To Ennetières
To Pérenchies

GLOSSARY.

Abbaye, Abb^e	Abbey.
Abreuvoir, Ab^r	Watering-place.
Abri de douaniers	Custom-shelter.
Aciérie	Steel works.
Aiguilles	Points (Ry.)
Allée	Alley, Narrow road
Ancien - ne, Anc^n - ne	Old.
Aqueduc	Aqueduct.
Arbre	Tree.
„ éventail	„ fan-shaped.
„ décharné	„ bare.
„ fourchu	„ forked.
„ isolé	„ isolated.
„ penché	„ leaning
Arbrisseau	Small tree.
Arc	Arch.
Ardoisière, Ard^re	Slate quarry.
Arrêt	Halt.
Asile	Asylum.
„ des / „ d' } aliénés	Lunatic asylum.
„ de charité / „ des pauvres / „ de refuge	Asylum.
Auberge, Aub^ge	Inn.
Aune	Alder-tree.
Bac	Ferry.
„ à traille	„
Bains	Baths.
Place aux bains	Bathing place.
Balise	Boom, Beacon.
Banc de sable	Sand-bank.
„ „ vase	Mud-bank.
Baraque	Hut.
Barrage	Dam.
Barrière	Gate, Stile.
(Machine à) Bascule	Weigh-bridge.
Bassin	Dock, Pond.
„ d'échouage	Tidal dock.
Bassin de radoub	Dry dock.
Bateau phare	Light-ship.
Blanchisserie	Laundry.
B.M. (borne milliare)	Mile stone.
B^k (borne kilométrique)	
Boulonnerie / Fab^e de boulons	Bolt Factory.
Bouée	Buoy.
Brasserie, Bras^ie	Brewery.
Briqueterie, Briq^ie	Brickfield.
Brise-lames	Breakwater.
Bureau de poste	Post office.
„ de douane	Custom house.
Butte	Butt, Mound.
Cabane	Hut.
Cabaret, Cab^t	Inn.
Câble sous-marin	Submarine cable.
Calvaire, Calv^e	Calvary.
Canal de desséchement	Drainage canal.
Canal d'irrigation	Irrigation canal.
Fab^e de caoutchouc	Rubber factory.
Carrière, Carr^e	Quarry.
„ de gravier	Gravel-pit.
Caserne	Barracks.
Champ de courses	Race-course.
„ „ manœuvres	Drill-ground.
„ „ tir	Rifle range.
Chantier	Building yard. / Ship yard. / Dock yard.
Chantier de construction	Slip-way.
Chapelle, Ch^le	Chapel.
Charbonnage	Colliery.
Château d'eau	Water tower.
Chaussée	Causeway. / Highway.
Chemin de fer	Railway.
Cheminée, Ch^ée	Chimney.
Chêne	Oak tree.
Cimetière, Cim^re	Cemetery.
Clocher	Belfry.
Clouterie	Nail factory.
Colombier	Dove-cot.
Coron	Workmen's dwellings.
Cour des / aux } marchandises	Goods yard.
Couvent	Convent.
Crassier	Slag heap.
Croix	Cross.
Darse	Inner dock.
Démoli - e	Destroyed.
Détruit - e, Dét^t - e	„
Déversoir	Weir.
Digue	Dyke, causeway.
Distillerie, Dist^ie	Distillery.
Douane / Bureau de douane	Custom-house.
Entrepôt de douane	Custom warehouse.
Dynamitière, Dynam^re	Dynamite magazine.
Dynamiterie	Dynamite factory.
Ecluse	Sluice, Lock.
Eclusette, Ecl^te	Sluice.
Ecole	School.
Ecurie	Stable.
Eglise	Church.
Emaillerie	Enamel works.
Embarcadère, Emb^re	Landing-place.
Estaminet, Estam^t	Inn.
Etang	Pond.
Fabrique, Fab^e	Factory.
Fab^e de produits chimiques	Chemical works.
Fab^e de faïence / Faïencerie	Pottery.
Ferme, F^me	Farm.
Filature, Fil^re	Spinning mill.
Fonderie, Fond^ie	Foundry.
Fontaine, Font^ne	Spring, fountain.
Forêt	Forest
Forme de radoub	Dry dock.
Forge	Smithy.
Fosse	Mine, Pit.
Fossé	Moat, Ditch.
Four	Kiln.
„ à chaux	Lime-kiln.
Four à coke	Coke oven.
Ganterie	Glove Factory.
Gare	Station.
Garenne	Warren.
Garnison	Garrison.
Gazomètre	Gasometer.
Glacerie / Fab^e de glaces	Mirror Factory.
Glacière	Ice factory.
Grue	Crane.
Gué	Ford.
Guérite	Sentry-box, Turret.
„ à signaux	Signal-box (Ry.)
Halte	Halt.
Hangar	Shed, Hangar.
Hôpital	Hospital.
Hôtel-de-Ville	Town hall.
Houillère	Colliery.
Huilerie	Oil factory.
Imprimerie, Impr^ie	Printing works.
Jetée	Pier.
Laminerie	Rolling mills.
Ligne / Laisse } de haute marée	High water mark.
„ de basse marée	Low „
Maison Forestière / M^on F^re	Forester's house.
Malterie	Malt-house.
Marbrerie	Marble works.
Marais	Marsh.
Marais salant	Saltern, Salt marsh.
Marché	Market.
Mare	Pool.
Meule	Rick.
Minière	Mine.
Monastère	Monastery.
Moulin, M^in	Mill.
„ à vapeur	Steam mill.
Mur	Wall.
„ crénelé	Loop-holed wall.
Nacelle	Ferry.
Orme	Elm.
Orphelinat	Orphanage.
Oseraies	Osier-beds.
Ouvrage	Fort.
Ouvrages hydrauliques	Water works.
Papeterie	Paper-mill.
Parc	Park, yard.
„ aérostatique	Aviation ground.
„ à charbon	Coal yard.
„ à pétrole	Petrol store.
Passage à niveau P.N.	Level-crossing.
Passerelle, Pas^lle	Foot-bridge.
Pépinière	Nursery-garden.
Peuplier	Poplar tree.
Phare	Light-house.
Pilier, Pil^r	Post.
Plaine d'exercice	Drill ground.
Pompe	Pump.
Ponceau	Culvert.
Pont	Bridge.
„ levis	Drawbridge.
Poste / Station } de garde-côte	Coast-guard station.
Poteau P^au	Post.
Poterie	Pottery.
Poudrière, Poud^re / Magasin à poudre	Powder magazine.
Prise d'eau	Water supply.
Puits	Pit-head, Shaft, Well.
„ artésien	Artesian well.
„ d'aérage / „ ventilateur	Ventilating shaft.
„ de sondage	Boring.
Quai	Quay, Platform.
„ aux bestiaux	Cattle platform.
„ aux / „ des } marchandises	Goods platform.
Raccordement	Junction.
Raffinerie	Refinery.
„ de sucre	Sugar refinery.
Râperie	Beet-root factory.
Remblai	Embankment.
Remise des / aux Machines	Engine-shed.
Réservoir, Rés^r	Reservoir.
Route cavalière	Bridle road.
Rubanerie	Ribbon Factory.
Ruine / Ruines / En ruine / Ruiné - e	Ruin.
Sablière	Sand-pit.
Sablonnière, Sablon^re	„
Sapin	Fir tree.
Saule	Willow tree.
Saunerie	Salt-works.
Scierie, Sc^ie	Saw-mill.
Sondage	Boring.
Source	Spring.
Sucrerie, Suc^ie	Sugar factory.
Tannerie	Tannery.
Tir à la cible	Rifle range.
Tissage	Weaving mill.
Tôlerie	Rolling mill
Tombeau	Tomb.
Tour	Tower.
Tourbière	Peat-bog, Peat-bed.
Tourelle	Small tower.
Tuilerie	Tile works.
Usine à gaz	Gas works.
„ électrique / „ d'électricité	Electricity works.
„ métallurgique	Metal works.
„ à agglomérés	Briquette factory.
Verrerie, Verr^ie	Glass works.
Viaduc	Viaduct.
Vivier	Fish Pond.
Voie de chargement / „ „ déchargement / „ „ d'évitement / „ „ formation / „ „ manœuvre	Siding.
Zinguerie	Zinc works.

Coron	Workmen's dwellings.
Cour des / aux marchandises	Goods yard.
Couvent	Convent.
Crassier	Slag heap.
Croix	Cross.
Darse	Inner dock.
Démoli - e	Destroyed.
Détruit - e, Dét - e	"
Déversoir	Weir.
Digue	Dyke, causeway.
Distillerie, Dist[ie]	Distillery.
Douane / Bureau de douane	Custom-house.
Entrepôt de douane	Custom warehouse.
Dynamitière, Dynam[re]	Dynamite magazine.
Dynamiterie	Dynamite factory.
Ecluse	Sluice, Lock.
Ecluset(te), Ecl[te]	Sluice.
Ecole	School.
Ecurie	Stable.
Eglise	Church.
Emaillerie	Enamel works.
Embarcadère, Emb[re]	Landing-place.
Estaminet, Estam[t]	Inn.
Etang	Pond.
Fabrique, Fab[e]	Factory.
Fab[e] de produits chimiques	Chemical works.
Fab[e] de faïence / Faïencerie	Pottery.
Ferme, F[me]	Farm.
Filature, Fil[re]	Spinning mill.
Fonderie, Fond[ie]	Foundry.
Fontaine, Font[ne]	Spring, fountain.
Forêt	Forest.
Forme de radoub	Dry dock.
Forge	Smithy.
Fosse	Mine, Pit.
Fossé	Moat, Ditch.
Four	Kiln.
" à chaux	Lime kiln.
Four à coke	Coke oven.
Ganterie	Glove Factory.
Gare	Station.
Garenne	Warren.
Garnison	Garrison.
Gazomètre	Gasometer.
Glacerie / Fab[e] de glaces	Mirror Factory.
Glacière	Ice factory.
Grue	Crane.
Gué	Ford.
Guérite	Sentry-box, Turret.
" à signaux	Signal-box (Ry.)
Halte	Halt.
Hangar	Shed, Hangar.
Hôpital	Hospital.
Hôtel-de-Ville	Town hall.
Houillère	Colliery.
Huilerie	Oil factory.
Imprimerie, Impr[ie]	Printing works.
Jetée	Pier.
Laminerie	Rolling mills.
Ligne / Laisse de haute marée	High water mark.
" de basse marée	Low " "
Maison Forestière / M[on] F[re]	Forester's house.
Malterie	Malt-house.
Marbrerie	Marble works.
Marais	Marsh.
Marais salant	Saltern, Salt marsh.
Marché	Market.
Mare	Pool.
Meule	Rick.
Minière	Mine.
Monastère	Monastery.
Moulin, M[in]	Mill.
" à vapeur	Steam mill.
Mur	Wall.
" crénelé	Loop-holed wall.
Nacelle	Ferry.
Orme	Elm.
Orphelinat	Orphanage.
Oseraies	Osier-beds.
Ouvrage	Fort.
Ouvrages hydrauliques	Water works.
Papeterie	Paper-mill.
Parc	Park, yard.
" aérostatique	Aviation ground.
" à charbon	Coal yard.
" à pétrole	Petrol store.
Passage à niveau P.N.	Level-crossing.
Passerelle, Pas[le]	Foot-bridge.
Pépinière	Nursery-garden.
Peuplier	Poplar tree.
Phare	Light-house.
Pilier, Pil[r]	Post.
Plaine d'exercice	Drill ground.
Pompe	Pump.
Ponceau	Culvert.
Pont	Bridge.
" levis	Drawbridge.
Poste / Station de garde-côte	Coast-guard station.
Poteau P[au]	Post.
Poterie	Pottery.
Poudrière, Poud[re] / Magasin à poudre	Powder magazine.
Prise d'eau	Water supply.
Puits	Pit-head, Shaft, Well.
" artésien	Artesian well.
" d'aérage / ventilateur	Ventilating shaft.
" de sondage	Boring.
Quai	Quay, Platform.
" aux bestiaux	Cattle platform.
" aux / des marchandises	Goods platform.
Raccordement	Junction.
Raffinerie	Refinery.
" de sucre	Sugar refinery.
Râperie	Beet-root factory.
Remblai	Embankment.
Remise des / aux Machines	Engine-shed.
Réservoir, Rés[r]	Reservoir.
Route cavalière	Bridle road.
Rubanerie	Ribbon Factory.
Ruine / Ruines / En ruine / Ruiné - e	Ruin.
Sablière	Sand-pit.
Sablonnière, Sablon[re]	"
Sapin	Fir tree.
Saule	Willow tree.
Saunerie	Salt-works.
Scierie, Sc[ie]	Saw-mill.
Sondage	Boring.
Source	Spring.
Sucrerie, Suc[ie]	Sugar factory.
Tannerie	Tannery.
Tir à la cible	Rifle range.
Tissage	Weaving mill.
Tôlerie	Rolling mill.
Tombeau	Tomb.
Tour	Tower.
Tourbière	Peat-bog, Peat-bed.
Tourelle	Small tower.
Tuilerie	Tile works.
Usine à gaz	Gas works.
" électrique / " d'électricité	Electricity works.
" métallurgique	Metal works.
" à agglomérés	Briquette factory.
Verrerie, Verr[ie]	Glass works.
Viaduc	Viaduct.
Vivier	Fish Pond.
Voie de chargement / " " déchargement / " " d'évitement / " " formation / " " manœuvre	Siding.
Zinguerie	Zinc works.

FRANCE.

ARMENTIERES.

36 N.W. 2.

EDITION 2.

Scale 1 : 10,000.

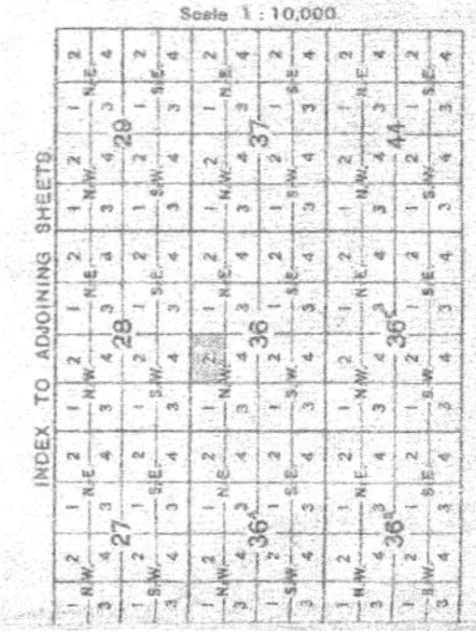

Army Form C. 2118.

Instructions regarding War Diaries and Intelligence Summaries are contained in F. S. Regs., Part II. and the Staff Manual respectively. Title pages will be prepared in manuscript.

WAR DIARY

~~or~~

~~INTELLIGENCE SUMMARY.~~

(Erase heading not required.)

Vol 29

Place	Date	Hour	Summary of Events and Information	Remarks and references to Appendices
			208th Field Coy R.E. — MAY 1918 —	

D. D. & L., London, E.C.
(A8004) Wt. W1771/M2031 750,000 5/17 Sch. 52 Forms/C2118/14

Instructions regarding War Diaries and Intelligence Summaries are contained in F. S. Regs., Part II. and the Staff Manual respectively. Title pages will be prepared in manuscript.

WAR DIARY

~~INTELLIGENCE SUMMARY.~~

(Erase heading not required.)

Army Form C. 2118.

208 Field Coy R.E.

Place	Date	Hour	Summary of Events and Information	Remarks and references to Appendices
PESELHOEK.	1st MAY 1918		1 Section worked with 1st Bn 102 Inf Bde on EAST POPERINGHE TRENCH SYSTEM and 2 sections with 2 Bns 102 Inf Bde on the BRANDHOEK TRENCH SYSTEM. — Work – making trenches defensible as quickly as possible, camouflaging, draining, clearing field of fire and wiring. One Section employed on marking with pickets two overland tracks between the POPERINGHE and BRANDHOEK SYSTEMS.	
"	2nd	"	102 Inf Bde from today are responsible for whole of work on the BRANDHOEK and POPERINGHE SYSTEMS within Bde Boundaries. One Bn & 1 Section R.E. were withdrawn from the BRANDHOEK SYSTEM & take over work on RESERVE TRENCH POPERINGHE SYSTEM and 3 defended localities between the Reserve & Support Trenches (by pioneers placed at disposal of the Bde for work on POPERINGHE SYSTEM).	
"	3rd		2 Farms reconnoitred with a view to converting them into strong points at G11a.22 and G17.c.5.7. in order to cover any withdrawal which might become necessary from the BRANDHOEK LINE to the POPERINGHE LINE. Section employed on overland tracks took over work of loopholing these farms. 2/Lt STATON proceeded to England on 7 days special leave.	

D. D. & L., London, E.C. (A8001) Wt. W1771/M2031 750,000 5/17 Sch. 52 Forms/C2118/14

Instructions regarding War Diaries and Intelligence Summaries are contained in F. S. Regs., Part II. and the Staff Manual respectively. Title pages will be prepared in manuscript.

WAR DIARY

~~INTELLIGENCE SUMMARY.~~

(Erase heading not required.)

Army Form C. 2118.

208 Field Coy R.E.

Place	Date	Hour	Summary of Events and Information	Remarks and references to Appendices
PESELHOEK	4th MAY 1918		Work as on 3rd — good progress made each Bn. finding out working parties of nearly 200. Fine R	
"	5th	—	103 Inf Bde relieved the 102 Inf Bde. — No working parties available — Company did no work. Heavy Rain R	
"	6th	—	Very wet. — Company and infantry working parties employed on drainage. R	
"	7th	—	103 Inf Bde extended to the right and took over the whole divisional front. Company took over all work of 207 Field Coy RE in addition to that in hand. — Work as on 6th R	
"	8th	—	Work stopped on the BRANDHOEK SYSTEM, and work started on 3 strong points between the BRANDHOEK and POPERINGHE SYSTEMS each for a garrison of 2 companies infantry at G11a.22, G17.c.5.7 and G23c 35.70. Strong points were wired by the CRE ~~Working Party~~ (Working party [illegible] RE [illegible]). Remainder of company with 1 Coy Pioneers & 2 Bns Infantry worked on the POPERINGHE SYSTEM. R	

D. D. & L., London, E.C. (A8001) Wt. W1771/M2031 750,000 5/17 Sch. 52 Forms/C2118/14

Instructions regarding War Diaries and Intelligence Summaries are contained in F. S. Regs., Part II. and the Staff Manual respectively. Title pages will be prepared in manuscript.

WAR DIARY

~~or~~

~~INTELLIGENCE SUMMARY.~~

(Erase heading not required.)

308 Field Coy RE

Army Form C. 2118.

Place	Date	Hour	Summary of Events and Information	Remarks and references to Appendices
PESELHOEK	9th MAY 1918		Work as on 8th. Enemy very quiet.	K.
"	10th		Company employed on Strong points & Poperinghe System. Working party appx. 600 infantry	K.
"	11th		Working party on the Poperinghe System concentrated on the Reserve Line and completed the digging of this trench between the divisional boundaries. About 6pm orders recd that Company would move on 12th under orders of 103 Inf Bde.	K.
HOUTKERQUE	12th		Company marched to HOUTKERQUE. Transport rejoined Company	K.
AFFRINGUES	13th		Dismounted personnel moved by motor bus to AFFRINGUES. - Transport by route march to St MOMELIN.	K.
"	14th		Company resting. Transport rejoined Company. K went round & proposed training area with GSO1 & 2	K.
"	15th		Company training. OC ~~saw~~ to 2nd Army re supply of RE Stores for the training of American Troops.	K.

D. D. & L., London, E.C. (A8001) Wt. W1771/M2031 750,000 5/17 Sch. 52 Forms/C2118/14

Instructions regarding War Diaries and Intelligence Summaries are contained in F. S. Regs., Part II. and the Staff Manual respectively. Title pages will be prepared in manuscript.

WAR DIARY

or

~~INTELLIGENCE SUMMARY.~~

(Erase heading not required.)

208 Field Coy RE

Army Form C. 2118.

Place	Date	Hour	Summary of Events and Information	Remarks and references to Appendices
AFFRINGUES	16th May 1918		1 Section erecting Nissen Huts for DHQ. – remainder training. Sites for 6 Bayonet Assault Courses and 6 30yd ranges for American Troops to be affiliated to 101 Inf Bde selected in LUMBRES AREA. K.	
"	17th	"	Sections 1 & 4 commenced work on Assault Courses and Ranges for 101 Inf Bde. – Sections camping on site of work. Sections 2 and 3 continued erection of NISSEN HUTS for DHQ. K.	
"	18th	"	Working party of 20 RAMC & 40 RE Signal Coy. assisted on DHQ Camp. Working party of 80 RAMC assisted Sections 1 and 4 on Assault Courses & Ranges – party camping on site. K.	
"	19th		Sites selected for 6 Assault Courses and 6 30yd Rifle Ranges for American Troops to be attached to 102 Inf Bde. Work started on 2 gas huts for 101 Inf Bde. Party of RAMC on DHQ Camp increased to 60. 2/Lt. STATON RE returned from leave. K.	

D. D. & L., London, E.C. (A5001) Wt. W1771/M2031 750,000 5/17 Sch. 52 Forms/C2118/14

Army Form C. 2118.

Instructions regarding War Diaries and Intelligence Summaries are contained in F. S. Regs., Part II. and the Staff Manual respectively. Title pages will be prepared in manuscript.

WAR DIARY

~~or~~

~~INTELLIGENCE SUMMARY.~~

(Erase heading not required.)

208 Field Coy RE.

Place	Date	Hour	Summary of Events and Information	Remarks and references to Appendices
AFFRINGUES	20TH MAY 1918.		Work as on 19th inst. Good progress being made.	K.
"	21st		Section 3 and one half of Sections 1 and 4. sent to commence work on Assault course and Rifle Ranges for 102 Inf Bde in BLEQUIN AREA. Working party of 80 RAMC obtained to assist. Parties camped on site of work. Site chosen near COLEMBERT for a 400 yds VICKERS GUN RANGE for 32 Targets. also for 3 30 yd Rifle & MG Ranges near LE WAST for American Troops affiliated to 103 Inf Bde. Arrangements made that officer of 18th NF Pioneers should take charge of this work with RAMC working party of 90 men. - work to commence on 23rd inst.	K.
"	~~22nd~~			
"	22nd	-	Work as on 21st. 1 NCO & 2 Sappers sent to COLEMBERT to assist on Range and to erect a 9 ft hut there.	K.
"	23rd	-	Work started on COLEMBERT RANGE. Progress on all work being seriously hampered owing to lack of motor transport and supply of materials.	K.

D. D. & L., London, E.C. (A8001) Wt. W1771/M2031 750,000 5/17 Sch. 52 Forms/C2118/14

Instructions regarding War Diaries and Intelligence Summaries are contained in F. S. Regs., Part II. and the Staff Manual respectively. Title pages will be prepared in manuscript.

WAR DIARY

~~or~~

~~INTELLIGENCE SUMMARY.~~

(Erase heading not required.)

Army Form C. 2118.

208 Field Coy RE.

Place	Date	Hour	Summary of Events and Information	Remarks and references to Appendices
AFFRINGUES	24th MAY		RAMC. working parties withdrawn after work. These parties worked exceptionally well, excellent progress having been made on the work to be done in the Div. Area. Columbert Range completed except for placing of targets.	
"	25th	-	Very Wet. American Infantry working parties obtained in lieu of RAMC. Site chosen for a bombing ground for 101 Inf Bde.	
"	26th	-	No work. Company had a holiday. Capt Chalmers proceeded on special leave to England.	
"	27th	-	Work started on bombing ground for 101 Inf Bde with American working party. Site chosen for a second bombing ground for same Bde. Other work as before.	
"	28th	-	Work started on second bombing ground for 101 Inf Bde also on Open air bathhouse at BLEQUIN. Crater blown for bombing ground 12 ft deep x 30 ft dia – charge 150 lbs ammonal. Failure of American working parties to turn up and the poor working of the men causing serious delays in progress.	

D. D. & L., London, E.C. (A8001) Wt. W1771/M2031 750,000 5/17 Sch. 52 Forms/C2118/14

Army Form C. 2118.

Instructions regarding War Diaries and Intelligence Summaries are contained in F. S. Regs., Part II. and the Staff Manual respectively. Title pages will be prepared in manuscript.

WAR DIARY
or
~~INTELLIGENCE SUMMARY.~~

(Erase heading not required.)

209 Field Coy RE.

Place	Date	Hour	Summary of Events and Information	Remarks and references to Appendices
AFFRINGUES.	29th MAY 1918.		2/Lt STATON RE sent to live with 103 Inf Bde to take charge of work in LE WAST – COLEMBERT area as 18th NF Pioneer officer no longer available. Reconnaissance made of COLEMBERT. M.G. Range with view to converting it into a rifle range – Also of BRECQUIN and ESCOEUILLES Army Rifle Ranges with view to lengthening range in each case to 600 yds.	
"	30th	–	Crater blown for second bombing ground in 101 Bde area 9 ft deep x 20 ft dia – charge 100 lbs ammonal. No American working parties available.	
"	31st	–	Work in 101 Bde Area completed except for second bombing ground which should have been completed but for poor work of American Infantry parties. Work in 102 Inf Bde areas will be completed tomorrow – only finishing touches required. Work on Duty Camp completed.	

D. D. & L., London, E.C.
(A8001) Wt. W1771/M2031 750,000 5/17 Sch. 52 Forms/C2118/14

Army Form C. 2118.

WAR DIARY

or

~~INTELLIGENCE SUMMARY.~~

(*Erase heading not required.*)

Instructions regarding War Diaries and Intelligence Summaries are contained in F. S. Regs., Part II. and the Staff Manual respectively. Title pages will be prepared in manuscript.

208 Field Coy R.E.

Place	Date	Hour	Summary of Events and Information	Remarks and references to Appendices
AFFRINGUES.	31st May. 1918 continued.		Honours received during the month of May.	
			855122 / Cpl. A. Simmons R.E. awarded Military Medal for gallantry on 21st March near CROISELLES.	
			2/Lt. C.O. Morris R.E. awarded Military Cross. for gallantry on 21st March near CROISELLES.	
			84787. Sgt. J. Rowlands. R.E. } 84808 Sgt. R Gould. R.E } Awarded military medal for gallantry at ARMENTIERES on 10th April.	
			Major J. Russell M.C. R.E. } Lt. H.H.C. Fowler M.C. R.E. } Awarded bar to military cross for operations at Armentieres during April.	
			2/Lt. F Hibbert. R.E. Awarded Military Cross for gallantry on 13th April near BAILLEUL.	
			James Russell Major R.E. OC 208 Field Coy R.E.	

D. D. & L., London, E.C. (A8001) Wt. W1771/M2031 750,000 5/17 Sch. 52 Forms/C2118/14

Instructions regarding War Diaries and Intelligence Summaries are contained in F. S. Regs., Part II. and the Staff Manual respectively. Title Pages will be prepared in manuscript.

WAR DIARY

or

~~INTELLIGENCE SUMMARY~~

(Erase heading not required.)

Army Form C. 2118.

VR 30

Place	Date	Hour	Summary of Events and Information	Remarks and references to Appendices
			208th Field Coy R.E. — June 1918 —	

2449 Wt. W14957/M90 750,000 1/16 J.B.C. & A. Forms/C.2118/12.

Instructions regarding War Diaries and Intelligence Summaries are contained in F. S. Regs., Part II. and the Staff Manual respectively. Title pages will be prepared in manuscript.

WAR DIARY
or
~~INTELLIGENCE SUMMARY.~~
(Erase heading not required.)

Army Form C. 2118.

208. Field Coy RE

Place	Date	Hour	Summary of Events and Information	Remarks and references to Appendices
AFFRINGUES.	1st June 1918.		Work on 102 Inf Bde Area completed. also on bathhouse at BIECQUIN. Rifle range at COLEMBERT for 32 targets up to range of 500 yds laid out with assistance of range officers from Second Army. Existing disused range at LE BREUIL reconnoitred with a view to constructing a VICKERS M.G. Range of 32 targets with firing points of 400 yds. Sites reconnoitred and chosen for 5 new Assault Courses and 5 30 yd ranges in area between LONGUEVILLE and LOTTINGHEM. These are required owing to BIECQUIN AREA being withdrawn from the 34th Div. One Bn 302 American Sapper Regiment arrived at BELLE for work on Ranges detailed above.	R.
"	2nd	—	No work. Company had a holiday. OC took OC American RE Bn round ~~sites of~~ work to be done and arranged camping grounds on works. 260. ARE detailed for work on Assault Courses and 30 yd Ranges and 340 on Ranges at COLEMBERT and LE BREUIL	R

Army Form C. 2118.

Instructions regarding War Diaries and Intelligence Summaries are contained in F. S. Regs., Part II. and the Staff Manual respectively. Title pages will be prepared in manuscript.

WAR DIARY
or
~~INTELLIGENCE SUMMARY.~~

(Erase heading not required.)

208 Field Coy RE

Place	Date	Hour	Summary of Events and Information	Remarks and references to Appendices
AFFRINGUES	3rd June 1918.		Sappers withdrawn from 101 & 102 Bde Areas, except small party in 101 Bd area to construct a third Bombing Ground, and distributed on new work to be done between LOTTINGHEM and LONGUEVILLE. Also parties sent ~~and~~ to hasten completion of bombing ground & 30 yd Ranges in 103 Inf Bde Area ~~between~~ HENNEVEUX and LE WAST. American Sappers commenced work on MG range at LE BREUIL – other parties detailed on 2nd inst marched to sites of work and camped.	R.
"	4th	–	Work started on Rifle Range at COLEMBERT and on the 5 Assault Courses and 30 yd Ranges between LOTTINGHEM & LONGUEVILLES. Lt BOWES with Section 2 proceeded to COLEMBERT to take charge of work there.	R.
"	5th	–	GSO.1 visited Colembert & Le Breuil Ranges and appeared satisfied with progress made	R.

D. D. & L., London, E.C. (A8001) Wt. W1771/M2031 750,000 5/17 Sch. 52 Forms/C2118/14

Instructions regarding War Diaries and Intelligence Summaries are contained in F. S. Regs., Part II. and the Staff Manual respectively. Title Pages will be prepared in manuscript.

WAR DIARY
or
~~INTELLIGENCE SUMMARY~~
(Erase heading not required.)

Army Form C. 2118.

208 Field Coy RE

Place	Date	Hour	Summary of Events and Information	Remarks and references to Appendices
AFFRINGUES	6th June 1918.		American Sappers 302. Regiment were withdrawn from works on Colembert and Le Breuil Ranges, also on Assault courses and 30yd Ranges in LOTTINGHEM-LONGUEVILLE Area: - no other working parties available. The American Sappers did exceptionally good work whilst working in conjunction with this Company.	R
"	7th	"	OC went round HARDINGHEM AREA with CRE 39th Div and took over all works and RE dump at BELLE - no men available to continue this work.	R
"	8th	"	30y Ranges and Bombing Grounds in HENNEVEUX - LE WAST AREA completed. Parties employed on these were sent to complete LE BREUIL MG. Range.	R
"	9th	"	Sunday - The Company did not work. Arrangements made that 2 American MG Coys would start work on COLEMBERT RANGE and one coy on LE BREUIL MG. Range tomorrow	R

Army Form C. 2118.

WAR DIARY
or
~~INTELLIGENCE SUMMARY~~
(Erase heading not required.)

Instructions regarding War Diaries and Intelligence Summaries are contained in F. S. Regs., Part II. and the Staff Manual respectively. Title Pages will be prepared in manuscript.

208 Field Coy R.E.

Place	Date	Hour	Summary of Events and Information	Remarks and references to Appendices
AFFRINGUES	10th June 1918.		Working parties as arranged on 9th commenced work on LEBREUIL and COLEMBERT RANGES	K
"	11th		GSO1 went round works and appeared satisfied with progress made. Capt Chalmers returned from leave to England	
"	12th	..	M G Range at LEBREUIL completed except for finishing touches. Arrangements made that party employed should now work on COLEMBERT RANGE	K
"	13th	..	American M.G. Parties on COLEMBERT RANGE very irregular. Only one Coy worked today instead of 3. Progress retarded – 600 men required daily to complete Range in 7 days as asked. American Infantry Working Parties started work on 3 of the 5 – 30 yd Ranges under construction in the LOTTINGHEM – LONGUEVILLE AREA to hasten completion. The 5 Assault Courses and remaining Ranges in this area are practically completed.	K

2449 Wt. W14957/M90 750,000 1/16 J.B.C. & A. Forms/C.2118/12.

Army Form C. 2118.

Instructions regarding War Diaries and Intelligence Summaries are contained in F. S. Regs., Part II. and the Staff Manual respectively. Title Pages will be prepared in manuscript.

WAR DIARY
or
~~INTELLIGENCE SUMMARY~~
(Erase heading not required.)

208 Field Coy. R.E.

Place	Date	Hour	Summary of Events and Information	Remarks and references to Appendices
AFFRINGUES	14th June 1918		G.S.O.1 went round works, and was satisfied with progress	[initials]
"	15th "		Work on Assault Courses and Rifle Ranges in LOTTINGHEM-LONGUEVILLE AREA completed. Also a 3rd Bombing Course in the LUMBRES AREA completed – Bath house started at LE BREUIL. 6 Cases of Spanish Fever occurred in the Company. This disease very prevalent in this area and will probably go right through the Company.	[initials]
"	16th "		Sunday. Day off. Parties on Assault Courses and Ranges in LOTTINGHEM-LONGUEVILLE Area withdrawn and redistributed i.e. Section 1 to COLEMBERT RANGE and SECTION IV to Coy HQ. 2 Companies RE ~~American~~ 303 American Regt arrived at COLEMBERT to work on Range in lieu of the MG Coys which had been withdrawn. Instructions recd that Company would move to SAMER AREA tomorrow and that all works and dumps ~~are~~ to be handed over to CRE 39th Div except LE BREUIL and COLEMBERT RANGES which were to be completed before leaving. OC – Field Coy RE 39th Div arrived to take over. – Copy of handing over report attached	[initials]

2449 Wt. W14957/M90 750,000 1/16 J.B.C. & A. Forms/C.2118/12.

Instructions regarding War Diaries and Intelligence Summaries are contained in F. S. Regs., Part II. and the Staff Manual respectively. Title pages will be prepared in manuscript.

WAR DIARY

or

~~INTELLIGENCE SUMMARY.~~

(Erase heading not required.)

208 Field Coy RE.

Army Form C. 2118.

Place	Date	Hour	Summary of Events and Information	Remarks and references to Appendices
SECQUIERES	17th June 1918.		Coy HQ and Section IV moved from AFFRINGUES to SECQUIERES. (SAMER AREA)	R.
"	18th "		M G Range at LE BREUIL completed. Section I rejoined Coy from COLEMBERT bringing 6 men suffering from Spanish Fever.	R.
"	19th.		Section III rejoined Coy from COLEMBERT – work on bathhouse at LE BREUIL handed over to CRE 39th Div. Two lorries attached from Second Army to transport materials for LE BREUIL and COLEMBERT RANGES rejoined their unit.	R
"	20th.		~~Section I~~ Sites chosen for 30yd Rifle Ranges and Assault Courses at AIX EN ERGNY and CAMPAGNE. Sections IV and I sent to camp on sites and to commence work tomorrow with parties arranged from Battns at these places. 32 target 500yd Rifle Range at COLEMBERT completed – 12 days actual work expended on this range with parties varying from 120 to 500 – Every credit is due to 2/Lt BOWES RE who was in charge.	R

D. D. & L., London, E.C. (A8091) Wt. W1771/M2031 750,000 5/17 Sch. 52 Forms/C2118/14

Instructions regarding War Diaries and Intelligence Summaries are contained in F. S. Regs., Part II. and the Staff Manual respectively. Title Pages will be prepared in manuscript.

WAR DIARY
or
~~INTELLIGENCE SUMMARY~~

(Erase heading not required.)

208 Field Coy RE

Army Form C. 2118.

Place	Date	Hour	Summary of Events and Information	Remarks and references to Appendices
LE CATELET	21st June 1918.		Company moved to LE CATELET. Section II rejoined Company from COLEMBERT. Work started on one 1507nd Rifle Range one 307d Rifle Range, and one Assault Course at CAMPAGNE. Unable to start work on site chosen at AIX-EN-ERGNY owing to owner of ground refusing permission. OC to CE First Army re supply of RE Stores.	
"			3 more cases of Spanish Fever.	R.
	22nd		Site chosen for Assault Course & 307d Range at WICKINGHEM but unable to come to agreement with owner. — Similarly at AIX-EN-ERGNY	R
"	23rd		Sunday – The Company did no work – Alternative sites for training grounds chosen at WICKINGHEM and at AIX-EN-ERGNY and all arrangements made to commence work tomorrow. Section IV moved to new site at AIX-EN-ERGNY. 2 Cases of Spanish Fever. OC to DHQ and met CRE 34th Div returned from leave.	R.
"	~~24th~~			

2449 Wt. W14957/M90 750,000 1/16 J.B.C. & A. Forms/C.2118/12.

Instructions regarding War Diaries and Intelligence Summaries are contained in F. S. Regs., Part II. and the Staff Manual respectively. Title Pages will be prepared in manuscript.

WAR DIARY

or

~~INTELLIGENCE SUMMARY~~

(Erase heading not required.)

Army Form C. 2118.

208. Field Coy R.E.

Place	Date	Hour	Summary of Events and Information	Remarks and references to Appendices
LE CATELET	24th June 1918		Assault Courses 30yd Range & Bombing Ground started for Bn at WICKINGHEM — also Assault Course and 30yd Range for Bn at AIX-EN-ERGNY. Bombing Ground started for Bn at CAMPAGNE.	K
"	25th "		CRE 34th Div went round works. Motor Cycle on loan to Company since coming to back areas was returned to DHQ. Without this cycle the work carried out by the Company could not have been accomplished.	K
"	26th		Obtained loan of motor cycle from Field Amb. Section III sent to assist Section I on Ranges and Assault Courses at CAMPAGNE. 2 Cases of Spanish Fever. Bath house started at WICKINGHEM.	K
"	27th		OC to DHQ and recd orders to move on 28th inst with 103 Inf Bde. Sections 1, 3 and 4 recalled from works at CAMPAGNE and AIX-EN-ERGNY. Work handed over to CRE 16th Div. — Copy of handing over report attached. A further 6 cases of Spanish Influenza. — 13 men now in hospital with this disease 12 men having returned during the last week.	K

Army Form C. 2118.

WAR DIARY
or
INTELLIGENCE SUMMARY
(Erase heading not required.)

208 Field Coy R.E.

Instructions regarding War Diaries and Intelligence Summaries are contained in F. S. Regs., Part II. and the Staff Manual respectively. Title Pages will be prepared in manuscript.

Place	Date	Hour	Summary of Events and Information	Remarks and references to Appendices
ASSINGHEM near ELNES.	28th June 1918.		Company moved to ASSINGHEM in the ELNES AREA. 5 Cases of Spanish Influenza to hospital.	K
NIEURLET	29th.		Company moved to NIEURLET in the St MOMELIN AREA 6 Cases Spanish Influenza to hospital	K
BAMBECQUE	30th.		Company moved to BAMBECQUE. – 20 mile march in excessive heat. A further 6 cases of Spanish Influenza.	K

James Russell
Major R.E.
OC 208 Field Coy R.E.

— COPY —

Handing – over Report

I. Work COMPLETED.

(a) Assault Courses – 17.

(b) 30 yd. Ranges – 26.

(c) Bombing Grounds – 3. In addition 3 craters have been blown for live bomb practice in the HENNEVEUX AREA and 2 bombing grounds were made in the BLECQUIN AREA under Brigade supervision.

(d) Gas Huts – 3.

II. Work UNDER CONSTRUCTION:–

(a) 32 Target rifle range at COLEMBERT with firing points at 200, 300, 400 + 500 yds. Labour :– 1 Section, R.E., 2 Coys American R.E., – approx 500 men.
Above party should complete work in 4 days. Necessary iron work is being made by 573 A.T. Coy, R.E., and 351 E + M Coy. R.E. at LUMBRES.
Notice boards are being made by 573 A.T. Coy, R.E.
It is probable that the iron work for holding the targets may not be completed within the time given but the targets can be nailed in position as a temporary measure.

(b) 32 Target M.G. RANGE at LE BREUIL.
Notice boards and danger flags only to be erected to complete range. Labour 1 Section, R.E.

(c) Gas Hut and TRENCHES at ESCOEUILLES.
Four days work required to complete Gas hut – Labour 4 R.E.
[illegible]
[illegible]

(d) BATH HOUSE, BOURSIN.

Work has just been started - labour 1 section RE, 6 spray set has been handed over to Area Comdt., BOURSIN.

III WORK PROPOSED.

(a) GAS HUT and TRENCHES at BLECQUIN.

(b) BATH-HOUSE at BLECQUIN - A 6 spray set has been delivered to the Area Commandant, BLECQUIN.

IV Maps showing sites of work enumerated in 1, 2 and 3 are being handed over by 3rd Division "G".

V. Stores:-

(a) Dumps are situated at BELLE and AFFRINGUES. A stock sheet for each dump will be handed over to C.R.E., 30th Div. on taking over.

All material at AFFRINGUES has been signed for by the Americans and includes training stores in miniature ranges, bayonet fighting discs etc.

Material at BELLE has not yet been signed for by the Americans. A note of material issued for the use of American units by this company since previously taking over from CRE, 20th Divis^n will be handed to C.R.E., 30th Divs^n on taking over the Dumps.

(b) All stores are obtained through CRE, 2nd Army Troops and Stores Officer 2nd Army.

(Sgd) James Russell
Major RE
O.C. 218th Fld. Co. RE.

Copy.

Handing Over Report

The following works are in an unfinished state and require completing in the CAMPAGNE-ERGNY AREA.

1/ **Assault Courses:-**

(a) LE FAY FME O.5.a.6.4 Sheet 36.
Sacks to be fixed to gallows. Pickets + wire to be erected for targets. Shell-holes to be blown representing "No Man's Land". Materials are on site, except sacks.

(b) Midway between CAMPAGNE and AIX-EN-ERGNY. O.15.c.0.0.
Gallows to be erected + sacks fixed – jumping off trench to be sandbagged. Pickets + wire for targets to be erected and ground in front of targets levelled. Shell-holes to be blown. Holes for charges are dug, also in (a). Materials for uprights of gallows only on site.

(c) At [illegible] of Aa River between CATELET and WICQUINGHEM. N.20.a central. Sacks to be fixed to gallows.

Note:- Sacks were promised today by Adjt 16th Divsn but did not arrive. Straw for sacks is at LE CATELET.

2. **30 Yd. Rifle ranges:-**

(a) LE FAY FME beside Assault Course.
Pickets + wire to hold targets and hut for stores to be erected – Only wire on site.

(b) O.15.c.0.0 – Bank to be squared [illegible] made shooting [illegible]. Pickets and wire for targets to be erected. Platform 2 ft high

(b) (cont) for firing point to be made. Hut to be erected for Stores. No materials on site.

(c) N.29.a. central – Hut for Stores to be erected – No materials on site.

3. 150 yd. Rifle Ranges.

(a) LE FAY FME including the 30 yd Range of (a) para 2 – Half overhead cover to be completed. 7 targets to be erected (one target is now erected to show design). One half of the revetting to be wired back and parapets levelled. Platform at 150 yds range to be completed by filling in existing revetting.
All materials + targets are in trench to be used for markers and have been handed over to Area Commdt, CAMPAGNE.

4. Bombing Courses.

(a) At S edge of wood N of HAPPE I.29.d.3.5. Completed except for deepening of Assembly trench + erection of hut for stores. No materials on site.

(b). 1000 yds S.W. of WICQUINGHEM, T.4.b.5.2 Complete except for hut for stores. – No materials on site.

Bath House, WICQUINGHEM, N.36.a.6.2.

Spray house only erected – Sprays are on site but are deficient of the following (a) Length of suction hose for pump. (b) One 5 ft length of 1" piping screwed at both ends. (c) Firebars for boiler grate. (d) Hot water container is lacking. – The central

tube requires two stays and soldering where it joins bottom of tank.
Note:- Above stores were promised today by Adjt., 16th Divl R.E. but did not arrive. No other materials are on site.

Dumps. At LE CATELET, N.22.a.0.0.
List of materials is accompanying report to C.R.E., 16 Div.
Materials are drawn through C.R.E. 16th Div. at SAMER.

(Sd) James Russell
Major R.E.
O.C. 208th Fld Coy. R.E.

Instructions regarding War Diaries and Intelligence Summaries are contained in F. S. Regs., Part II. and the Staff Manual respectively. Title Pages will be prepared in manuscript.

WAR DIARY
or
~~INTELLIGENCE SUMMARY~~

(Erase heading not required.)

Army Form C. 2118.

Vol 31

Place	Date	Hour	Summary of Events and Information	Remarks and references to Appendices
			208th Field Coy., R.E.	
			July, 1918.	

2449 Wt. W14957/M90 750,000 1/16 J.B.C. & A. Forms/C.2118/12.

Army Form C. 2118.

Instructions regarding War Diaries and Intelligence Summaries are contained in F. S. Regs., Part II. and the Staff Manual respectively. Title Pages will be prepared in manuscript.

WAR DIARY
or
INTELLIGENCE SUMMARY

(Erase heading not required.)

208 Field Coy RE.

Place	Date	Hour	Summary of Events and Information	Remarks and references to Appendices
BAMBECQUE	1st July 1918.		Company resting. Another 6 men to hospital with Spanish Influenza. CRE called.	K
"	2nd	–	2/Lt BOWES and 2/Lt STATON with 6 NCOs and 30 men proceeded to POPERINGHE to act as Caretakers of the East POPERINGHE LINE in the IInd Corps Area. Remainder of Coy. Resting. 3 men to hospital with Spanish Influenza.	K.
"	3rd	–	Sections I & IV and remainder of II & III training. No cases of Spanish Influenza. 19 men returned from hospital. OC visited E. Pop. LINE. 2nd Lt C. W. ANDREWS joined Coy as reinforcement.	K
"	4th	–	Coy training. No further cases of ~~[illegible]~~ Influenza.	K
"	5th	–	Coy training. OC to St OMER with CRE and reconnoitred sites for 6 emergency pontoon bridges over Canal between St OMER and WATTEN.	K

Army Form C. 2118.

Instructions regarding War Diaries and Intelligence Summaries are contained in F. S. Regs., Part II. and the Staff Manual respectively. Title Pages will be prepared in manuscript.

WAR DIARY
or
~~INTELLIGENCE SUMMARY~~
(Erase heading not required.)

208 Field Coy RE

Place	Date	Hour	Summary of Events and Information	Remarks and references to Appendices
BAMBECQUE	6th July 1918		Coy training.	K.
F27b.8.5.	7th	"	Coy moved to Camp on S. side of road halfway between PROYEN and POPERINGHE at F27b.8.5. Sheet 27.	K.
"	8th	"	Officers and men on E. Poperinghe Line rejoined company.	K.
"	9th	"	2/Lt BOWES and 2/Lt STATON with 8 NCOs proceeded to PROYEN as instructors to 2/4th Bn SOMERSET L.I. being trained as pioneers. Coy training.	K.
"	10th	"	H and remaining Officers reconnoitred WEST POPERINGHE SWITCH LINE S of PROYEN - POPERINGHE ROAD and submitted proposals for employment of 4 Bns American Infantry on this sector of trenches. – Work to commence on 12th. Coy training.	K.
"	11th	"	G.O.C. 34th Div. inspected Coy and appeared satisfied with turn out. Work of American Infantry on WEST POPERINGHE SWITCH cancelled.	K.
"	12th		Coy started work on WEST POP. SWITCH without working party. Owing to heavy rain only drainage possible.	K.

2449 Wt. W14957/M90 750,000 1/16 J.B.C. & A. Forms/C.2118/12.

Instructions regarding War Diaries and Intelligence Summaries are contained in F. S. Regs., Part II. and the Staff Manual respectively. Title Pages will be prepared in manuscript.

WAR DIARY ~~or~~ INTELLIGENCE SUMMARY

(Erase heading not required.)

Army Form C. 2118.

208 Field Coy RE

Place	Date	Hour	Summary of Events and Information	Remarks and references to Appendices
F27.6.85. Sheet 27.	13th July 1918		Continued work on WEST. POPERINGHE SWITCH LINE – revetting firebays to 4'-6" cover, duckboarding and thickening parapet.	R
"	14th		Sunday. The Coy did no work. Recd instructions that 101 Inf Bde would occupy W.P.S. Line on 16th inst and would work under supervision of Company.	R
	15th		Sited and taped out three communication trenches to be worked on by 101 Inf Bde. Orders recd during afternoon that this work was cancelled and that the Division would move by train commencing 16th.	R
"	16th		Company instructed in the working of the LEWIS. GUN, and teams fired on range – each section and HQ now provided with a Lewis Gun	R
"	17th		Coy marched to PROVEN STATION and entrained leaving Proven at 7am. – Route BOULOGNE – NOYELLES – CHARS.	R

2449 Wt. W14957/M90 750,000 1/16 J.B.C. & A. Forms/C.2118/12.

Instructions regarding War Diaries and Intelligence Summaries are contained in F. S. Regs., Part II. and the Staff Manual respectively. Title Pages will be prepared in manuscript.

WAR DIARY ~~or~~ INTELLIGENCE SUMMARY

(Erase heading not required.)

208 Field Coy R.E.

Army Form C. 2118.

Place	Date	Hour	Summary of Events and Information	Remarks and references to Appendices
VILLEMETRIE (near SENLIS N.E. of PARIS)	18th July 1918		Detrained at SURVILLIERS and marched at 12 noon to VILLEMETRIE.	
VAUMOISE.	19th	"	Transport marched at 5.45am to VAUMOISE. – Dismounted personnel to same place by bus at 7am.	
"	20th	"	Coy recd further instruction in working of Lewis Gun	
PUISEUX	21st	"	Marched at 12.15 am to PUISEUX with 102 Inf/Bde	
Moulin de Villers Hélon	22nd	"	Left PUISEUX at 10am and marched to MOULIN de VILLERS HÉLON taking over accommodation and relieving 19/2 Field Coy. French R.E. working on the left sector of the 38th French Div front. Transport billeted at LA GRANGE FME near LONGPONT. 34th Div relieved the 38th French Div on front between TIGNY and COUTREMAIN.	
"	23rd	"	34th Div attacked in conjunction with the French on either flank. Division advanced about 1000 yards – troops on either flank held up. Company standing by till situation cleared. Work allotted to Coy as follows – Clear and repair road MONTREBOEF FME – TIGNY – HARTENNES-ET-TAUX – DROIZY. No work done owing to failure to advance	

Instructions regarding War Diaries and Intelligence Summaries are contained in F. S. Regs., Part II. and the Staff Manual respectively. Title Pages will be prepared in manuscript.

WAR DIARY
or
INTELLIGENCE SUMMARY
(Erase heading not required.)

Army Form C. 2118.

208 FIELD Coy RE

Place	Date	Hour	Summary of Events and Information	Remarks and references to Appendices
MOULIN de VILLERS HÉLON	24th July 1918.		Road MONTREBOEF FME – TIGNY reconnoitred. Road badly blocked by fallen trees and being in full view of the enemy no work could be done on it during daylight. Party proceeded to work at night.	R
"	25th	–	Road cleared during night to halfway between MONTREBOEF FME and TIGNY. 2 Sections worked on horse transport tracks LONGPONT – MOULIN de VILLERS HELON – MONTREBOEF FME. Sergt Gould. (Section IV) wounded by shellfire	R
"	26th	–	TIGNY ROAD cleared during night to within 100 yds of Cross Roads immediately N of PARCY-TIGNY. – Road reconnoitred to a point 500 yds West of TIGNY appr. 200 yds inside "No mans Land." Work on horse transport tracks continued	R
BOIS de NADON	27th	"	TIGNY Road cleared to front line with the exception of one large tree. Owing to enemy shelling of previous day 3 large trees had to be removed from length of road previously cleared. Instructions recd that division will be relieved during night. 2 Sections worked on horse transport tracks till midday. Company marched at 8-30 pm to BOIS de NADON and was joined there by transport	R

2449 Wt. W14957/M90 750,000 1/16 J.B.C. & A. Forms/C.2118/12.

Instructions regarding War Diaries and Intelligence Summaries are contained in F. S. Regs., Part II. and the Staff Manual respectively. Title Pages will be prepared in manuscript.

WAR DIARY
or
INTELLIGENCE SUMMARY
(Erase heading not required.)

208 Field Coy RE.

Army Form C. 2118.

Place	Date	Hour	Summary of Events and Information	Remarks and references to Appendices
Bois. de Nadon.	28th July. 1918.		CRE called about 10.30am and explained that the Division would march to the Bois. de la. Baillette during the night and attack in a N.E direction at dawn. - Field Coys to be at the B. de la. Baillette by dawn. Later orders instructed Field Coys to march to Geromenil Fme and await further orders.	
Billy-sur. Ourcq.	29th	..	Coy marched at 2am arriving at rendezvous at 4am. Transport less toolcarts & limbers remained at the Bois-de-Nadon. 34th Bri attacked in conjunction with French Troops at 4.10am. At 8am. company proceeded to clear and repair Road. Billy-sur-Ourcq - Oulchy la Ville - Oulchy le Chateau. Road allotted to company cleared and repaired for motor lorries by 6pm. Some shelling at Cross Roads between Geromenil Fme and Oulchy-la Ville and on road between Oulchy la Ville and Oulchy le Chateau.	
"	30th	..	Improved road. Billy-sur-Ourcq to Oulchy-le Chateau. 3 sections working by day - one section at night. Successful reconnaissance made with view to supply of water in forward area in the event of an advance.	

2449 Wt. W14957/M90 750,000 1/16 J.B.C. & A. Forms/C.2118/12.

Instructions regarding War Diaries and Intelligence Summaries are contained in F. S. Regs., Part II. and the Staff Manual respectively. Title Pages will be prepared in manuscript.

WAR DIARY
or
INTELLIGENCE SUMMARY
(Erase heading not required.)

Army Form C. 2118.

208 FIELD Coy RE

Place	Date	Hour	Summary of Events and Information	Remarks and references to Appendices
BILLY-SUR OURCQ.	31st July 1918.		Company employed as before on maintenance and improvement of road BILLY-SUR-OURCQ to OULCHY ~~[illegible]~~ le CHATEAU. Capt. W. Chalmers RE left company to be attached to Chief Engineer Fifth Army	

James Russell
Major RE
OC 208 Field Coy RE.

2449 Wt. W14957/M90 750,000 1/16 J.B.C. & A. Forms/C.2118/12.

Instructions regarding War Diaries and Intelligence Summaries are contained in F. S. Regs., Part II. and the Staff Manual respectively. Title Pages will be prepared in manuscript.

Original

Army Form C. 2118.

WAR DIARY
or
~~INTELLIGENCE SUMMARY~~

(Erase heading not required.)

Vol 32

Place	Date	Hour	Summary of Events and Information	Remarks and references to Appendices
			208th Field Coy RE — August 1918 —	

2449 Wt. W14957/M90 750,000 1/16 J.B.C. & A. Forms/C.2118/12.

Army Form C. 2118.

WAR DIARY
or
~~INTELLIGENCE SUMMARY.~~
(Erase heading not required.)

208 Field Coy R.E.

Instructions regarding War Diaries and Intelligence Summaries are contained in F. S. Regs., Part II. and the Staff Manual respectively. Title pages will be prepared in manuscript.

Place	Date	Hour	Summary of Events and Information	Remarks and references to Appendices
BILLY SUR OURCQ	1st Aug. 1918		34th Div continued the attack – objective – ridge N.E. of GRAND ROZOY. Objective taken early and a French Division passing through the 34th Div continued the pursuit. At 8am 2 Sections proceeded to maintain road to OULCHY-LE-CHATEAU already repaired, and to clear and repair the main CHATEAU THIERRY – SOISSONS ROAD between the Divisional boundaries – the remaining 2 Sections to OULCHY-LA-VILLE to await further orders. At 9.00 am OC with CRE visited forward area. After reconnaissance CRE instructed the 2 Sections in reserve to assist 207 Field Coy RE to clear the main road through GRAND ROZOY. Shelling which was negligible during the morning commenced shortly after this party got onto work. Work was completed by 4.30pm. Casualties 3 Sappers wounded.	R.
BOIS de la BAILLETTE.	2nd	"	Company detailed to maintain all roads W. of and including CHATEAU-THIERRY – SOISSONS Road inside the Divisional Boundaries. Coy proceeded to work at 8am. 3 Sections withdrawn at 11am and proceeded to BEUGNEUX to clear the Battlefield. Party did not return to billets till 9pm. At 7pm orders recd to prepare to move forward reporting when ready to move. At 11am Coy marched to E end of the Bois de la BAILLETTE and bivouaced arriving about 2am on 3rd inst.	R.

Instructions regarding War Diaries and Intelligence Summaries are contained in F. S. Regs., Part II. and the Staff Manual respectively. Title pages will be prepared in manuscript.

WAR DIARY
or
~~INTELLIGENCE SUMMARY.~~
(Erase heading not required.)

Army Form C. 2118.

208 Field Coy R.E.

Place	Date	Hour	Summary of Events and Information	Remarks and references to Appendices
Bois de la BAILLETTE	3rd Aug 1918.		Transport joined Company about 4 am. At 1pm Coy proceeded to complete clearance of battle-field at BEUGNEUX, but found all units burying their own dead and returned to billets about 6pm after completely searching the battle-field.	
			Lt H.A.C. FOWLER M.C. R.E. decorated with the Croix de Guerre (Citation de l'Armée) by the Divisional Commander for act of gallantry performed at GRAND ROZOY on the 1st inst.	R.
CHEVREVILLE	4th	"	Coy moved by bus to CHEVREVILLE. – transport by road to NEUFCHELLES.	R.
"	5th	"	Transport rejoined Company.	R.
LE PLESSY BELVILLE	6th	"	Coy marched to LE PLESSY BELVILLE and entrained at 6pm.	R.
BERGUES.	7th	"	Arrived BERGUES 9pm. Dismounted personnel marched to ZEGGERS-CAPPEL	R.
ZEGGERS-CAPPEL	8th	"	Transport rejoined Company about 6 am. Coy resting. Leave improved – one place per day allotted to the Coy.	R.
"	9th	"	Preparing for inspection by CRE.	R.
"	10th	"	Coy inspected by CRE who expressed entire satisfaction	R.
"	11th	"	Sunday – resting.	R.

(A9175) Wt W2358/P360 600,000 12/17 D. D. & L. Sch. 52a. Forms/C2118/15.

Instructions regarding War Diaries and Intelligence Summaries are contained in F. S. Regs., Part II. and the Staff Manual respectively. Title pages will be prepared in manuscript.

WAR DIARY
or
~~INTELLIGENCE SUMMARY.~~
(Erase heading not required.)

Army Form C. 2118.

208 Field Coy R.E.

Place	Date	Hour	Summary of Events and Information	Remarks and references to Appendices
WORMHOUDT ~~ZEGGERS CAPPEL~~	12th Aug 1918		Baths. Commenced training. At 6pm recd orders to march to WORMHOUDT and proceed on 13th inst to POPERINGHE Area to work under C.E. II Corps. Arrived WORMHOUDT 9.30pm.	R
POPERINGHE.	13th	"	Sappers marched to and bivouacked on POPERINGHE CANAL 1 mile N of POPERINGHE. – transport to SCHOOL CAMP, St JANSTER BIEZEN. One Sapper wounded shellfire.	R
"	14th	"	OC and officers reconnoitred VLAMERTINGHE LINE immediately S of VLAMERTINGHE and selected sites for 7. 20 man shelters. OC visited sites selected with CE II Corps during afternoon. Coy HQ and 3 Sections moved to vicinity of LAWRENCE CAMP 2 miles due E. of POPERINGHE and bivouacked. One section remained at POPERINGHE CANAL and was joined by transport from St JANSTER BIEZEN.	R
"	15th	"	Work commenced on 3 shelters in the VLAMERTINGHE Support Line – one section employed on each – remaining section supplying stores. Men proceeding to and from work by light railway. Lt STATON promoted substantive Lieutenant from [illegible].	R
"	16th	"	Lack of stores hindering work and excavations for the remaining 4 shelters chosen started. CRE called and stated that Coy would relieve the 458 Field Coy RE working on right sector of the 49th Div front immediately E of YPRES on night 20/21st.	R

Instructions regarding War Diaries and Intelligence Summaries are contained in F. S. Regs., Part II. and the Staff Manual respectively. Title pages will be prepared in manuscript.

Army Form C. 2118.

WAR DIARY
or
~~INTELLIGENCE SUMMARY.~~
(Erase heading not required.)

208 Field Coy R.E.

Place	Date	Hour	Summary of Events and Information	Remarks and references to Appendices
POPERINGHE.	17th Aug.		Framework for 3 shelters now on sites and good progress being made.	K
"	18th	"	Sunday - Resting. OC & Lt Hibbert visited 458 Field Coy RE and went round works.	K
"	19th	"	Handed over work on the VLAMERTINGHE LINE to 61st Field Coy RE	K
YPRES	20th		Relieved 458 Field Coy RE. 2 Sections billeted on island in YPRES MOAT - Coy HQ and 2 Sections at Machine Gun Sidings ½ mile S of YPRES. Transport at A30 Central.	K
"	21st	"	The following work started:- By day - (1) Bde HQ Mty Farm. (2) MG Emplacement in the BRIELEN LINE near Coy HQ. (3) Strengthening cellars in the ECOLE YPRES (4) 2 MG Emplacements in the YPRES DEFENCE LINE (5) Concrete O.P for Artillery in house on the YPRES MENIN ROAD. By Night - (1) Revetting and thickening parapet and parados of the Support Line.	K
"	22nd	"	CRE called re organisation of work. Coy to be responsible for work of the Coy of Pioneers allotted to the Right Bde in the line. Reconnoitred the BRIELEN SYSTEM of trenches with view to completion. In addition to work as on 21st the strengthening of Coy HQ was started. Lt. Fowler proceeded on 1 month's leave to UK.	K

(A9175) Wt W2358/P360 630,000 12/17 D. D. & L. Sch. 52a. Forms/C2118/15.

Instructions regarding War Diaries and Intelligence Summaries are contained in F. S. Regs., Part II. and the Staff Manual respectively. Title pages will be prepared in manuscript.

WAR DIARY

~~or~~

~~INTELLIGENCE~~ SUMMARY.

(*Erase heading not required.*)

Army Form C. 2118.

208 Field Coy R.E.

Place	Date	Hour	Summary of Events and Information	Remarks and references to Appendices
YPRES.	23rd Aug. 1918.		Reconnoitred front and support line within the Bde Boundaries with view to obtaining flank defence on right and to organise work on three defended localities in each line. Work as on 22nd. Lt H.H.C. Fowler MC RE promoted A/Capt from 31st July 1918 and to be Second in Command of the company	R.
"	24th	"	Commenced work on the BRIELEN Front and Support Lines with 250 infantry from the Reserve Bde. Other work as on 23rd inst. 13 Sappers detailed for demolitions with 209 Fd Coy	
"	25th	"	Sunday, no work. A semi permanent party of 2 off & 50 ORs infantry from Bde reported for attachment and were instructed to keep work on wolting front and support lines supplied with materials by push trolley from YPRES. — one half party detailed for each line — work to commence on 26th.	R.
"	26th	"	Forward work reorganised. Pioneers split into three parties of 1 platoon, 2 platoons and 1 platoon for work on the 3 defended localities in the Front Line with 4 Sapper NCOs to supervise — 2 parties each of ½ Section RE and one Coy infantry from the Support Battn to work ~~[illegible]~~ on 2 defended localities in the Support Line — the third defended locality with flank defence not yet being approved.	R.

(A9175) Wt W2358/P360 600,000 12/17 D. D. & L. Sch. 52a. Forms/C2118/15.

Instructions regarding War Diaries and Intelligence Summaries are contained in F. S. Regs., Part II. and the Staff Manual respectively. Title pages will be prepared in manuscript.

WAR DIARY

~~or~~

~~INTELLIGENCE~~ SUMMARY.

(*Erase heading not required.*)

208 Field Coy RE

Army Form C. 2118.

Place	Date	Hour	Summary of Events and Information	Remarks and references to Appendices
YPRES	27th Aug 1918.		No work done on front and Support lines during previous night owing to Gas being released by the division on our right. O.C. 61st Field Coy RE arrived to take over works and was shown round the line	R
A.30.Central	28th	"	Coy moved to A30. Central on relief by 61st Field Coy RE. Copy of handing over report attached.	R
WIPPENHOEK	29th	"	OC and Officers proceeded to SCHERPENBERG AREA and took over works of 237 Field Coy RE 41st Div. Coy left A30 Central at 8pm - arriving in new area at midnight and relieved 237 Field Coy RE.	R
"	30th	"	Company employed on back area work. Commenced work as taken over. OC reconnoitred WESTOUTRE LINE and forwarded to CRE proposal for employment of 400 infantry from Reserve Bde for improving existing trenches.	R
"	31st		Proceeded to work as usual. Sappers recalled at midday as enemy retiring and the Division now in possession of KEMMEL HILL. Coy in Reserve. At 9pm orders recd to send one Section to each of the 2 forward Bde. for attachment at once. - Also that remainder of	

(A9175) Wt W2358/P360 600,000 12/17 D. D. & L. Sch. 52a. Forms/C2118/15.

Instructions regarding War Diaries and Intelligence Summaries are contained in F. S. Regs., Part II. and the Staff Manual respectively. Title pages will be prepared in manuscript.

WAR DIARY

~~or~~

~~INTELLIGENCE SUMMARY.~~

(Erase heading not required.)

Army Form C. 2118.

208 Field Coy RE

Place	Date	Hour	Summary of Events and Information	Remarks and references to Appendices
			(Continued).	
WIPPENHOEK.	31st Aug 1918.		Company to march immediately to the WESTOUTRE LINE and Bivouac – transport to move forward to area one mile S of RENINGHELST. Moves completed at 1am on 1st ~~Aug~~ SEPT.	R

James Russell
Major RE
OC 208 Field Coy RE

(A9175) Wt W2358/P360 600,000 12/17 D. D. & L. Sch. 52a. Forms/C2118/15.

WEEKLY WORKS REPORT
208th Field Coy R.E.
Week ending 6 P.M. 28/8/18.

I FRONT LINE (a) 130 yds parapet made bullet proof I 15 d. 8.1 to I 15 d. 85.40. (Pioneers)

(b) Improving trench I 21 d 15. to I 21 b 15.30. — one nights work only in cleaning trench. (Pioneers)

(c) Improving trench I 16 a 65.40 to I 16 a. 35.00. — one nights work only thickening parados. (Pioneers)

(d) Improving duckboard track I 15 b. 41 to I 16 a. 65.40. — one nights work only. (Pioneers)

II SUPPORT LINE. (a) Revetting parapet. I 15 b. 5.3 to I 15 b 6.8 20 yds hurdles erected. Infantry & R.E.

(b) Revetting parados and thickening earth on parapet and parados from I 15 c 85.65. to I 15 c. 3.4. — 126 yds parados revetted with hurdles 170 yds parados earthing up 80% complete 50 yds parapet " " " "

Infantry & R.E.

III OTHER WORK in FORWARD ZONE.

(a) Artillery O.P. Menin Road. I 9. c 9.4. — Concrete raised 4'6". Camouflage completed. (R.E. & R.A.)

(b) Strengthening cellars at the Ecole — brick wall at entrance completed — Sandbag wall blocking [illegible] knocked in [illegible] raised to 5' [illegible] 12 [illegible] roof erected. (R.E.)

(c). M.G. Emplacement I.15.a.5.8. – Trench between emplacement and shelter pumped out and revetted. Camouflage over trench raised. Earth built up round emplacement. Shelter strutted. – Note further drainage and cover on shelter required – RE and M.G.s.

(d). 2 new M.G. Empl^{ts} at I.13.b.25.90. Trench connecting emplacements revetted (RE and M.G.s.)

IV. INTERMEDIATE ZONE

(a) BRIELEN SYSTEM. Front line. 80^{y} parapet thickened & bullet proof at H.12.a.2.6.
260^{y} hurdles erected on parados. } H.6.a.2.6. to
40 yds parados half thickened } H.6.a.3.1.
110^{y} duckboards relaid
(Infantry from Reserve Bde. & RE)

(b) ~~Brielen system~~ Support line. H.5.b.5.8 & H.6.b.5.
80^{y} existing trench revetted 30^{y} parapet thickened & bullet proof. 100^{y} trench cleared 28^{y} duckboards laid.
(Infantry from Reserve Bde & RE)

(c). New M.G. Empl^{t} H.12.a.8.1. Roofs camouflaged. Floor completed. Concrete and walls erected to 4th course of blocks. Ironwork of roof assembled. (RE and M.G.s.)

(d). Completing roof of dugouts at M.G. Siding H.12.a.3.5. – Burster course 70% completed. (RE & RAMC)

(e). 5th HQ. BOESTAY CASTLE. Strengthening shelter of officers sleeping accommodation. 40% complete.

(f). Bde. HQ. Machine Gun Farm.
(1). Brigade office. – 9 cub. yds. concrete placed on roof. Steel rails laid and reinforcement of roof completed.

f) (2). Officers mess. Walls and reinforcement of roof completed ready for concrete (Infantry & RE)

(3) Artillery HQ. Thickening cover over Signal Office 10% completed. (RE and RGA)

Note. The 50 attached infantry were employed in carrying rations & supplying front and support lines with working materials.

Clement Russell
Major RE
OC 508 Field Coy RE

28/6/16.

CRE
34th Div.

Ref Map.
SOISSONS. 1/80000.

Ref your W 121. The role of the 208 Field Coy RE throughout the recent active operations was the upkeep of communications.

This company relieved the 19/2 Compagnie du Genie working in the left sector of the 38th French Div. Front between TIGNY and PARCY-TIGNY on the night 22/23rd July – Sappers bivouacing at the MOULIN DE VILLERS HELON with transport at LA GRANGE FME LONGPONT.

The 34th Div attacked in the early morning of the 23rd inst – the company standing by for orders from 5 am. Owing to the infantry failing to advance sufficiently no work was done.

On the 24th the company proceeded to clear the road from MONTREBOEUF FME towards TIGNY, and to repair it for motor transport. No work was possible during daylight as the road was wholly under enemy observation. By the morning of the 27th this road was repaired and cleared to the front line with the exception of one large tree across it. – enemy shelling brought down several trees daily. A reconnaissance during the previous night showed the road to be in a fit state to take motor lorries to within 500 yds of TIGNY.

At dusk on the 27th the Company marched

of the BOIS de NADON and bivouaced.
Instructions were received that the 34th Bn would attack in conjunction with French Troops on either flank in a N.E. direction from the Bois de la BAILLETTE during the early hours of the 29th.
At 2am sappers with tool carts and limbers marched to GEROMENIL FME. arriving there at 4am with instructions to await further orders. At 8am the company proceeded to clear and repair road - BILLY-SUR-OURCQ — OULCHY LA VILLE — OULCHY LE CHATEAU. Enemy shelling interfered considerably with the work, particularly between OULCHY LA VILLE and OULCHY LE CHATEAU. The work alloted to the company was completed by 6pm and the road in a fit state to take motor lorries up to and through OULCHY LE CHATEAU.
During the next two days the road was further improved by carting and placing as much stone as possible from BILLY-SUR-OURCQ where the Company was accommodated.
But for this precaution the bad weather experienced on the 2nd August would undoubtedly have rendered the portion of this road in the vicinity of GEROMENIL FME. unfit for motor transport and greatly hindered the advance on that day.
On the morning of the 1st August the attack was continued with great success. One section was employed on improving and maintaining the road already mentioned - another section on clearing and repairing the CHATEAU THIERRY - SOISSONS ROAD inside the Divisional boundaries -

– the remaining two sections being held in reserve.

After reconnaissance by the CRE these sections were instructed to assist 207 Field Coy RE to clear the main road through GRAND-ROZOY. Enemy shelling which was negligible during the morning commenced shortly after the party got to work. In spite of it the work allotted was completed by 4.30pm.

During subsequent days until relief on the 4th inst the company maintained all roads West of, and including the CHATEAU THIERRY – SOISSONS ROAD within the Divisional boundaries. On the night of the 2nd the company with all transport moved forward to the E end of the BOIS de la BAILLETTE and bivouaced.

Casualties throughout the operations were 1 NCO and 3 Sappers wounded.

12/8/18.

James Russell
Major RE
OC 208 Field Coy RE

HANDING OVER NOTES.

208. FIELD Coy R.E.

FRONTAGE. – E of YPRES. – boundaries are shown on attached map. The forward zone comprises 3 lines of trenches. ie Front line – Support line – Reserve line or YPRES DEFENCE LINE. All three lines are held by a system of posts organised in three separate localities in each line. The trenches are more or less continuous throughout but in many poor condition. The present policy is to make good the trenches in the above mentioned localities ~~only~~ first and finally to complete the whole system. Only front and support lines are being worked on at present. In order to mislead the enemy thoroughly, revetting is being completed throughout but parapet and parados only patched up when required. There is ~~only~~ one C.T. on the whole sector front which leads to the support line only. The average cover is about 3 ft. The front line is reached by walking overland. Parties of two or three can do this in safety if present conditions continue.

ORGANISATION OF WORK. (a). Trench System in forward Zone.

(b). Work other than trenches in forward Zone.

(c) Work in Intermediate Zone.

one section and one company pioneers are allotted to (a). ½ section to (b) – the other ½ of this section is looked up as a permanent demolition party –, 2 sections to C.

<u>List of Work</u>. (A). Trench System in Forward Zone.

<u>1</u>. Improving <u>trench</u> front line trench from I.21 b. 1.2. to I.21 d. 19.85. – 1 RE NCO at night 1 platoon pioneers

<u>2</u>. Improving front line trench from I 15 d 95.50 to I 15 d 8.2 – 2 RE NCO at night. 2 platoons pioneers.

<u>3</u>. Improving front line trench from I 16. a. 8.5 to I 16 a. 6.4 – 1 RE NCO 1 NCO at night 1 platoon pioneers less 6 men. at night.

<u>4</u>. Preparing double duck board track from I 15 b. 45.15 to front line at I 16. a. 6.4. – 1 NCO & 6 pioneers referred to in <u>3</u>. at night.

<u>5</u>. Improving support line trench from I 15. b. 5.2 to I 15. b. 15.00 – ½ section RE at night 1 Coy Infantry from Support Bn.

<u>6</u>. Improving support line trench from I 15.c. 66 to I 15 c. 30. 35. – ½ section RE at night 1 Coy Infantry from Support Bn.

A permanent infantry party of 1 officer & 25 men keep front line supplied with material from St Pierre Dump I 14 a. 89 by push trolley to I. 15. b. 5.1. A similar party supplies materials by night to the Support Line to the same extent. The third locality which is held in the support line is at I.4.a.1.6. but work is not ~~[illegible]~~ started as it is not yet decided what Bde. Flank defence is required which cannot be determined at this point. It is suggested that the support line should be constructed & run through OTAGO and HAURAWATU Camps as indicated on the ground yesterday.

6. Work on the Main Trenches in Forward Zone

1. Artillery O.P. MENIN ROAD in house at I.9.c.9.5. Roughly 30% completed concrete work. — 1 NCO. 4 Sappers working by day. — carrying party of 8. RFA at night.

2. ECOLE. — Strengthening cellars — renewing and strengthening timbering. 1 NCO & 6 Sappers working by day. — carrying party of 12 to 20 infantry from garrison by night.

3. MG EMPT I.15.a.5.8. Strengthening shelter — throwing up earth round. MG EMPT — drainage. — 2 Sappers. 4 MGunners working by night.

(e) Work in INTERMEDIATE ZONE.

1. BRIELEN SYSTEM. FRONT LINE. H.6.a.2.6 towards S. Revetting traverses and throwing up earth from borrow pit. — 1/2 Section RE. and 200 infantry from Reserve Bde. day work

2. BRIELEN SYSTEM. SUPPORT LINE. H.5.b.3.8. running SOUTH. Cleaning out existing trench, revetting and duckboarding — 1/2 Section RE and 50 men [illegible] day work.

3. BRIGADE HQ. Machine Gun Farm. H.5.c.9.9. Sketches and details of work attached. Concrete materials are supplied by light railway to site of work by day. – 1 Section RE less 5 sappers. 1 platoon from reserve Bn and 20 RF working party by day.

4. Bty HQ HG Sidings. Earmarked for a dressing station. – Laying concrete on roof. – 2 RE and 20 RAMC [illegible] on site working by day.

5. Res. Bn HQ. [illegible] CASTLE. H.11.b.8.3. – Strengthening officers sleeping quarters. 1 RE & 1 platoon from Reserve Bn working by day.

6. MOIR MG Empt. H.12.a.8.1. Erection in progress. – 2 sappers & 7 M. Gunners working by day.

WORK PROPOSED. (A) TRENCH SYSTEM in FORWARD ZONE.

1. Improvement of communication along [illegible] line where it runs parallel to N bank of the ZILLEBEKE LAKE. This portion of trench is enfiladed from the South.

2. Continuation of support line through OTAGO and MANAWATU CAMPS or erection of MOIR MG Empts inside existing NISSEN HUTS to give flank defence.

(B) Work other than Trenches in Forward Zone.

1. Erection of concrete shelter at I.20.d.90.65. Camouflage has been indented for and work is to start as soon as this [illegible]. Particulars of work are attached.

attached map shows approved sites for 19 shelters between the Right Bde Boundary and the MENIN ROAD. Sites for 18 only are marked on the ground between above mentioned limits. The error is at site B.6. which should be marked No. 10 & No. 11 on the ground but is actually marked No. 10 only.

2. Screen & hide entrance to ECOLE at I 9 c 8.2. – material indented for.

3. Screen & hide pathway to ECOLE from ECOLE ALLEY at I 9 c 2.3. – material indented for.

4. Tunnel under WARRINGTON ROAD where RAILWAY LINE ~~[illegible]~~ meets road. (not urgent)

c. WORK IN INTERMEDIATE ZONE.
– 1. BRIELEN SYSTEM. Support line to be dug from H 5 d. 6 7 to H 11 d. 7.8.

DEMOLITIONS: List attached with instructions re firing. This Coy supplies 2 NCOs and 11 Sappers who live on sites. They are under the command of the demolition officer detailed from the Field Coy of the LEFT BRIGADE.

BILLETS: 2 Sections and 2 officers are accommodated in Shelters on Island at I 14. a. 4. 2. HQ and 2 Sections at Machine Gun Siding H 12. a. 3 5. Transport at A. 30. Central.

28/8/18.

James Russell
Major R.E.
OC 204 Field Coy RE

STORES.

1 The main Divisional Dump is CULODDEN DUMP near VLAMERTINGHE. and all materials are drawn from there.

2. Light Railways deliver materials indented for to any point on the light railway. Attached map shows detraining stations.

3 A representative of the light railways calls daily at Coy HQ between 2pm and 3pm and collects indents. The materials are supplied the same night if available at CULODDEN Dump.

4 Bdes. & Battns send indents direct to Field Coy HQ stating detraining points. Indents for materials required the same night must be at Coy HQ by 12 noon.

6 Indents for daily requirements only should be submitted and not bulk indents as trucks at night are limited.

[illegible]
[illegible]
[illegible]

28/8/18.

LIST OF MAPS, SKETCHES &c
HANDED OVER TO 61ST FIELD COY R.E.

(a). 2 White prints 1/5000 YPRES showing work in hand.

(b) 1 Tracing showing Bde Boundaries.

(c) ST JULIEN TRENCH MAP 1/10000 5 Copies (one 1 to Bde showing work done and 1 to CRE showing work done.

(d) YPRES TRENCH MAP 1/10000. 5 Copies. (with 1 copy to Bde and 1 to CRE)

(e). Instructions, Sketch of shelter and plan showing sites of concrete shelters to be erected in the YPRES DEFENCE LINE.

(f). List of demolitions and copy of instructions

(g). 1 copy of instructions for erection of HOIR MG EMPT.

(i) Sketches of work at Machine Gun Farm.

(j) Bde defence scheme.

(k) Map showing Light Railway System

(L) Position Cells.

(M) Sketch of TANK TRAP

(O) List of materials delivered to CULLODEN DUMP.

Received
E.A.D. Richmond Capt R.E.
o/O.C. 61st & 82 Coy R.E.

James Russell
Major R.E.
[illegible]

28/8/17

Instructions regarding War Diaries and Intelligence Summaries are contained in F. S. Regs., Part II. and the Staff Manual respectively. Title pages will be prepared in manuscript.

WAR DIARY

~~or~~

~~INTELLIGENCE SUMMARY.~~

(Erase heading not required.)

Army Form C. 2118.

9/8 33

Place	Date	Hour	Summary of Events and Information	Remarks and references to Appendices
			— 208th Field Coy, R.E., —	
			— September 1918. —	

(A9175) Wt W235⁸/P360 600,000 12/17 D. D. & L. **Sch. 52a.** Forms/C2118/15.

ORIGINAL.

Instructions regarding War Diaries and Intelligence Summaries are contained in F. S. Regs., Part II. and the Staff Manual respectively. Title pages will be prepared in manuscript.

I

WAR DIARY
or
~~INTELLIGENCE SUMMARY.~~
(Erase heading not required.)

Army Form C. 2118.

208 Field Coy RE

Place	Date	Hour	Summary of Events and Information	Remarks and references to Appendices
WESTOUTRE	1st SEPT. 1918.		CRE called about 9am and instructed that the remaining 2 sections in reserve should work on the LA CLYTTE – KEMMEL – MESSINES ROAD with A and B Coys Pioneers in 2 Reliefs, making the road fit for motor transport, and pushing forward as far as possible. 1 Sect RE and 1 Coy Pioneers started work in old "No mans land" at 11 am. OC reconnoitred road to present front line, about 1¾ miles E of KEMMEL, and reported that present parties would take two days to ~~complete~~ get road through – improvement later would be required. Remaining Sect RE and Coy Pioneers relieved first party at 4pm and continued work till 9pm making road good to old German Front Line. Instructions recd at midnight that all available sections of Field Coys & Pioneers would concentrate on the above mentioned road on 2nd inst working in 3 reliefs – 1st Relief 2 Sections 208 F Coy RE and 1 Coy of Pioneers from 8am to 12 noon. ~~Other Sections~~ Section attached to Left Bde rejoined Coy as B.G.C. Bde did not want them. Section with right Bde remained but did no work as line advancing.	

(A9175) Wt W2358/P360 600,000 12/17 D. D. & L. Sch. 52a. Forms/C2118/15.

Instructions regarding War Diaries and Intelligence Summaries are contained in F. S. Regs., Part II, and the Staff Manual respectively. Title pages will be prepared in manuscript.

II

WAR DIARY
or
INTELLIGENCE SUMMARY.
(Erase heading not required.)

Army Form C. 2118.

208 Field Coy R.E.

Place	Date	Hour	Summary of Events and Information	Remarks and references to Appendices
WESTOUTRE	2nd SEPT. 1918.		2 Sects proceeded to work as instructed on 1st inst — one Section remaining in Reserve. Pioneer Coy was 1 hour late at rendezvous. At end of relief Road ~~was~~ through to crest immediately E of Kemmel village. OC reported to CRE that 2nd relief would complete road E of to KEMMEL village, and suggested 3rd relief rendezvousing at 8 pm instead of at 4 pm so that it could work by night and get road through to present front line — Road beyond Kemmel Village in fairly good order with scattered shell holes only. On instructions from CRE arranged reliefs with 209 Field Coy RE and OC Pioneers as suggested. CRE called about 7 pm and instructed Coy to improve ~~[illegible]~~ Kemmel Road with 1 Coy pioneers on 3rd inst — keeping 1 Sect in reserve. Section with Right Bde making new Bde HQ on S. Slope of Kemmel Hill.	R.
	3rd SEPT.		2 Sections 71 Coy pioneers commenced work on & improving KEMMEL Road at 2 pm relieving 207 Field Coy RE. Section with Right Bde rejoined Coy about 3 pm being instructed by B.G.C. to cease work on new Bde HQ.	

(A9175) Wt W2358/P360 600,000 12/17 D. D. & L. Sch. 52a. Forms/C2118/15.

Instructions regarding War Diaries and Intelligence Summaries are contained in F. S. Regs., Part II. and the Staff Manual respectively. Title pages will be prepared in manuscript.

WAR DIARY or ~~INTELLIGENCE SUMMARY.~~

(Erase heading not required.)

208 Field Coy RE

Army Form C. 2118.

Place	Date	Hour	Summary of Events and Information	Remarks and references to Appendices
WESTOUTRE	3RD SEPT 1918.		(Continued). CRE called at 10pm and instructed OC to be at Bde HQs LITTLE KEMMEL at 6am on 4th inst with 2 Sections to be attached to Bde during attack on WYTSCHAETE RIDGE.	R
"	4th	"	Attack partial success only. – Sections attached to Bde did no work owing to fluctuating fighting and returned to camp. Remaining 2 Sections and one Coy Pioneers worked on the LACLYTTE – KEMMEL – WYTSCHAETE ROAD and opened road for ambulance traffic to the front line. Road through KEMMEL VILLAGE shelled greatly hindering work.	R
"	5th	"	Sections attached to Bde worked as follows – one on improving Bde HQ at LITTLE KEMMEL – one on strengthening and increasing accommodation at Bn HQ in ROSSIGNOL WOOD. The other 2 Sections and one Coy Pioneers worked on LACLYTTE – KEMMEL ROAD. Lt STATON and Sgt. ROWLANDS proceeded to ROUEN for one month to attend an R.E. course of instruction.	R.
	6th		Work reorganised – Company now to work with Left Brigade. Reconnoitred Left Bde area for a combined C.T. and Track from KEMMEL VILLAGE to the	

(A9475) Wt W2358/P360 600,000 12/17 D. D. & L. Sch. 52a. Forms/C2118/15.

IV

Army Form C. 2118.

Instructions regarding War Diaries and Intelligence Summaries are contained in F. S. Regs., Part II. and the Staff Manual respectively. Title pages will be prepared in manuscript.

WAR DIARY or ~~INTELLIGENCE SUMMARY.~~

(Erase heading not required.)

208 Field Coy RE

Place	Date	Hour	Summary of Events and Information	Remarks and references to Appendices
	6th Sept		(Continued)	
Westoutre	1918.		front line, also for existing shelters or suitable sites for 3 Battn HQs and 3 Coy HQs. – the Coy HQs to be sufficiently large to accommodate Battn HQs if necessary. – Existing shelters requiring improving were decided on for Battns at ① Parrain Fme. ② York House ③ St Patricks Church. – 2 existing Coy HQs, one only requiring improving were decided on in front line, and a site chosen for the third near Alberta Dugouts. It was decided to reclaim the old CT commencing on the Vierstraat Road near La Polka and running E through Saskatchewan Fort to Alberta Dugouts. Work was carried on as on 5th inst. The party on the La Clytte – Kemmel Road started screening it. K.	
"	7th	–	1 Section worked on Bde HQ Little Kemmel – 1 Section on York House and St Patricks Church – 1 Section on new Coy HQ at Alberta Dugouts and one section with C Coy Pioneers on C.T. reconnoitred yesterday. Work on the La Clytte – Kemmel Road was handed over to 209 Field Coy RE. K.	
"	8th	.	Work as on 7th inst. The interbrigade boundary was altered so that Parrain Fme passed to the Right Bde, and site for a new Bn HQ now required. K.	

Army Form C. 2118.

Instructions regarding War Diaries and Intelligence Summaries are contained in F. S. Regs., Part II. and the Staff Manual respectively. Title pages will be prepared in manuscript.

WAR DIARY or INTELLIGENCE SUMMARY.

(Erase heading not required.)

208 Field Coy R.E.

Place	Date	Hour	Summary of Events and Information	Remarks and references to Appendices
WESTOUTRE	9th Sept 1918.		OC went round area with B.G.C. 102 Inf Bde and decided on the site for the 3rd Battn HQ near YORK HOUSE – work not to be started till YORK HOUSE and St PATRICKS CHURCH completed.	R
"	10th Sept.		Work progressing satisfactorily	R
"	11th "		Supply of duckboards running out. – commenced salving from disused trenches and old camps	R
"	12th		Bad weather retarding progress on C.T. CRE called and instructed Company to move to the vicinity of LA CLYTTE. – 2 fine days would be given to complete new camp.	R
"	13th		Coy making new camp at M6c9.2 near LA CLYTTE.	R
"	14th		As on 13th inst.	R
LA CLYTTE.	15th		Sunday – no work. Company moved to LA CLYTTE.	R
"	16th		In addition to works previously detailed a new duckboard track was commenced from the LA CLYTTE – KEMMEL ROAD to Bde HQ at LITTLE KEMMEL	R
"	17th		Work as on 16th inst – Short of duckboards.	R
"	18th		VISUAL SIGNALLING O.P. commenced on top of LITTLE KEMMEL. Instructions	

(A9175) Wt W2358/P360 600,000 12/17 D. D. & L. Sch. 52a. Forms/C2118/15.

Instructions regarding War Diaries and Intelligence Summaries are contained in F. S. Regs., Part II. and the Staff Manual respectively. Title pages will be prepared in manuscript.

WAR DIARY
or
INTELLIGENCE SUMMARY.
(*Erase heading not required.*)

Army Form C. 2118.

208 Field Coy RE

Place	Date	Hour	Summary of Events and Information	Remarks and references to Appendices
LA CLYTTE	18th Sept 1918		(Continued) received from CRE that St PATRICKS CHURCH was now to be made to accommodate a Bde HQ and to be ready for occupation by noon on 21st inst — Also that York House as a Bn HQ ~~was~~ to be ready for occupation at the same time. — Other work to be stopped if necessary.	K.
"	19th "		Work on Coy HQ at ALBERTA DUGOUTS temporarily stopped and section fully employed on St PATRICKS CHURCH as second shift. Section employed at Bde HQ, in addition to work in hand, commenced work on Artillery Bde HQ near LITTLE KEMMEL taken over from 207 Field Coy RE. Copy of weekly works report attached	K.
"	20th "		Work as on 19th inst — progress good.	K.
"	21st		St Patricks Church and York House ready for occupation — improvements suggested if labour available and work handed over to 207 Field Coy RE. Work in hand in Right Bde Area taken over from 207 Field Coy RE with instructions to work on urgent work only. CRE held a conference of Field Coy & Pioneer Commanders re distribution of work	K.

(A9175) Wt W2358/P569 600,000 12/17 D. D. & L. Sch. 52a. Forms/C2118/15.

Army Form C. 2118.

Instructions regarding War Diaries and Intelligence Summaries are contained in F. S. Regs., Part II. and the Staff Manual respectively. Title pages will be prepared in manuscript.

VIII

WAR DIARY
or
INTELLIGENCE SUMMARY.
(Erase heading not required.)

208 Field Coy R.E.

Place	Date	Hour	Summary of Events and Information	Remarks and references to Appendices
LA CLYTTE	22nd Sept 1918.		Work reorganised as follows to meet requirements in view of a probable enemy retirement — 1½ Sections on Coy HQ at ALBERTA DUGOUTS being prepared for a Battn HQ — ½ Section on REGENT St DUGOUTS being prepared for an Inf Bde and an Artillery Bde HQ — ½ Section with one Coy Pioneers distributed equally on C.T. to ALBERTA DUGOUTS, C.T to REGENT St DUGOUTS, duckboard track from LA CLYTTE-KEMMEL Road to Bde HQ at LITTLE KEMMEL — 1½ Sections on Inf Bde HQ and Artillery Bde HQ at LITTLE KEMMEL being prepared as advanced Divisional HQ.	K
"	23rd	"	Work as on 22nd inst. Capt FOWLER MC RE returned from leave	K
"	24th	"	Duckboard track to LITTLE KEMMEL completed and party set free employed on Adv. DHQ at LITTLE KEMMEL. O.P. on Little KEMMEL completed — weather proof only. CRE held conference of Coy Commanders and OC Pioneers re work to be done and moves in view of probable enemy retiral.	K
"	25th	"	Bad weather hindering work. Enemy shelled C.T. to Regent St Dugouts making several direct hits. Dump of duckboards formed at LA POLKA.	K
"	26th	"	Work as detailed on 22nd. Copy of weekly works report attached	K

(A9175) Wt W2358/P360 600,000 12/17 D. D. & L. Sch. 52a. Forms/C2118/15.

Instructions regarding War Diaries and Intelligence Summaries are contained in F. S. Regs., Part II. and the Staff Manual respectively. Title pages will be prepared in manuscript.

WAR DIARY
or
INTELLIGENCE SUMMARY.
(Erase heading not required.)

Army Form C. 2118.

208 Field Coy RE

Place	Date	Hour	Summary of Events and Information	Remarks and references to Appendices
LACLYTTE	27th Sept 1918.		OC handed over Company to Capt H.H.C. Fowler M.C. R.E. and proceeded on leave to England.	
			Captain H.H.C. Fowler R.E. assumed command of the Company.	
			C.Ts to Regent St Dug Out & Alberta Dugout again received direct hits & were repaired, dump of duckwalks enlarged at La Polka & dump formed at Spey Farm, wood pickets & wire also added to both dumps for marking out track forward immediately infantry advanced	HHCF
			One shelter at Regent St Dug Out hit & partly repaired, large shell hole at N.29.a.2.8 repaired during the night. Work as detailed on the 22nd carried on & completed.	
	28th		Coy standing by for orders to proceed to work on repairing road from Kemmel to Wytschaete & to carry on forward on the Oosttaverne road if possible, also to carry C.Ts forward. No orders to move received, but C.R.E. gave orders to start work at dawn on the 29th.	HHCF
	29th		Repairing road from Kemmel to Wytschaete, making 3 timber track deviations round	

(A9175) Wt W2358/P360 600,000 12/17 D. D. & L. Sch. 52a. Forms/C2118/15.

Instructions regarding War Diaries and Intelligence Summaries are contained in F. S. Regs., Part II. and the Staff Manual respectively. Title Pages will be prepared in manuscript.

IX

WAR DIARY
or
INTELLIGENCE SUMMARY

(Erase heading not required.)

Army Form C. 2118.

Place	Date	Hour	Summary of Events and Information	Remarks and references to Appendices
LA CLYTTE	29th	Sept 1918	Continued. Craters blown by the enemy, filling in numerous shell holes 3 sections RE + 3 platoons Pioneers engaged at first, the reserve section RE + reserve platoon Pioneers ordered out to assist about 10 am About 10 am CRE gave orders for Coy to move to N.15.b.2.7 & horse line to shift up to M.6.c.9.2. Location of craters (i) N.29.b.2.5, (ii) N.24.d.1.2, (iii) N.19.c.4.5 (i) Consisted of 1 large round hole about 20' across. (ii) 4 small craters not quite merging into each other (iii) 4 " " merging into each other & completely destroying the roadway for 50'-0". Traffic (horse) using road by 3 pm. Actual work 9 hrs.	HHCF
CHEAPSIDE N.15.b.2.7	~~29th~~ 30th		Heavy rain fell during night 28/29th considerably depreciating roadway. Whole Coy + 'C' Coy Pioneers worked from 11.30 am – 7 pm on same stretch & made it fit for light motor traffic; horse traffic of 30th Division used it all day, & greatly impeded work. Heavy rain all day showed that the drainage could be improved. This portion road between KEMMEL & WYTSCHAETE to be taken over by Xth Corps on the morrow.	HHCF

Herbert H C Fowler
Capt RE
o/c 208 Field Coy.

2449 Wt. W14957/M90 750,000 1/16 J.B.C. & A. Forms/C.2118/12.

208TH FIELD COMPANY, R.E.
No. ....
Date. ....

Weekly Works Report.
208th Fld. Co. R.E.
Week Ending 19/9/18.

Works Completed — Nil —

Work in Hand. (a) Duckboard track and C.T from N.21.d.90.95 to N.23.a.15.75. – 300 yds double track laid. – 250 yds single track laid – 15 A frames placed in trench where single track laid at wet places.

(b) Duckboard track from N.14.d.25.15 to Bde H.Q. N.20.a.2.5. 600 yds single track laid with bearers to take a double track – formation for track practically completed.

(c) Bde. H.Q. N.20.a.2.5. (1) 50 yds duckboards laid. (2) 70% excavation for shelter as sleeping accomodation for B.G.C. completed – (This work delayed for lack of working parties) –. (3) Headcover to Mess and Office 75% completed. (4) 0 Dog kennels erected. (5) Roofs of 3 shelters opened up, leaks traced and repaired. (6) Entrances to 2 shelters revetted. (7) Front of one shelter opened up and roof repaired. (8) Area in front of Bde H.Q drained.

(d) Artillery Bde. H.Q. N.20.d.4.2 – 2 English shelters strutted and ends fitted ready for headcover.

(e) Bn H.Q. N.16.c.0.2 – 4 shelters now occupied – work on each as follows:– (1) Entrance revetted and sandbagged – sides sandbagged – Extra row of pitprops placed on roof as burster. (2) Entrance revetted and sandbagged. – One side strengthened with pitprops. (3) Entrance revetted and sandbagged. Sides strengthened with pit-props (4) Strengthening roof supports. This H.Q could now be occupied by a Bn – work nearly completed.

(f) Bn H.Q. N.16.c.?.0 – Entrances to 2 small shelters cleared. ½ T.M. bomb in one shelter

(Contd)

removed – other shelter still full of bombs – Work on this H.Q temporarily stopped.

(g) Bn. H.Q., N.16.d.2.4. – 2 Entrances cleared one of which is sandbagged – Floor drained – strutting of roof nearly completed – Flooring 25% completed. – Clearance of new shelter 15'×15' at N. end commenced.

NOTE. This is being converted into a Bde H.Q. Total accommodation. 1 compartment 15'×8' for mess – one compartment 34'×15' at one end and 10' at other end being divided into 4 compartments for B.G.C., B.M. + S.C, Clerks, Signals. – one compartment approx 15'×15' now being cleared for orderlies – One French shelter outside for cookhouse (not splinter proof)

(h) Coy H.Q. N.23.d.2.9. – 21 ft. of French Shelter erected. Materials collected for roof. Work temporarily stopped.

(i) Soup Kitchen. N.23.d.2.7 – 2 Shelters cleared for making and serving soup and as sleeping accommodation for 2 men. – Work temporarily stopped.

(j) Road from LA POLKA CORNER to junction of V.C. Road and VIERSTRAAT Road was cleared and repaired for the passage of limbers before work on road was taken on by the Pioneers.

NOTE. The Company did not work on 13th, 14th + 15th insts.

(Sgd) James Russell
Major R.E.
O.C. 208th Fld. Coy. R.E.

19/9/1918.

WEEKLY WORKS REPORT

208 FIELD COY R.E.

WEEK ENDING 26/9/18

WORKS. COMPLETED. (1) ST PATRICKS CHURCH. N16d.2.4. made ~~ready~~ fit for occupation by an Inf Bde. H.Q.

(2). YORK HOUSE. N16c9.2 made ~~ready~~ fit for occupation by a battalion H.Q.

(3). Duckboard track from N14d.25.15 to Bde HQ N.20.d.2.5. and continued to Artillery Bde HQ. N20d.4.2. – single track completed with leaves for a double track if necessary. – appx. 600 yds track laid during week.

~~Note~~. (4) Weatherproof O.P. on top of LITTLE KEMMEL N20d.35.65

NOTE. (1) and (2) handed over to 207 Field Coy R.E. for improvement.

WORKS IN. HAND. (1) Bde HQ. N20d.2.5. (a) 2 English Shelters 12'×9' erected – fronts sandbagged – splinter proof roofs provided.

(b). 2 Kitchens erected.

(c). Sites for 3 Armstrong Huts excavated.

(d). Vent shaft to one dugout cleared and fitted with stove pipe.

(e). Gas blankets fitted to all dugouts.

(f). Duckboard approaches laid.

(g) No 1 Mess. provided with one coat of paint

(2). Artillery Bde HQ. N20d.4.2.

(a) Splinter proof roofs put on 2 Existing English Shelters.

(b) 2 English Shelters 12'×9' erected and made splinter proof.

(c) Existing Shelter for Signals made Splinter Proof

WORKS IN HAND (CONTINUED). (2). (d). Kitchens relined.
(e). Several weather proof shelters cleared for occupation.

(3) REGENT ST DUGOUTS. N29.c.4.3. – Taken over from 207 Field Coy R.E. on 22nd inst. –
(a). Traverse in front of 5 shelters half finished when taken over now finished.
(b) Floors ~~[illegible]~~ fitted to 2 shelters.
(c). Partitions in 2 dugouts in course of erection – will be complete tomorrow.
(d). Existing duckboard track in front of dugouts improved and additional duckboards laid.
Note. Gas blankets have been fitted by 207 Field Coy R.E.
Dugouts are now fit for occupation by an Inf Bde H.Q. and affiliated Artillery Bde H.Q.

(4). Coy HQ. N23d.29. (a) Shelter 27'×9' which had iron work only erected. is now floored, partitioned and made splinter proof.
(b) Shelter appx. 8'×10' cleared out, re strutted, floored and bunked.
Note.– Gas curtains will be fitted tomorrow.–
Is now habitable as a Bn. H.Q.

(5). REGENT. ST. C.T. – Duckboards laid to N28d.80.65. – pickets and wire continued from ~~that~~ point to Regent ST Dugouts thence along BEAVER ST to appx. N29.c.7.8. –
Appx 400 yds duckboards laid and 500 yds pickets & wire erected since taking over from 207 Field Coy R.E. on 22/9/18.

WORKS. IN. HAND. (CONTINUED.)

(6). FORT SASKATCHEWAN. C.T. Duckboards laid to N.23.c.60.60. – pickets and wire continued to. N23 d 2.8. – appx 600 yds trench cleared out and duckboards laid during week.

(7). A dump of appx 500 duckboards pickets and wire has been established on the VIERSTRAAT Road between LA. POLKA CORNER and commencement of FORT SASKATCHEWAN. C.T.

(8). A dump of ? duckboards, pickets and wire has been established at SPY FME. Note. C Coy Pioneers should report number of duckboards.

(9). 546 Duckboards salved during week.

26/9/18.

James Russell
Major R.E.
OC 208 Field Coy R.E.

— Original —

Army Form C. 2118.

Instructions regarding War Diaries and Intelligence Summaries are contained in F. S. Regs., Part II. and the Staff Manual respectively. Title pages will be prepared in manuscript.

WAR DIARY
or
INTELLIGENCE SUMMARY.
(*Erase heading not required.*)

Vol 34

Place	Date	Hour	Summary of Events and Information	Remarks and references to Appendices
			208th Field Coy R.E.	
			— October 1918 —	

(A9175) Wt W2358/P360 600,000 12/17 D. D. & L. **Sch. 52a.** Forms/C2118/15.

Instructions regarding War Diaries and Intelligence Summaries are contained in F. S. Regs., Part II. and the Staff Manual respectively. Title Pages will be prepared in manuscript.

WAR DIARY

~~or~~

~~INTELLIGENCE SUMMARY~~

(Erase heading not required.)

208 Field Coy R.E.

Army Form C. 2118.

Place	Date	Hour	Summary of Events and Information	Remarks and references to Appendices
HOLLEBEKE	1st	October 1918	Received 'Warning Order' that Division would move. " Orders to move to HOLLEBEKE AREA received at 6.30 am One officer sent forward to reconnoitre camp & horse lines Dismounted personnel arrived at St ELOI as per march table at 10.40 am, marched to billet at O.4.c.4.3 (Sheet 28 1/40,000) & at once proceeded to make up roadway to WHITE CHATu. to park transport, all the surrounding country being cut up by shell fire. Coy transport arrived during afternoon, roads blocked by transport moving up.	
	2nd	"	3 Sects repairing timber track between St ELOI & HOLLEBEKE, from O.10.a.7.9 to O.10.a.9.8 1 Sect in reserve.	
	3rd	"	Whole Coy cleaning & repairing road between HOLLEBEKE & TENBRIELEN from P.14.a.6.7 to P.15.a.0.7 Verbal orders from C.R.E. one officer reported to 41st Div to arrange repair of road in P.2.b, [illegible] found 41st Division R.E. had [illegible] work in hand [illegible] transport parked on road.	
	"	"	2 Sects repairing timber track at O.10.b.5.7 especially the centre joint in the double portion. 1 Sect. with 3 Platoons 7th Somerset Pioneers in conjunction with 41st Divisional R.E. mending road & laying new slab track at P.2.b.95.10 1 Sect in reserve. 1 Platoon 7th Somerset in reserve. C.E. Coy, 1 officer & 6 O.R. reconnoitring roads & water supply in Div! area, report sent to C.R.E.	
	5th	"	Lieut. F. Hebbert M.C. R.E. proceeded on leave to U.K. 4 Sects with 2 Platoons 7th Somerset Pioneers repairing ZANVOORDE – KLEIN ZILLEBEKE Road at J.32.c.2.7, road practically impassable here, 41st Div! R.E. working on road EAST of [illegible] 2 Platoons 7th Somerset laying 6" layer of brick & debris off road in ZANDVOORDE to P.3.a.4.0.	
	6th	"	4 Sects working on roadway between P.3.a.0.2 & CHURCH at ZANDVOORDE laying a layer of brick & debris off road, filling in worst places & strengthening sides of road with fascines & pickets. Enemy fired about 10 rounds shrapnel over this portion of road about 09.15, no casualties. Winter time came into force at 01.00 hours, Coy time put back 1 hour.	

2449 Wt. W14957/M90 750,000 1/16 J.B.C. & A. Forms/C.2118/12.

Instructions regarding War Diaries and Intelligence Summaries are contained in F. S. Regs., Part II. and the Staff Manual respectively. Title Pages will be prepared in manuscript.

Army Form C. 2118.

WAR DIARY

~~or~~

~~INTELLIGENCE SUMMARY~~

(Erase heading not required.)

208 Field Coy R.E.

Place	Date	Hour	Summary of Events and Information	Remarks and references to Appendices
HOLLEBEKE	7th	October 1918	Work continued on portion of road between ZANDVOORDE CHURCH, Road junct at P.3.a.0.2 & P.2.d.7.5. The greater portion of this stretch is under direct observation & periodically shelled, less by day than by night, consequently as 10 groups from 103 Bde were indented for as working party, it was decided to work in two '4' hour reliefs, 08.00 – 12.00 & 12.00 – 16.00. 2 Sects & 5 groups 1st relief & 2 Sects with 5 groups 2nd relief. Men were spread out well & progress was good, road between ZANDVOORDE & P.3.a.0.2 being quite fit for horse traffic, but extensive repairs to surface & sides of road are required between P.3.a.0.2 & P.2.d.7.5. No casualties to men or transport.	[illegible]
	8th	"	Lieut. J. F. Sh[illegible] returned from R.E. Course at ROUEN. Owing to Brigade relief no working parties available today. Parties for 9th inst. arranged with 102nd Brigade. 4 Sections continued work on road as for the 7th. Rain which fell during night 7th/8th showed clearly how important it is to clear top layer of mud & rubbish off good road in village of ZANDVOORDE. Roads in close vicinity of ZANDVOORDE intermittently shelled all day, no casualties.	[illegible]
	9th	"	Work continued on above portion of road in two reliefs, viz. 1 Sect R.E. with 5 groups Infantry 08 – 12.00, 2 Sects R.E. with 5 groups Infantry 12.00 – 16.00. Progress in getting top layer of mud & debris off road – good. Very little brick rubble to be found in ZANDVOORDE, & that little there is has to be dug out & carried to road to load up limbers. 1 Sect. R.E. constructing new Plank siding between UP & DOWN roads at O.12.b.7.6 to facilitate entry of wagons to REFILLING POINT. Two sappers pumping out concrete buildings for 102 Bde H.Q. O.6.d.9.9. 4 G.S. limbers from 102 Bde with Coy Transport carting materials to works.	[illegible]
	10th	"	Work continued on road between ZANDVOORDE CHURCH & P.2.d.7.5. in two reliefs. 2 Sects. R.E. with 5 Groups 102 Bde Infantry 08.00 – 12.00 " " " 12.00 – 16.00. Progress good between P.3.a.0.2 & P.3.a.9.0, soft places being dug out & filled with brick. Coy transport & 4 G.S. limbers from 102 Bde carting material.	[illegible]
	11th	"	As for 10th, bottlenecks being widened, two bad places being slabbed	[illegible]

2449 Wt. W14957/M90 750,000 1/16 J.B.C. & A. Forms/C.2118/12.

Instructions regarding War Diaries and Intelligence Summaries are contained in F. S. Regs., Part II. and the Staff Manual respectively. Title Pages will be prepared in manuscript.

WAR DIARY

or

~~INTELLIGENCE SUMMARY~~

(Erase heading not required.)

Army Form C. 2118.

208 Field Coy R.E.

Place	Date	Hour	Summary of Events and Information	Remarks and references to Appendices
HOLLEBEKE	12th	OCTOBER 1918	No working parties or transport supplied by Brigade today owing to Brigade going up into the Line tonight. 4 R.E. Section continued working road as for 10th inst. 2 Sappers fixing pickets at dangerous places along road between HOLLEBEKE CHATEAU – KORTEWILDE – P.15.d.2.7 to P.10.d.2.4 to prevent lorries running off road in the dark. CRE held conference of Field Coy Commdrs at 20 Div H.Qrs re R.E. work on J. day.	[illegible]
"	13th	"	Coy resting under CRE orders, O/C reconnoitring work laid down for Coy in CRE's Operation Orders No 114. also with Section Officers concerned reconnoitring assembly positions for section attached to 102 Bde for J day. Maintenance party patrolling road through HOUTHEM, KORTEWILDE, P.14.a & b, P.15.a also road through P.8.c & d. Visited 102 Bde & fixed time for Section & ½ Coy Pioneers to report on J day.	[illegible]
"	14th		J day. Infantry attacked at H hour 05.35 with limited objectives. 1 Sect reported to 102 Bde at 07.35 to consolidate YELLOW (DEFENSIVE) LINE. A half Coy of Somerset L.I. (Pioneers) were to have reported at same time to assist, but failed to appear at RENDEZ VOUS. The Sect was given One Coy of Infantry to dig line & a series of posts & M.G. positions were constructed supporting each other between Q.4.b.5.4 & Q.9.c.95.00. This Sect remained with Brigade. Pontoon & trestle wagons were loaded up & animals hooked in ready to move by 05.30 to bridge the River Lys if required. Wagons & Bridging detachment standing by all day. 1 Section in Reserve standing by. 2 Sappers with 2 Pontoon wagons from 207 Pontoon Park repairing road at P.2.d.7.5. C.O. returned from leave to U.K.	[illegible]
	15th	"	Infantry advanced to the W bank of the River Lys and occupied MENIN. 2/Lt ANDREWS made daring reconnaissance of the River at MENIN with view to bridging. 2 Sections with all pontoon equipment moved to KRUISEECKE. Forward Section	

2449 Wt. W14957/M90 750,000 1/16 J.B.C. & A. Forms/C.2118/12.

Instructions regarding War Diaries and Intelligence Summaries are contained in F. S. Regs., Part II. and the Staff Manual respectively. Title Pages will be prepared in manuscript.

WAR DIARY

or

~~INTELLIGENCE SUMMARY~~

(Erase heading not required.)

208 FIELD Coy RE

Army Form C. 2118.

Place	Date	Hour	Summary of Events and Information	Remarks and references to Appendices
HOLLEBEKE	15th Oct. 1918		(Continued) with 102 Inf Bde worked on YELLOW DEFENCE LINE S of GHELUWE with A Coy. Somerset L.I. Pioneers which had reported on previous evening. Remaining sections worked on road at ZANDVOORDE. 2/Lt BOWES proceeded on leave to ENGLAND.	
GHELUWE	16th	"	Coy moved at dawn to KRUISEECKE, but on arrival were further instructed to proceed to GHELUWE to which bridging detachment had already proceeded. Infantry crossed river at MENIN but were unable to advance owing to MG fire. 2nd/Lt Andrews made a further reconnaissance of the river and sent back useful information. The Division sidestepped to a sector immediately E of MENIN. The bridging detachment plus one pontoon from 209 Field Coy RE moved to an area 1½ miles N.E. of MENIN at 4pm while attached to 101 Inf Bde.	
"	17th	"	102 Inf Bde were relieved and 2nd Lt Andrews with ~~Section~~ IV rejoined the Coy. Lt STATON i/c of bridging detachment erected a pontoon and trestle bridge to take horse transport and field guns across the River Lys at a point 2 miles E of MENIN. At this point the river is 90ft wide and as the pontoon equipment was ~~not~~ sufficient, a ~~boat~~ trestle was improvised made from	

Instructions regarding War Diaries and Intelligence Summaries are contained in F. S. Regs., Part II. and the Staff Manual respectively. Title Pages will be prepared in manuscript.

WAR DIARY

~~or~~ ~~INTELLIGENCE SUMMARY~~

(Erase heading not required.)

Army Form C. 2118.

208 Field Coy RE

Place	Date	Hour	Summary of Events and Information	Remarks and references to Appendices
GHELUWE	17th Oct 1918.		(Continued). timber found in an enemy RE Dump close at hand. There was no enemy interference. Remainder of Coy standing by. Word received that C.S.M. MINTER had died in hospital on 13th inst.	R
"	18th	"	2 Sections with 2 platoons pioneers repaired road from GHELUWE to WEVELGHEM. – A special endeavour being made to complete crater blown in road at KIJKUITHOEK. This was made fit for transport at 10 pm. Remaining 2 Sections with 2 platoons pioneers standing by. Forward roads were reconnoitred to main railway E of LAUWE. All East of the River LYS were found in excellent condition; 3 very large craters had been blown in the MENIN – WEVELGHEM ROAD. These were being repaired by ~~209~~ 207th Field Coy RE. 2nd Lt DAVIDSON was admitted to hospital sick.	R
STE ANNE.	19th	"	Coy moved with 102 Inf Bde to KRUISHOEK in early morning – thence to SCHEERBAK E of the River LYS. – Thence to AELBEKE and finally to STE ANNE. Raining and extremely dark before final billets reached when Coy ~~arrived~~ at 1/4 hrs notice to move. Pontoon wagons were left behind to be loaded by 209 Field Coy RE when they dismantled bridge erected on 17th inst.	R

2449 Wt. W14957/M90 750,000 1/16 J.B.C. & A. Forms/C.2118/12.

Instructions regarding War Diaries and Intelligence Summaries are contained in F. S. Regs., Part II. and the Staff Manual respectively. Title Pages will be prepared in manuscript.

WAR DIARY
or
INTELLIGENCE SUMMARY
(Erase heading not required.)

Army Form C. 2118.

208 Field Coy RE

Place	Date	Hour	Summary of Events and Information	Remarks and references to Appendices
STE ANNE	20th Oct. 1918		Company now on 2 hours notice to move. Forward roads to BELLEGHEM were reconnoitred and found in good repair except at one point. A party went out and repaired this.	R
"	21st	"	Coy still on 2 hours notice to move. Coy resting.	R
"	22nd		As on 21st.	R
BELLEGHEM	23rd		Coy moved with 102 Inf Bde to Area 2 miles E of BELLEGHEM and relieved the 124 Inf Bde on the front 500 yds W of the BOSSUYT-COURTRAI CANAL between BOSSUYT and KNOKKE. Roads to SAINT-GENOIS parallel to the Canal were reconnoitred and found fit for one way motor traffic. 2nd LIEUT C.L. FOX RE joined company as reinforcement from RE Base. Lt F.E. HIBBERT MC RE returned from leave, and proceeded to D.H.Q. to take over duties of Adjt RE 34th Div to which he had been appointed. Pontoon equipment rejoined the Company.	R
"	24th	"	The 41st Div on left of the 102 Bde attacked at 2 am in a S.E. direction E of the BOSSUYT-COURTRAI CANAL. As soon as 41st Div reached canal crossing 1000 yds S.E. of KNOKKE the 102 Bde was to cross canal and attack in a S.E. direction on right of 41st Div. The 41st Div failed. Attack of 102 Bde Cancelled	

2449 Wt. W14957/M90 750,000 1/16 J.B.C. & A. Forms/C.2118/12.

Instructions regarding War Diaries and Intelligence Summaries are contained in F. S. Regs., Part II. and the Staff Manual respectively. Title Pages will be prepared in manuscript.

WAR DIARY ~~or~~ INTELLIGENCE SUMMARY

(Erase heading not required.)

Army Form C. 2118.

208 Field Coy R.E.

Place	Date	Hour	Summary of Events and Information	Remarks and references to Appendices
BELLEGHEM	24th Oct 1918		(Continued)	
			One section employed converting Stokes Mortar Bombs into Smoke Bombs to be fired by Stokes Mortars. – 1 Sect and 1 Coy Pioneers less 20 men on the BELLEGHEM – DRIES ROAD, a portion of which badly cutting up owing to excessive lorry traffic. – 2 Sections and 20 pioneers collecting bridging material, and standing by as bridging party.	
			At 7pm bridging party proceeded to a farm 1 mile N.W. of DRIES preparatory to bridging the BOSSUYT – COURTRAI CANAL between MOEN and BOSSUYT during attack planned for the 25th inst.	
			As information gained showed canal to be an aqueduct with very high banks it was decided to use barrel rafts as a temporary means of getting the infantry across.	
"	25th	"	A subsidiary attack at 3 am was arranged to take BOSSUYT and establish bridgeheads over the Canal between BOSSUYT and railway crossing Canal 2000 yds N of BOSSUYT.	
			Bridging detachment moved to POELDRIESCH and were in position with necessary materials at 2 am. The attack captured BOSSUYT, but failed to gain the W Canal bank. At 8.30 am the enemy counterattacked	

2449 Wt. W14957/M90 750,000 1/16 J.B.C. & A. Forms/C.2118/12.

Instructions regarding War Diaries and Intelligence Summaries are contained in F. S. Regs., Part II. and the Staff Manual respectively. Title Pages will be prepared in manuscript.

WAR DIARY
or
INTELLIGENCE SUMMARY
(*Erase heading not required.*)

Army Form C. 2118.

208 Field Coy RE.

Place	Date	Hour	Summary of Events and Information	Remarks and references to Appendices
BELLEGHEM	25th Oct 1918		(Continued) and strongly established himself in houses at Locks 4 and 5 in vicinity of above mentioned railway on W side of Canal. Attacks at 9am failed to dislodge him. By advance of troops in a SE direction from MOEN on E side of Canal during the afternoon the enemy was forced to retire from Locks 4 and 5. On reconnaissance being made to bridge enemy footbridges were found intact at BOSSUYT, Lock 4, and midway between these places. Bridging party was therefore not required. It remained in the open at POELDRIESCH from 2am to 5pm, a large portion of which time it was under heavy M.G. and shell fire. Casualties – 3 Sappers wounded. 2/Lt ANDREWS reconnoitred original road crossing at MOEN and found bridge and far abutment completely destroyed. Owing to high banks and low level of water (water 2 to 3 ft deep only) pontoon bridging was found to be impracticable and very long trestles or crib piering necessary. Span 60 ft. Road crossing 1000 yds S of KNOKKE was found undamaged and fit for motor transport. At night Lt STATON made a careful reconnaissance of road crossing	

2449 Wt. W14957/M90 750,000 1/16 J.B.C. & A. Forms/C.2118/12.

Instructions regarding War Diaries and Intelligence Summaries are contained in F. S. Regs., Part II. and the Staff Manual respectively. Title Pages will be prepared in manuscript.

WAR DIARY ~~or~~ ~~INTELLIGENCE SUMMARY~~

(Erase heading not required.)

Army Form C. 2118.

208 Field Coy RE

Place	Date	Hour	Summary of Events and Information	Remarks and references to Appendices
BELLEGHEM	25th Oct 1918		(Continued) at Lock 5 when it was decided to construct a bridge for horse transport using rails from railway close at hand - Span 23 ft. The Attached Coy of Pioneers were employed on roads. Remaining two sections RE moved to forward billets during the afternoon and relieved the Bridging Party.	R
"	26th	"	Roads E of Canal were reconnoitred and found in fair condition. Arrangements made to repair them where necessary and to erect horse transport bridge at Lock No 5 during night 26/27th. Orders received that 36th Div would relieve 102 Inf Bde on night 26/27th. Coy handed over to 203 Field Coy RE and concentrated at Coy HQ.	R
STE ANNE	27th	"	~~Coy moved.~~ CRE stopped leave for ORs for one week owing to the delay in men returning from leave. Working strength of Coy appx 50.	R
			Coy moved with 102 Inf Bde to STE ANNE. One trestle of the pontoon equipment handed over to 36th Div RE in replacement of one heavy lift in bridge in area to be taken over by 54th Div	R
OYGHEM	28th	"	Coy moved with 102 Inf Bde to OYGHEM. One pontoon wagon badly ditched by a motor lorry and broken beyond repair.	R

2449 Wt. W14957/M90 750,000 1/16 J.B.C. & A. Forms/C.2118/12.

Instructions regarding War Diaries and Intelligence Summaries are contained in F. S. Regs., Part II. and the Staff Manual respectively. Title Pages will be prepared in manuscript.

WAR DIARY

or

~~INTELLIGENCE SUMMARY~~

(Erase heading not required.)

Army Form C. 2118.

208 Field Coy RE

Place	Date	Hour	Summary of Events and Information	Remarks and references to Appendices
OYGHEM	29th Oct 1918		Coy ordered to move with 102 Inf Bde to HARLEBEKE. At same time instructions received to construct a trestle bridge over the RIVER LYS for motor lorries to replace a pontoon bridge 1000 yds S.W. of DESSELGHEM. Sanction asked and obtained for Coy and affiliated Pioneer Coy to remain at OYGHEM. Site of bridge and dumps of material reconnoitred. At midday Coy with Pioneers started work on necessary diversion of roadway at site. About 3pm instructions rec'd that no work be done on bridge until further orders. Sections and Pioneers withdrawn. At night further orders received to proceed with bridge. Span at point selected 101 ft. – greatest depth of water 13 ft. – height of highest bank 10 ft. It was decided to ramp the high bank and construct bridge with roadway 6 ft above water level. This necessitated legs of longest trestle to be 17 ft long. Material available and suitable as follows – legs 9"x9", transoms 10"x9", roadbearers 9"x4", bracing 9"x3", ledgers 9"x3" and 15"x3" (long), decking 9"x3½" – bays to be 10 ft span. River bottom sound earth with coating of 6" mud. – 9" sinkage allowed.	

HK

2449 Wt. W14957/M90 750,000 1/16 J.B.C. & A. Forms/C.2118/12.

Instructions regarding War Diaries and Intelligence Summaries are contained in F. S. Regs., Part II. and the Staff Manual respectively. Title pages will be prepared in manuscript.

WAR DIARY
or
~~INTELLIGENCE SUMMARY.~~
(Erase heading not required.)

Army Form C. 2118.

208 Field Coy RE

Place	Date	Hour	Summary of Events and Information	Remarks and references to Appendices
OYGHEM.	30th Oct 1918		1 Section & 3 platoons pioneers employed on road deviation to bridge 3 Sections & 1 platoon pioneers collecting and sorting material for bridge. All available pontoon equipment handed over to 207 Field Coy RE This Company to replace equipment when pontoon bridge being replaced by trestle bridge is dismantled. OC to conference of CRE re attack of 34th Div in conjunction with the French on 31st inst. — Company to continue work on bridge	R
"	31st "		Construction of bridge started. 4 trestles made and one trestle launched. As suitable timber for roadbearers not available in sufficient quantity it was decided to substitute 7 metre rails for the 9 centre spans making a flat bridge ramped down at both abutments. Pioneers completed road diversion, and started improvement of roads along bank of river and road approaching bridge. 2nd Lt BOWES returned from leave.	R

James Russell
Major RE
OC 208 Field Coy RE

Army Form C. 2118.

VR 35

Instructions regarding War Diaries and Intelligence Summaries are contained in F. S. Regs., Part II. and the Staff Manual respectively. Title pages will be prepared in manuscript.

WAR DIARY
~~or~~
~~INTELLIGENCE~~ ~~SUMMARY.~~
(*Erase heading not required.*)

Place	Date	Hour	Summary of Events and Information	Remarks and references to Appendices
			208th Field Coy., R.E.	
			November 1918.	

(A9175) Wt W2358/P360 600,000 12/17 D. D. & L. **Sch. 52a.** Forms/C2118/15.

Instructions regarding War Diaries and Intelligence Summaries are contained in F. S. Regs., Part II. and the Staff Manual respectively. Title pages will be prepared in manuscript.

WAR DIARY
or
INTELLIGENCE SUMMARY.
(*Erase heading not required.*)

208 Field Coy R.E.

Army Form C. 2118.

Place	Date	Hour	Summary of Events and Information	Remarks and references to Appendices
OYGHEM	1st Nov 1918		Company employed building a trestle bridge across the River Lys near OYGHEM to take 3 ton motor lorries. 4 trestles now launched. It was decided to use pairs of roadbearers in order to weigh down and stabilize the bridge – Suitable timber for roadbearers in any case not available. Affiliated Coy Pioneers employed on roads approaching bridge.	H.
"	2nd.		One trestle launched yesterday gave a lot of trouble owing to a large stone in the bed of the river. This now rectified. One additional trestle launched.	H.
"	3rd.		34th Div moved to a new area but Company left behind with affiliated Coy of Pioneers to complete bridge – Two more trestles launched	H.
"	4th.		One trestle only launched. Trouble experienced in ~~[illegible]~~ getting trestle into position owing to rapid current. A Sapper fell into the river. Sapper AHMOND immediately dived to rescue the man with all his clothes on. A rescue was effected. Leave reopened for ORs.	H.

(A9175) Wt W2353/P360 600,000 12/17 D. D. & L. Sch. 52a. Forms/C2118/15.

Instructions regarding War Diaries and Intelligence Summaries are contained in F. S. Regs., Part II. and the Staff Manual respectively. Title pages will be prepared in manuscript.

WAR DIARY
or
INTELLIGENCE SUMMARY.
(*Erase heading not required.*)

208 Field Coy RE

Army Form C. 2118.

Place	Date	Hour	Summary of Events and Information	Remarks and references to Appendices
OYGHEM.	5th Nov. 1918		Remaining two trestles launched. OC inspected bridge. 2nd Lt. Andrews proceeded on leave to England.	K
"	6th	"	Bridge adjusted and packed where necessary – Roadbearers laid. Pioneers making good progress on roads.	K
"	7th		Decking completed. River rose 4ft during the night. Bridge was inspected by CRE and GOC 34th Div who appeared satisfied. Heavy rain	K
"	8th	"	Bridge completed and opened for motor traffic. Pontoon bridge, replaced by trestle bridge, dismantled. River still high. 2nd Lt C.W. ANDREWS RE awarded the Military Cross for gallantry at MENIN on 15th and 16th Oct. 1918.	K
"	9th	"	Company employed removing obstruction caused by destroyed bridge where road from OYGHEM to DESSELGHEM crosses the River Lys. Obstruction damming the river app. 12 inches. Pioneers employed on roads which are in bad state owing to recent very heavy rain.	
"	10th	"	Sunday – a holiday. About 20.30 hrs. strong rumours received that enemy had accepted armistice terms	K

Instructions regarding War Diaries and Intelligence Summaries are contained in F. S. Regs., Part II. and the Staff Manual respectively. Title pages will be prepared in manuscript.

WAR DIARY
or
INTELLIGENCE SUMMARY.
(*Erase heading not required.*)

208 Field Coy R.E.

Army Form C. 2118.

Place	Date	Hour	Summary of Events and Information	Remarks and references to Appendices
OYGHEM	11th Nov. 1918		Company training. Word received during morning that enemy had accepted terms and armistice would commence at 11.00 hours.	R.
"	12th	"	Company training. Instructions received to rejoin Division at MOORSEELE on 14th inst. Lt. STATON. RE proceeded on leave to England. OC. to No 7 Pontoon Park re replacement of damaged pontoons.	R.
"	13th	"	Coy. training. 2 new pontoons obtained from No 7 Pontoon Park in lieu of damaged ones sent there for repair. Orders recd Cancelling move on 14th inst	R.
ROLLEGHEM.	14th	"	Orders recd in early morning to move during afternoon to ~~[illegible]~~ ROLLEGHEM rejoining 102 Inf Bde in that area. Coy marched at 13 hours arriving in new area at 17 hrs. One sick mule left behind - ADVS notified.	R.
QUESNOY	15th	"	Coy marched with 102 Inf Bde to POTTES - CELLES area crossing the River SCHELDT at HELCHIN.	R.
BEAUFAUX.	16th	"	Coy marched with 102 Inf Bde to RENAIX area.	R.
"	17th		Coy resting. Coy attended Bde Thanksgiving Service	R.
BRUYERE	18th	"	Marched to BRUYERE. Bde moved to FLOBECQUE Area.	R.
"	19th		Coy resting.	R.

(A9175) Wt W2358/P360 600,000 12/17 D. D. & L. Sch. 52a. Forms/C2118/15.

Instructions regarding War Diaries and Intelligence Summaries are contained in F. S. Regs., Part II. and the Staff Manual respectively. Title pages will be prepared in manuscript.

WAR DIARY
or
INTELLIGENCE SUMMARY.
(*Erase heading not required.*)

Army Form C. 2118.

208 FIELD Coy R.E.

Place	Date	Hour	Summary of Events and Information	Remarks and references to Appendices
BRUYÈRE	20th Nov. 1918.		Commenced training. 3½ hours devoted to military training, remainder recreation – organised football, shooting etc. – 3, 30yd ranges and one 200yd range found close to billets.	A.
"	21st "		Training. CRE called.	A.
"	22nd "		R. attended conference at 102nd Bde HQ re training and organisation of sports and competitions within the Brigade. 2/Lt. Andrews returned from leave.	A.
"	23rd "		GOC 34th Div inspected Company and expressed satisfaction with turnout. Information received that Lt. F. STATON RE 208 Field Coy was appointed Group Education Officer for the Group comprising the three Field Coys and the Pioneer Battn and CQMS BURDETT RE 208 Field Coy Group Sub education officer for the 3 Field Coys, under the educational scheme being organised for the period of the Armistice and Demobilization.	
"	24th "		Sunday – day off. Educational Scheme explained to the Company and taken up with enthusiasm. An average entry of 2 subjects per man throughout the Coy, also numerous instructors available for the practical trades	A.
"	25th "		Training. Unable to find field in area suitable for wagon drill	A.
"	26th "		Coy visited LESSINES STONE QUARRIES and were shown round by Quarries manager.	A.

(A9175) Wt W2358/P360 600,000 12/17 D. D. & L. Sch. 52a. Forms/C2118/15.

Instructions regarding War Diaries and Intelligence Summaries are contained in F. S. Regs., Part II. and the Staff Manual respectively. Title pages will be prepared in manuscript.

WAR DIARY
or
INTELLIGENCE SUMMARY.
(Erase heading not required.)

Army Form C. 2118.

208 Field Coy RE

Place	Date	Hour	Summary of Events and Information	Remarks and references to Appendices
BRUYÈRE	27th Nov			
"	28th		Training. Inter section competitions in football and shooting in progress.	R
"	29th			
"	30th		CRE called re road between ELLEZELLES and FLOBECQUE and asked that a few men should work on it – Setts giving way in two places owing to excessive lorry traffic and recent wet weather. – 2 Sections sent to work on it – material for filling holes obtained from railway cutting near Coy. billets.	R

James Russell
Major RE
OC 208 Field Coy RE.

Originals

Army Form C. 2118.

Instructions regarding War Diaries and Intelligence Summaries are contained in F. S. Regs., Part II. and the Staff Manual respectively. Title pages will be prepared in manuscript.

WAR DIARY
~~or~~
~~INTELLIGENCE SUMMARY.~~
(Erase heading not required.)

Place	Date	Hour	Summary of Events and Information	Remarks and references to Appendices
			V 8	36
			208th Field Coy R.E.	
			December 1918	

(A9175) Wt W2358/P360 600,000 12/17 D. D. & L. Sch. 52a. Forms/C2118/15.

Instructions regarding War Diaries and Intelligence Summaries are contained in F. S. Regs., Part II. and the Staff Manual respectively. Title pages will be prepared in manuscript.

WAR DIARY
~~or~~
~~INTELLIGENCE SUMMARY.~~
(Erase heading not required.)

Army Form C. 2118.

208 Field Coy R.E.

Place	Date	Hour	Summary of Events and Information	Remarks and references to Appendices
BRUYÈRE	1st Dec 1918		Sunday – day off. Coy attended Bde. Church Service. K.	
"	2nd	"	Coy employed on road between ELLEZELLES and FLOBECQUE. Road cutting up very badly indeed. In places lorries have run off the setts and made deep ruts in the soft bordering, leaving the setts unsupported. These are fast becoming disintegrated. OC visited 102 Inf Bde HQ and asked for working party of 300 infantry to drain road. A message also sent to the CRE for a supply of road metal – 50 to 100 tons – necessary to save road. No material available in the immediate vicinity. K.	
"	3rd	"	Coy employed as on 2nd inst with working party of 300 men. Party worked during morning only. – organised games and shooting in afternoon. K.	
"	4th	"	Working party on road reduced to 100 infantry as no road metal available. Lt. Staton who returned from leave on 3rd inst commenced duties as Group Education Officer, being relieved of all other work. K.	
"	5th	"	Work on road continued. Infantry party did not turn up. K.	
"	6th	"	200 Infantry employed on road which is daily becoming worse. Information rec'd from CRE that no material is available, and that matter had been	

(A9175) Wt W2358/P560 600,000 12/17 D. D. & L. Sch. 52a. Forms/C2118/15.

Army Form C. 2118.

WAR DIARY
~~INTELLIGENCE SUMMARY.~~
(Erase heading not required.)

208 Field Coy RE

Instructions regarding War Diaries and Intelligence Summaries are contained in F. S. Regs., Part II. and the Staff Manual respectively. Title pages will be prepared in manuscript.

Place	Date	Hour	Summary of Events and Information	Remarks and references to Appendices
BRUYÈRE	6th Dec 1918.		(Continued) placed in hands of Belgian Civil authorities. Orders recd from Bde that company would move to a new area on 8th inst. All works and training for 7th inst cancelled.	K.
"	7th	"	Order to move cancelled. Work on road proceeded with. No infantry asked for as no material available. Shooting competition finished – Best shot Lt A.P. Clark	K.
"	8th	"	Sunday – day off. Coy attended Church Parade at FLOBECQUE	K.
"	9th	"	All sections employed on maintenance of road so far as possible without materials	K.
"	10th	"	Information recd that Coy would probably move on 12th inst – Nothing definite. Work as on 9th	K.
"	11th	"	Representative party of Officers & 25 Ors attended medal presentation parade at FLOBECQUE when Military Cross Ribbon presented by Div Commander to 2/Lt. C. ANDREWS MC RE. Remainder of company cleaning and loading wagons etc for forthcoming move.	K.
SILLY	12th		Coy marched with 102 Inf Bde to SILLY – 15 miles on setts. Severe on men	K.
	13th		Resting.	
SOIGNIES.	14th		Marched to SOIGNIES – No incidents	K.
"	15th		Resting. Coy attended Church Parade	K.
HAINE ST PAUL	16th		Marched to HAINE ST PAUL. Very Wet	K.

Instructions regarding War Diaries and Intelligence Summaries are contained in F. S. Regs., Part II. and the Staff Manual respectively. Title pages will be prepared in manuscript.

WAR DIARY
or
~~INTELLIGENCE SUMMARY.~~
(Erase heading not required.)

Army Form C. 2118.

208 FIELD Coy R.E.

Place	Date	Hour	Summary of Events and Information	Remarks and references to Appendices
MONCEAU	17th DEC 1918		Marched to MONCEAU. Coy marching exceedingly well.	
CHATELET	18th		Marched to CHATELET. Very wet day. CRE called.	
LESVES	19th		Marched to LESVES. Shocking billets – unable to occupy part of the [illegible] Sections billeted in buildings earmarked for schools. Official complaint made to CRE who promised that Coy would move to better area.	
	20th		Resting. Very wet. Reconnaissance of roads & bridges in LESVES area started.	
	21		Coy improving billets. Unofficially informed that Coy will probably move in a few days. Very wet.	
	22nd		Coy improving billets. Shortage of timber a serious drawback. Reconnaissance of roads & railways in area completed. Roads in excellent condition – railways all mined by enemy. Very wet.	
	23rd		207 Field Coy RE left LESVES. Coy moved to 207 Field Coy RE billets except HQ and one section. Greatly improved billets although not satisfactory [illegible] for winter.	
	24th		Coy preparing for Xmas. The first man (coalminer) to be demobilized.	

WAR DIARY

~~or~~

~~INTELLIGENCE SUMMARY.~~

(Erase heading not required.)

Army Form C. 2118.

Instructions regarding War Diaries and Intelligence Summaries are contained in F. S. Regs., Part II. and the Staff Manual respectively. Title pages will be prepared in manuscript.

Place	Date	Hour	Summary of Events and Information	Remarks and references to Appendices
[illegible]	24th Dec 1918		(Continued) proceeded to England	K
	25th		Xmas. Coy well satisfied with the dinner provided. Some men proceeded to England to be demobilized.	K
	26th		Coy had a holiday to recover from Xmas	K
	27th		Coy training — military and recreational. Demobilization Forms Z 16 completed for each man in the Company.	K
	28th		Coy training. Demobilization form Z 8 for Coy completed and forwarded. Major RUSSELL handed over Coy to Capt FOWLER MC RE and proceeded on 14 days special leave to England	Maj [illegible]
	29th		Coy attended Divine Service	[illegible]
	30th		Coy training - military & recreational. Held Court of Enquiry as [illegible] ordered by CRE 3rd Division re responsibility for loss of 2 bicycles. 2 Lt Andrews temporarily attached 20 Fd Coy. 1 Sect with Lt Cameron on attachment to 102 Bde	[illegible]
	31st		Sections with 102 Bde making latrines, rest of Coy making latrines, washing bays and recreational training. Lt Hibbert reported from 3rd Div Rest Camp.	[illegible]

[illegible signature]
Capt
O/C 28 Field Coy

(A9175) Wt W2358/P360 600,000 12/17 D. D. & L. **Sch. 52a.** Forms/C2118/13.

ORIGINAL.

Instructions regarding War Diaries and Intelligence Summaries are contained in F. S. Regs., Part II. and the Staff Manual respectively. Title pages will be prepared in manuscript.

WAR DIARY

~~or~~

~~INTELLIGENCE SUMMARY.~~

(Erase heading not required.)

Army Form C. 2118.

Vol 37

Place	Date	Hour	Summary of Events and Information	Remarks and references to Appendices
			— 208th Field Coy, R.E. —	
			— January 1919. —	

(A9175) Wt W2358/P360 600,000 12/17 D. D. & L. Sch. 52a. Forms/C2118/15.

Instructions regarding War Diaries and Intelligence Summaries are contained in F. S. Regs., Part II. and the Staff Manual respectively. Title pages will be prepared in manuscript.

WAR DIARY

~~or~~

~~INTELLIGENCE~~ SUMMARY.

(*Erase heading not required.*)

1/.

Army Form C. 2118.

208 Field Coy R.E.

Place	Date	Hour	Summary of Events and Information	Remarks and references to Appendices
LESVES	1st Jan. 1919		Coy training, military & recreational. 2/Lt Fox transferred to 209 Field Coy	
	2 "		" " " " 1 Off + 28 O.R. to CHARLEROI by lorry. HHCB	
	3 "		" training route march, lecture for Coy. finished. 2/Lt Anderson	
			rejoined from 209 Field Coy. HHCB	
	4th "		Coy training, military recreational. Coy played 207 at Rugby & beat them 9-3 HHCB	
	5th		Coy attended Divine Service. Coy played 209 at Soccer & beat them 7-3 HHCB	
	6th		Coy training, military recreational, 2 Off + 24 OR to CHARLEROI by lorry. HHCB	
	7th		Coy training, military recreational, Sapper Oates for demobilisation 'Serving Soldier'.	
			4 Reinforcements from Base, Erecting Spray Bath, Fixing German Cauldrons HHCB.	
	8th		Coy training military recreational, Started Riding Class for Sappers 6 O.R. inoculated	
			Two lectures (1) French (2) Map Reading. Work continued on Spray Bath / Cauldrons HHCB.	
	9th		Coy training military recreational, Riding Class, 4 O.R. inoculated, work continued	
			on Bath, handed over to Lt F. Hibbert MC RE & proceeded on leave to U.K. HHCB.	
	10th		Coy training, military & recreational, Mounted duties class for dismounted men, work continued on	
			Bath 4 Reinforcements from Base work continued on Snow ploughs, 1 section detached improving billets 102 Inf Bde. H	
			Lieut C. Bowes proceeded as Billeting Officer for RE in new area. H	
	11th		Coy training, military & recreational, Mounted duties Class work continued on snow ploughs. Bath set	
			completed & Coy bathed. Lieut. J.F. STATON to Concentration Camp for demobilization Group 43,	
			2 - OR. to Concentration Camp for demobilization Group 43, Musical Entertainment for men in evening. H	

(A9175) Wt W2358/P360 600,000 12/17 D. D. & L. Sch. 52a. Forms/C2118/15.

Instructions regarding War Diaries and Intelligence Summaries are contained in F. S. Regs., Part II. and the Staff Manual respectively. Title pages will be prepared in manuscript.

WAR DIARY ~~or~~ ~~INTELLIGENCE SUMMARY~~. 2.

(Erase heading not required.)

Army Form C. 2118.

208th Field Coy R.E.

Place	Date	Hour	Summary of Events and Information	Remarks and references to Appendices
LESVES	12th Jan 1919		Holy Communion + Church Parades, 1 section bathed, Football match between Coy + civilians in afternoon, 1 - OR to Hospital	H
	13th		Coy training military + recreational, 3 - O.Rs to Concentration Camp for demobilization "PIVOTAL".	H
			4 - O.Rs inoculated, lecture by M.O. RE to half company, 25 men by motor lorry to visit CHARLEROI	H
			Football match between N.C.Os + sappers in afternoon. H	
	14th		Coy training military + recreational 5 - O.Rs to Concentration Camp for demobilization Group 1 + 30	H
			lecture by M.O. RE to 1 section + drivers, bathing parades for company, 3 Reinforcements reported from Base	H
			Games in afternoon H	
	15th		Coy training military + recreational 9 - O.Rs to Concentration Camp for demobilization.	
			Circulars on Demobilization + Reconstruction read out to Coy, mounted duties class for sappers, 1 - OR on leave to U.K.	H
	16th		Coy training military + recreational, mounted duties class for sappers, 2nd Lt. Davison and No 1 Section rejoined Coy from detachment	H
	17th		Coy training military + recreational mounted duties class for sappers, Lt. J. Hibbert + Orderly Room Sergeant attended lecture on Demobilization at Army H.Q., circular on Reconstruction read to Coy.	H
	18th		Coy training military + recreational, mounted duties class for sappers, bathing parades, 1 - OR on leave to U.K. Instruction on demobilization read out to men.	H

(A9175) Wt W2355/P360 600,000 12/17 D. D. & L. **Sch. 52a.** Forms/C2118/15.

Instructions regarding War Diaries and Intelligence Summaries are contained in F. S. Regs., Part II. and the Staff Manual respectively. Title pages will be prepared in manuscript.

WAR DIARY ~~or~~ ~~INTELLIGENCE SUMMARY.~~

3.

(*Erase heading not required.*)

Army Form C. 2118.

208th Field Coy. R.E

Place	Date	Hour	Summary of Events and Information	Remarks and references to Appendices
LESVES	19th Jan.	1919	Holy Communion & Church Parades, games in afternoon.	H
	20th		Coy training Military & Recreational, mounted duties course for sappers, completed snow plough except for iron runners.	H
	21st		Coy training Military & Recreational, mounted duties course for sappers, preparing for move on 22nd inst, 1 - mule to 44th Mobile Vet. Section.	H
	22nd		Coy left LESVES at 7.30am, marched to ~~[illegible]~~ AUVELAIS and entrained, departing at 3.50pm	H
BONN	23rd		Coy detrained at BEUEL near BONN at 11.30am and marched to billets at GRAU RHEINDORF	H
	25th		Coy training military and recreational, mounted duties course for sappers, Football match between this Coy. and 209 Field Co. R.E.	H
	26th		Holy Communion, Church Parades, games, voluntary church service in evening	H
	27th		Coy training military & recreational, mounted duties course for sappers, games in afternoon all animals malleined & classified by A.D.V.S.	H
	28th		Coy training military ~~& recreational~~ all animals inspected by A.D.V.S, Football match in afternoon between this Coy & 5th Batt. Canadian Engineers	H
	29th		Coy training military & recreational, all animals reclassified by Corps Adviser	H
	30th		Coy training military & recreational, preparation for move, lecture by Commander Viscount Broome R.N. on "Work of Navy"	H

(A9175) Wt W2358/P360 600,000 12/17 D. D. & L. Sch. 52a. Forms/C2118/15.

Instructions regarding War Diaries and Intelligence Summaries are contained in F. S. Regs., Part II. and the Staff Manual respectively. Title pages will be prepared in manuscript.

WAR DIARY

~~or~~

~~INTELLIGENCE~~ SUMMARY.

(Erase heading not required.)

4.

Army Form C. 2118.

208th Field Coy. R.E.

Place	Date	Hour	Summary of Events and Information	Remarks and references to Appendices
BONN	31st Jan.		Company moved to TROISDORF.	
TROISDORF				
			[signature] Lieut R.E. O.C. 208th Fd. Co. R.E.	

(A9175) Wt W2358/P360 600,000 12/17 D. D. & L. Sch. 52a. Forms/C2118/15.

Army Form C. 2118.

Instructions regarding War Diaries and Intelligence Summaries are contained in F. S. Regs., Part II. and the Staff Manual respectively. Title pages will be prepared in manuscript.

WAR DIARY

~~or~~

~~INTELLIGENCE SUMMARY.~~

(Erase heading not required.)

Place	Date	Hour	Summary of Events and Information	Remarks and references to Appendices
			Vol 38	
			208th Field Coy R.E.	
			February 1919.	

(A9175) Wt W2358/P360 000,000 12/17 D. D. & L. Sch. 52a. Forms/C2118/15.

Instructions regarding War Diaries and Intelligence Summaries are contained in F. S. Regs., Part II. and the Staff Manual respectively. Title pages will be prepared in manuscript.

WAR DIARY
or
~~INTELLIGENCE SUMMARY.~~
(Erase heading not required.)

Army Form C. 2118.

208th Field Coy. R.E.

Place	Date	Hour	Summary of Events and Information	Remarks and references to Appendices
TROISDORF	1st Feb 1919		Coy training, military & recreational games in afternoon	[initials]
	2nd "		Holy Communion & Church Parades.	[initials]
	3rd "		Coy training, military & recreational. Football match in afternoon between this Coy and 7/4th Batt. Somerset Light Infantry	[initials]
	4th "		Coy moved to WAHLSCHIED — Lt Hibbert left the Coy – on leave to England.	[initials]
	5th to 13th "		Improving billets, erecting latrines & cook-houses. An inspection of the front-line "D" sub-sector of the Cologne Bridge-head was carried out between the 9th & 13th Feby & details of a proposed system of defence submitted to G.O.C. 103 Inf Brigade on the 13th Feby.	[initials]
	14th "		1 Section of sappers under a Sergt. sent to SEELSCHIED for work with 2/4th Queens erecting latrines, cookhouses, ovens, incinerators, sentry boxes etc.	[initials]
	14th to 28th		Company cleaning & painting wagons, preparing & painting notice boards for limit of Cologne Bridge-head, constructing boxing ring & laying out recreation ground. During this time a reconnaissance of roads & bridges ~~in~~ in "D" sub-area was carried out & drawings & reports submitted to C.R.E 34th Divn on 23rd Feby. 1919.	[initials]
	19th "		The Company's billets etc were inspected by G.O.C. 34th Divn.	[initials]
	20th "		O.C. Company took over duties of Dist. Commandant Wahlscheid (in addition to duties as O.C. Coy.)	[initials]

[signature] Lieut. R.E.
O.C. 208th Field Coy R.E.

SECRET.

D.A.G.,
3rd Echelon

Enclosed please find War Diary for March 1919. (Original)
Kindly acknowledge receipt.

(by Registered Post)

K. [illegible] Major R.E.,
OC. 208th Field Coy R.E.

Instructions regarding War Diaries and Intelligence Summaries are contained in F. S. Regs., Part II, and the Staff Manual respectively. Title pages will be prepared in manuscript.

34

WAR DIARY
or
INTELLIGENCE SUMMARY.
(Erase heading not required.)

Army Form C. 2118.

208th Field Coy. R.E

Vol 39

Place	Date	Hour	Summary of Events and Information	Remarks and references to Appendices
WAHLSCHIED	March 1919 1st		Lieut. F. HIBBERT M.C. R.E. having returned from leave & O.K. resumed command of Coy. CRE & Adjt 34th Division inspected work on baths etc in SEELSCHIED area. Making notice boards, targets etc.	H
	2nd		O.C. to inspect work at SEELSCHIED. LT. R. DAVISON to take charge of forward work & to live at SCHMITTEN. Football match in afternoon	H
	3rd		O.C. met G.S.O.1 34 Div. & 103rd Inf Bde Commander, to site posts & pill boxes in Defence line near SEELSCHIED. Coy working on baths, delousers, latrines etc at SEELSCHIED & notice boards, targets etc at WAHLSCHIED	H
	4th		O.C. met 103 Bde Commander & O.C. 8th Batt. Scottish Rifles to site posts & pill boxes in Defence line near NEUNKIRCHEN. Coy working on baths, etc at SEELSCHIED & notice boards targets etc at WAHLSCHIED	H
	5th		Coy working as for 4th inst. O.C. to SEELSCHIED to allot work in Defence line to officers. 2nd LT. ANDREWS & 2nd Lt FRYER to live at SCHMITTEN.	H
	6th		Coy working as for 5th inst. 3 NCOs & 22 men proceeded to SCHMITTEN on detachment for work on Defence line. LT. C. BEWES proceeded to No 1 Concentration Camp COLOGNE for demobilization	H
	7th		Work on Defence line at SEELSCHEID commenced	H
	7th		Coy. working on erection of baths, latrines etc in SEELSHEID area, working also on Pill boxes & wiring in Defence line. 4 – O.Rs proceeded to No 1 Concentration Camp Cologne for demobilization	H
	8th		Coy. working as for 7th inst.	

(A9175) Wt W2358/P360 600,000 12/17 D. D. & L. Sch. 52a. Forms/C2118/15.

Instructions regarding War Diaries and Intelligence Summaries are contained in F. S. Regs., Part II. and the Staff Manual respectively. Title pages will be prepared in manuscript.

WAR DIARY
or
INTELLIGENCE SUMMARY.
(Erase heading not required.)

Army Form C. 2118.

208 Field Coy R.E

Place	Date	Hour	Summary of Events and Information	Remarks and references to Appendices
	March 1919			
	9th		Church Parades + games in afternoon. 2 - ORs to No1 Concentration Camp Cologne for demobilization	[initials]
	10th		Coy working on erection of baths, latrines, etc in SEELSCHEID area, also working on Defence Line at SEELSHEID and NEUNKIRCHEN. 9 - ORs to No1 Concentration Camp Cologne for demobilization	[initials]
	11th		Coy working as for 10th inst.	[initials]
	12th		Coy working as for 11th inst. Veterinary Officer inspected several mules.	[initials]
	13th		Coy working as for 12th inst. 2 officers + 1 batman of 4th Batt. Suffolk Regt joined for attachment	[initials]
	14th		Coy working as for 13th inst.	[initials]
	15th		Coy working as for 14th inst. 3 - ORs to No1 Concentration Camp Cologne for demobilization	[initials]
	16th		Church Parades, games in afternoon	[initials]
	17th		Coy working on erection of latrines, bunks etc in SEELSCHEID area also working on Defence Line 4 German civilian carpenters commenced work	[initials]
	18th		Coy working as for 17th. C.R.E 34th Division inspected works at SEELSCHEID	[initials]
	19th		Coy working as for 18th. Major K.I. GOURLAY M.C, R.E assumed command of the Coy.	[initials]
	20th		Coy. working as for 19th	[initials]
	21st		" " 20th "Lt Cowell R.E joined for duty	[initials]
	22nd		" " 21th	[initials]

(A9175) Wt W2358/P360 600,000 12/17 D. D. & L. Sch. 52a. Forms/C2118/15.

Instructions regarding War Diaries and Intelligence Summaries are contained in F. S. Regs., Part II. and the Staff Manual respectively. Title pages will be prepared in manuscript.

WAR DIARY
or
INTELLIGENCE SUMMARY.
(Erase heading not required.)

Army Form C. 2118.

Place	Date	Hour	Summary of Events and Information	Remarks and references to Appendices
WAHLSCHEID SEELSCHEID.	24th - 29th		Coy working on Defence Line erecting wire & Moir pillboxes. Bunks & latrines be being made for Infantry Outposts. System of W.P.s changed on 25th. 6 German Carpenters employed.	
" "	29th		21 NCO's + O R left for No 1 Concentration Camp Cologne	
" "	30th		Church parades at Seelscheid. 40 O R joined from 4th Suffolks for employment as sappers & drivers.	
" "	31st		Work on Defence Line & on improving infantry billets. Erection of Nissen huts started to house 4 Sussex Q M Stores. Preparations for moving coy to SEELSCHEID begun.	

W H Gourlay
May 19
OC 208 Coy RE.

(A9175) Wt W2354/P360 600,000 12/17 D. D. & L. Sch. 52a. Forms/C2118/15.

SECRET East

208TH
FIELD COMPANY,
R.E.
No. B/4/32
Date. 1/5/19

D.A.G.
British Army of the Rhine

Enclosed please find War Diary for April 1919 (Original)

Kindly acknowledge receipt

(by Registered Post)

R.M. Cooper.
Capt. R.E.
a/O.C. 208th Field Coy. R.E.

APRIL 1919

Instructions regarding War Diaries and Intelligence Summaries are contained in F. S. Regs., Part II. and the Staff Manual respectively. Title pages will be prepared in manuscript.

WAR DIARY

~~or~~

~~INTELLIGENCE SUMMARY.~~

(Erase heading not required.)

Army Form C. 2118.

Place	Date	Hour	Summary of Events and Information	Remarks and references to Appendices
WAHLSHEID	1 – 6		Detachment working at SEELSHEID. Defence wire & Billets for 101 Bde.	
SEELSHEID	7th		Coy Hqrs move to Upper SEELSCHEID. Detachment of Drivers left at WAHLSCHEID	
	11th		Lieut A/Capt COOPER RE joins & takes over 2nd in Command.	
	17th		3rd Bde takes over from 1st Bde Move complete today.	
"	18		Lieut A/Capt HIBBERTMORE RE demobilized	
"	7–29		Work for 3rd Bde. Defence wire, work on billets infantry & R.E. Huts	
"			erected for Mounted Section.	
"	21		Holiday. Detachment from WAHLSCHEID join Coy.	
"	22–30		Work for 3rd Bde, DEFENCE wire, work on billets, Painting & erecting Notice	
			Boards for Brigade area – Working Parties supplied by 51st B.R. Sussex Regt.	
	21st		LIEUT. W.S.C. Anderson RE joins –	

R.M. Cooper. Capt. RE.
for O.C. 208th. Field Coy R.E.

Instructions regarding War Diaries and Intelligence Summaries are contained in F. S. Regs., Part II. and the Staff Manual respectively. Title pages will be prepared in manuscript.

May.

WAR DIARY
or
INTELLIGENCE SUMMARY.
(Erase heading not required.)

Army Form C. 2118.

Place	Date	Hour	Summary of Events and Information	Remarks and references to Appendices
SEELSCHEID	1st – 22nd		Work on Defence Line & improvements to Infy Billets.	
	10th		Maj Gourlay assumes command on return from U.K.	
	19th		Capt Cooper takes over command while Maj Gourlay acting as C.R.E.	
	24th		Maj Gourlay takes over company	
	23 to 31		Overhauling of equipment & transport. Mounted section made up to full strength of ~~[illegible]~~ personnel from Dismounted Men. 1 hours Military Training a day.	

H Gourlay
Maj RE
OC 208 Coy RE

Instructions regarding War Diaries and Intelligence Summaries are contained in F. S. Regs., Part II. and the Staff Manual respectively. Title pages will be prepared in manuscript.

WAR DIARY
or
~~INTELLIGENCE SUMMARY.~~
(Erase heading not required.)

Army Form C. 2118.

Place	Date	Hour	Summary of Events and Information	Remarks and references to Appendices
OBR-ZEIT. near SEELSCHEID. GERMANY.	JUNE. 1-17		Coy. employed on Improvements to Co. Billets, Checking, cleaning, overhauling Co Equipment and Vehicles, Training of Dismounted + Mounted Sections. Painting and erecting Direction Boards for Roads Crossings in area of 3rd. Eastern Infantry Brigade, and on works detailed by C.R.E. and G.O.C. 3rd Eastern Inf Bde.	
	3.		Inspection of Coy. and Co. Billets by G.O.C. Eastern Division.	
	3.		Honours + Awards. Kings Birthday Honours List. 3.6.1919. D.S.O. Major K.I. Gourlay. M.C. RE, ORs. M.S.M. Sergt. C. Burdett. RE. Sergt. G. Smith. RE.	
	18.		Coy. moved into Close Billets at OBR-ZEIT. on J-2. DAY.	
	21.		Coy. took part in Route March of 3rd. Eastern Infan. Brigade.	
	18-28		Coy. "Standing To" for Operations in the event of the Peace Treaty not being signed by the German Government. Works - Fixing Water troughs and Pumps for Water Supply arrangements 3rd East. Infan. Brigade. - Training.	
	28.		The Peace Treaty was officially signed by the German representative in Paris at 16.00 hrs.	
	30.		A. Day. The 3rd. East. Infan. Brigade resumed normal billets. Coy resumed usual works. + Training.	
	30.		Maj. K.I. Gourlay. D.S.O. M.C. RE. assumed the duties of C.R.E. during the CRE's absence on leave to the U.K.	

P.M. Cooper. Capt RE
o/c. 208th. Field Co RE.
30. 6. 1919

Army Form C. 2118.

Instructions regarding War Diaries and Intelligence Summaries are contained in F. S. Regs., Part II. and the Staff Manual respectively. Title pages will be prepared in manuscript.

WAR DIARY
or
~~INTELLIGENCE SUMMARY.~~
(*Erase heading not required.*)

Place	Date	Hour	Summary of Events and Information	Remarks and references to Appendices
	JULY		WORKS. 208th FIELD. Co. R.E.	
SEELSCHEID	1-31		The Company was employed on the following Works.	
GERMANY			Rifle Range BRUCKHAUSEN, Erecting FIELD OVENS for Battalions 3rd.	
			EASTERN Infantry BRIGADE, Erection of Baths at SELIGENTHAL, Salving	
			R.E. material on Outpost Line + in the BRIGADE AREA, on preparing	
			GROUNDS for the Horse SHOWS of the 3rd. EASTERN BRIGADE, and for	
			the EASTERN DIVISION - + on other small works detailed by the CRE	
			EASTERN DIVISION + B.G.C 3rd. Eastern Infantry Brigade.	
			TRAINING. The following training has been carried out,	
			Physical Training, Gas, Musketry, SECTION DRILL. + Mounted Training.	
	4th		Capt P.M. Cooper. proceeded on leave to U.K + LIEUT. W.L.C Anderson assumed command	Moves Officers
	9th.		Lt. R. Dawson " " " " "	
	24th		Capt P.M. Cooper rejoined from leave in U.K.	
	30th		Lt. R. Dawson rejoined from leave in U.K.	
	31st.		ii Lieuts. W.G Dyer + C.A Mead left to join the 3rd. and 2nd. Infan. Bdes for training.	
	3rd		GENERAL HOLIDAY throughout the X CORPS.	
	19th		HOLIDAY + PEACE CELEBRATIONS	
	31st.		DIVISIONAL Horse SHOW. The Co was awarded FIRST PRIZE for R.E. Tool Cart + team.	

P. M. Cooper Capt. RE. O/C. 208th. FIELD Co. RE

(A9175) Wt W235/P360 600,000 12/17 D. D. & L. Sch. 52a. Forms/C2118/15.

www.ingramcontent.com/pod-product-compliance
Lightning Source LLC
Chambersburg PA
CBHW080853010526
44117CB00014B/2245
* 9 7 8 1 4 7 4 5 1 6 9 4 5 *